Rangers Football Club:
1998 - 2015

A descent into chaos, a resultant chaos, and an emergence from chaos

W B Howieson

www.publishnation.co.uk

Front cover image courtesy of *The Scottish Sun*

This club has been scrutinised at various levels over the last few years in particular and no doubt Rangers will continue to be examined in the years ahead, which will be no bad thing. But let's please have intelligent debate rather than the ill-informed nonsense that's been filling the newspapers, websites and airwaves.

Walter Smith[1]

---

[1] In Foreword by Walter Smith (Page 12) to Franklin, W. S., Gow, J. D. C., Graham. C., and McKillop, A. (Eds.). (2013). Follow We Will THE FALL AND RISE OF RANGERS. Edinburgh: Luath Press Limited.

Dedication

To Mary

Not a bad bone in her body — just not.

Contents

Page Number

List of Figures

List of Tables

About the Author

Brian Howieson is a business academic — he is Professor of Organisational Leadership and Associate Dean for Business Engagement at Stirling Management School, The University of Stirling.

Originally from Ayrshire, he attended secondary school in Cumbernauld before reading Mechanical Engineering at the University of Edinburgh. He was then commissioned into the Royal Air Force in 1987 and — as a Navigator/Weapon System Officer — completed tours of duty on the Nimrod MR2 and Nimrod R aircraft. He saw active service in the Gulf War (1990/1991), Kosovo War (1999) and United Nations Air Operations in Northern and Sothern Iraq (1999/2000). He was a United Kingdom Ministry of Defence, Defence Fellow (2002).

He has MBA and MPhil degrees from Heriot-Watt University in Edinburgh and completed his PhD in Leadership at the University of Edinburgh.

After the Royal Air Force, he worked for The Royal College of Physicians and Surgeons of Glasgow before entering academia mid-career. He travels extensively and has lectured and presented in all continents on the globe.

Prior to Covid-19, he was a Season Ticket Holder at Falkirk Football Club — he continues to support this League One team today. He also teaches on the Scottish Football Association's UEFA Professional License and A and B Licenses.

Preface

As a 'football watcher' and business academic, the events that took place at Rangers Football Club during the period 2011 - 2015 fascinated me. I was not sure if it was because such an institution could fail or the almost Shakespearean sense of tragedy but I wanted to write this book to attempt to understand what happened and to record this understanding from an objective and independent standpoint. I do say attempt — I am not a corporate lawyer. Moreover, I do not have a background in finance or accountancy. Rather, I come to this story 'cold.' I have attempted to understand what happened by drawing on a variety of literatures that are available in the public domain. These literatures included the print and broadcast media and the extensive information that is available at Companies House.

The actual interest in this story first developed in March 2010. I remember well — when travelling to the Barley Bree Restaurant in Crieff for lunch on 6 March 2010 — hearing on BBC Radio Scotland that a businessman called Andrew Ellis wanted to buy Rangers. This caught my immediate attention — it seemed like Sir David Murray had owned and operated Rangers forever. Were we now witnessing a change of ownership/direction? As the story — indeed drama — unfolded, the name of Craig Whyte emerged. Previously unknown in Scotland except, perhaps, to those in the corporate financial community, Whyte ultimately purchased Rangers Football Club via his acquisition of 85% of the shares in The Rangers Football Club plc. In this respect, I also remember returning from Stirling on a Friday evening on 6 May 2011 — and listening to Clyde Superscoreboard — when Jim Delahunt (the, then, radio show's anchor) stated that a company called Wavetower had purchased Rangers.

Little did any of us know that spring evening what was about to unfold for this football club. Simply, a further descent into chaos, a resultant chaos and a slow (but at times difficult) recovery from chaos that would last for some four years. On 6 March 2015 — with so-called regime change — we started to witness renewal.

In this book, I endeavour to explain and narrate this most chaotic period in this Football Club's 150-year history.

WBH

Foreword

Brian Howieson's book applies a forensic approach to the most extraordinary and notorious episode in Scottish football history — the financial folly at Ibrox and consequent implosion in 2012, which saw a pillar of the sport north of the border forced to refashion its sporting credentials at the lowest level of the professional leagues.

Yet in 1990, Rangers could claim to be the foremost football club, not only in Scotland but in the United Kingdom at a time when the sport in Britain had taken a battering. Rangers' status was, in part, the consequence of good governance at Ibrox and, in part, the outcome of avoidable calamities elsewhere.

The genesis of Rangers' prosperity was, paradoxically, the Ibrox Disaster of January 2, 1971, in which 66 supporters were killed and over 200 injured. In the aftermath, Willie Waddell — in his capacities as the club's general manager and vice-chairman — supervised an overhaul of the stadium based on the model of Borussia Dortmund's Westfalenstadion, which saw the construction of three new stands and left the small Main Stand enclosure as the only standing area. Waddell was able to accomplish this transformation because Rangers Pools was the largest club-based football pools operation in the UK and underwrote the estimated £6 million cost of implementing stadium reconstruction between 1978 and 1981.

In 1986 Rangers made another bold investment when the then chairman, David Holmes, recruited Graeme Souness to act as player-manager in place of Jock Wallace. It was a particularly timely move because English clubs were banned from European football in the aftermath of the Heysel Disaster and, although Souness had never played Scottish club football, his aura as former captain of Liverpool was crucial in persuading a string of England internationals, including captain Terry Butcher and goalkeeper Chris Woods, to move to Ibrox along with the likes of Mark Hateley, Ray Wilkins, Gary Stevens and Trevor Steven.

This was a reversal in direction of the traditional flow of talent across the border and Rangers' position was further strengthened by the Hillsborough Disaster in 1989 and the publication of the Taylor Report in 1990. Although the Taylor Report did not have force of law in Scotland, the Scottish Football Association accepted its recommendations in their entirety. At a stroke, virtually every British football club was obliged to find the means to undertake stadium reconstruction — collectively, a civil engineering project comparable with the Channel Tunnel. Rangers, though, were well ahead of the game and when it was decided to reconstruct the Main Stand to incorporate a Club Deck of around 6000 seats, £2 million of the cost was paid for by a grant from the Football Trust and £8.5 million was raised from the sale of debentures to supporters.

David Murray, as he then was, had come into the picture in November 1988 when — urged on by Souness — he bought Rangers from the club's Nevada-based owner, Laurence Marlborough. That season proved to be the first of Rangers' nine successive title-winning campaigns, first under Souness and then Walter Smith. For the reasons stated above, Murray had acquired Rangers at a particularly opportune moment in the history of their relationship with their Glasgow arch-rivals. Within a few months, the signing of Mo Johnston broke a long-standing and self-imposed taboo on signing Roman Catholic players, opening access to an abundant pool of talent.

Off the field, meanwhile, Celtic were run by a small group of families, whose stewardship stretched back to the foundation of the club but who lacked the financial resources needed to reconstruct Celtic Park — which had the biggest area of standing terracings of any British stadium — to the standards required post-Hillsborough.

While Celtic's trajectory led to the business coming within minutes of bankruptcy in 1994, Rangers became contenders in the 1993 Champions League and qualified for the group stage through home and away victories over Leeds United, the English champions. Rangers' superiority to Celtic on and off the field seemed almost impregnable, yet the factors that would bring about a complete reversal of fortunes were already at play.

For a start, the colossal expenditure required for stadium reconstruction south of the border had driven England's top clubs into a breakaway from the Football League, underwritten by a lucrative broadcast rights deal with Sky. Next, Celtic were saved from administration by Fergus McCann, who acted as guarantor for the club's £7 million debt and underwrote a share issue which raised £14 million and contributed to the reconstruction of an all-seated Parkhead with 53,000 season ticket holders.

In Europe, Rangers now had to compete with English clubs whose access to annual revenue was consistent and substantial and who could contend for European trophies. As Murray tried to keep pace — and especially after Dick Advocaat became manager in 1998 — Rangers' overdraft became swollen, a process made inevitable by Murray's proclamation that 'For every five pounds Celtic spend, we will spend ten". The hazard inherent in the formula was best illustrated by Celtic's purchase of John Hartson for £6 million and Rangers' acquisition of Tore Andre Flo for £12 million. Hartson scored 88 goals in 146 appearances while Flo netted 34 goals in 68 appearances. In other words, Hartson cost half but his yield was more than double that of Flo. Under Advocaat, who displayed an advanced state of entitlement when it came to demanding cash, Rangers spent £40 million on players — an unprecedented sum for a Scottish club — but won only two of the four available Scottish titles during his tenure. This was the period when Joe Lewis, through his ENIC group investment in Rangers (which just happened to be £40 million), discovered that he could not restrain Murray's spending spree.

It is also the period which Brian Howieson chose to begin his detailed examination of what he describes as "an organisational descent into chaos, a resultant organisational chaos, and an emergence of an organisation from this chaos." Those words encompass the Krakatoa-like explosion of debt at Murray's holding company to very nearly £1 billion, the collision with HM Revenue and Customs over the Employee Benefit Trusts used to pay players (the Big Tax Case), the decision by Murray's bankers to jettison Rangers and the change of ownership — encapsulated by the toss of a £1 coin across the boardroom table — to Craig Whyte, a hitherto little-known figure who claimed to have "billions of pounds under management" via his Liberty Trust and Wavetower companies, whose HQ turned out to be a Portakabin on a Swiss industrial estate.

Brian Howieson has rendered a refreshingly, non-partisan account of an almost incredible series of events which continue to reverberate at the time of writing with the admission, by the Crown Office, of malicious prosecution of Rangers' administrators — amidst costs to the public pocket of £40 million or more — and allegations that HMRC's estimate of the club's tax debt was double what it should have been because of mistakes in the calculation.

This astounding passage in Scottish football history, a tale of hubris and folly on a colossal scale, deserves a dispassionate, meticulous analysis. That is what Brian Howieson has delivered, undoubtedly to the gratitude of future historians of the game.

Roddy Forsyth

Acknowledgements

It is important that I place on record my sincere gratitude to several people who have helped me in this writing project.

At the book's conception stage, Richard Wilson (BBC), Keith Jackson (The Daily Record), Roger Hannah (The Scottish Sun) and James Traynor (then Level 5 PR) kindly agreed to meet with me to discuss my ideas and thoughts. Indeed, it was Roger who helped me with the Title of this book — see Chapter One. In addition, Roddy Forsyth (Scottish football correspondent for BBC Radio 5 Live and the Telegraph Group) was very willing to offer e-mail insight whenever I enquired. Thank you.

Thank you too to Keith Walker — Business and Management Subject Librarian — at Edinburgh Napier University who was a great help in guiding me though the Nexis® database.

At the drafting stage, I had several critical friends: Matthew Bonnett, James Brown, Billy Gilmore, Mike Sanderson, and James McMillan. I am grateful for the time and effort that these fine gentlemen afforded me. I also thank Rachel Findlay and (again) Matthew Bonnett for their insight, analysis and understanding with the Annual Reports and Accounts of The Rangers Football Club plc and the five Duff & Phelps Administrators' Reports respectively.

Formerly of DC Thomson Media, Craig Houston (who discussed this project with me on several train journeys to/from Dundee) and Steve Finnan (Author, Football nostalgia book) — Steve was a key champion from conception to delivery. I also thank David Morrison at PublishNation and Gus Campbell at Gus Campbell Graphic Design for his assistance with my diagrams.

Finally, for key football insights and friendship for almost 20 years: Graham Gettie and Fraser Stroak. True gentlemen.

Key Personnel

Name	Position/Role
Adam, Hugh:	Director, The Rangers Football Club plc (25 August 1988 – 24 June 1992 and 8 December 1993 – 30 September 2000).
Advocaat, Dick:	Manager, Rangers Football Club (1 June 1998 – 12 December 2001).
Ahmad, Imran:	Director, The Rangers Football Club Limited (14 June 2012 – 29 May 2013).
Allan, Gary QC:	Panel Member of Scottish Football Association Disciplinary Tribunal.
Ashley, Mike:	Shareholder, Rangers International Football Club plc. Chief Executive Officer of Frasers Group plc (formerly Sports Direct International). Previous owner of Newcastle United Football Club.
Bain, Martin:	Chief Executive Officer, The Rangers Football Club plc (11 February 2005 – 23 May 2011).
Betts, Phil:	Director of The Rangers Football Club plc (6 May 2011 – 20 January 2012).
Blin, Frank:	Former Executive Chairman of accountancy firm PricewaterhouseCoopers Scotland and proposed Director of Rangers International Football Club plc.

Name	Position/Role
Bryan, Ron:	Worked at Octopus Investments (owner of Ticketus).
Cadbury, George:	Worked on a venture for Merchant Capital (part of Merchant House Group) to finance a 'deal' for The Rangers Football Club plc.
Calloway, Lord:	Scottish advocate and judge. Panel Member of Scottish Football Association Appellate Tribunal.
Cartmell, Philip:	Director, Rangers International Football Club plc (7 December 2012 – 8 July 2013).
Cohen, Malcolm:	Binder, Dijke and Otte Joint Liquidator.
Cowan, Allan:	Previously Chairman at Partick Thistle Football Club. Panel Member of Scottish Football Association Appellate Tribunal.
Clark, Paul:	Duff & Phelps Joint Administrator.
Crighton, Norman:	Director, Rangers International Football Club plc (14 November 2013 – 9 December 2014).
Downes, Bob:	Deputy Chairman of the Environmental Protection Agency and Member of Scottish Football Association Independent Committee.

Name	Position/Role
Drysdale, Eric:	Director of Raith Rovers Football Club and Panel Member of Scottish Football Association Disciplinary Tribunal.
Easdale, James:	Director, Rangers International Football Club plc (9 July 2013 – 25 February 2015).
Early, Aidan:	Business colleague of Craig Whyte.
Easdale, Sandy:	Director, The Rangers Football Club Limited (11 September 2013 – 9 March 2015).
Ellis, Andrew:	London-based property developer who was linked with a takeover of The Rangers Football Club plc in March 2010. Director of The Rangers Football Club plc (20 January 2012 – 1 June 2012) and Director, The Rangers FC Group Limited (20 October 2010 – 21 August 2013).
Farr, Nigel:	Business acquaintance of Phil Betts in City of London who introduced Craig Whyte to Ron Bryan at Octopus Investments (owner of Ticketus).
Findlay, Donald QC:	Defence Counsel for Craig Whyte, Director and former Deputy Chairman of The Rangers Football Club plc (16 August 1991 – 31 May 1999).
Flint, Charles QC:	Member of Scottish Premier League Commission (with Nimmo Smith).

Name	Position/Role
Gilligan, John:	Director, Rangers International Football Club plc (6 March 2015 – 27 May 2017).
Gilmore, David:	Worked for trust company in Guernsey that administered the Employee Benefit Trust for Murray International Holdings Limited. Suggested possible sale of The Rangers Football Club plc to Andrew Ellis.
Glennie, Lord:	Senator of the College of Justice and Principal Commercial Judge in the Court of Session. Offered a Judicial Review of the Appellate Tribunal's decision at the Court of Session.
Graham, Craig:	Chairman of Spartans Football Club and a partner at KPMG. Panel Member of Scottish Football Association Appellate Tribunal.
Green, Charles:	Director, The Rangers Football Club Limited (29 May 2012 – 31 May 2013) and Chief Executive Officer, Rangers International Football Club plc (4 December 2012 – 31 May 2013).
Greig, John:	Former Rangers Captain and Manager. Director, The Rangers Football Club plc (6 February 2004 – 16 October 2011). Honorary Life President from 23 May 2015.

Name	Position/Role
Grier, David:	Financial Advisor at Menzies Corporate Restructuring, which became part of Duff & Phelps.
Harte, Ian:	Director, Rangers International Football Club plc (7 December 2012 – 10 October 2013).
Hodge, Lord:	Deputy President of the Supreme Court of the United Kingdom.
Houston, Craig:	Sons of Struth spokesman.
Irvine, Jack:	Executive Chairman Media House International Limited.
Johnston, Alastair:	Chairman, The Rangers Football Club plc (26 August 2009 – 6 May 2011). Director, Rangers International Football Club plc (5 June 2017 – to present).
Kennedy, Brian:	Businessman – made unsuccessful bid for The Rangers Football Club plc.
King, David:	Director, The Rangers Football Club plc (30 March 2000 – 1 June 2012); Chairman/Director Rangers International Football Club plc (18 March 2015 – 27 March 2020).
Lambias, Derek:	Director and Chief Executive Officer, Rangers International Football Club plc (2 November 2014 – 6 March 2015).
Kingsnorth, Colin:	Executive Director at Laxey Partners Limited.
Leach, Barry:	Director, Rangers International Football Club plc (5 January 2015 – 6 March 2015).

Name	Position/Role
Letham, George:	One of 'The Three Bears.' Director, The Rangers Football Club Limited (15 January 2021 – to present).
Levvy, Daniel:	Director, The Rangers Football Club plc (21 February 1997 – 27 August 2004).
Lothian, Niall:	Past President of the Institute of Chartered Accountants in Scotland and Member of Scottish Football Association Independent Committee.
Mather, Craig:	Sporting Director/Chief Executive Officer Rangers International Football Club plc (24 April 2013 – 6 October 2013).
Martin, Roy, QC:	Oversaw independent investigation relating to allegations made by Craig Whyte concerning Rangers International Football Club's former Chief Executive Officer (Charles Green) and former Commercial Director (Imran Ahmad).
McCoist, Ally:	Manager, The Rangers Football Club (1 June 2011 – 21 December 2014).
McColl, Jim:	Monaco-based Scottish businessman and entrepreneur.
McClelland, John:	Director, The Rangers Football Club plc (14 September 2000 – 16 October 2011).

Name	Position/Role
McDowall, Kenny:	Interim Manager, The Rangers Football Club (21 December 2014 to 12 March 2015).
McGill, Mike:	Murray International Holdings Limited Finance Director. Director, The Rangers Football Club plc (16 October 2009 – 6 May 2011).
McKenzie, Rod:	Lawyer for Harper Macleod.
McIntyre, Donald:	Director, The Rangers Football Club plc (12 June 2006 – 7 October 2011).
Miller, Bill:	American businessman who offered to purchase the business and assets of The Rangers Football Club plc for £25M.
Morgan, Chris:	London lawyer who represented Blue Pitch Holdings investment in Rangers International Football Club plc.
Muir, Donald:	Turnaround specialist/corporate doctor. Lloyds Banking Group-appointed Director, The Rangers Football Club plc (16 October 2009 – 6 May 2011).
Murning, Alistair:	Freelance journalist and Panel Member of Scottish Football Association Disciplinary Tribunal.
Murdoch, Scott:	Proposed Director to Rangers International Football Club plc.
Murray, Sir David:	Principal shareholder, The Rangers Football Club plc (23

Name	Position/Role
	November 1988 – 6 May 2011).
Murray, Paul:	Director, The Rangers Football Club plc (20 September 2007 – 23 May 2011); Chairman/Director Rangers International Football Club plc (6 March 2015 – 2 May 2018).
Murray, Malcolm:	Chairman/Director, Rangers International Football Club plc (7 December 2012 – 8 July 2013).
Newlands, John:	London financier. Gave evidence at trial of Craig Whyte.
Nimmo Smith, Lord:	Former Senator of the College of Justice, a judge of the Supreme Courts of Scotland, sitting in the High Court of Justiciary and the Inner House of the Court of Session. Involved in two separate inquiries that commenced in the spring of 2012: the Scottish Football Association Independent Committee; and the Scottish Premier League Commission.
Odam, Douglas:	Secretary, The Rangers Football Club plc (27 November 2002 – 1 December 2003); Finance Director, The Rangers Football Club plc (30 March 2000 – 1 December 2003).

Name	Position/Role
Park, Douglas:	One of 'The Three Bears.' Director, Rangers International Football Club plc (6 March 2015 – 3 August 2015 and 16 November 2015 – to present). Chairman, Rangers International Football Club plc (27 March 2020 – to present).
Rafat, Rizvi:	Reported as a convicted criminal and, at one time, wanted by Interpol.
Regan, Stewart:	Scottish Football Association Chief Executive Officer.
Russell, Ali:	Chief Operating Officer, The Rangers Football Club plc (June 2011 – February 2012).
Shanks, Ian:	Senior Lloyds Banking Group Manager.
Smart, Bryan:	Director, Rangers International Football Club plc (7 December 2012 – 16 October 2013).
Smith, Gordon:	Director of Football, The Rangers Football Club plc (June 2011 – February 2012).
Smith, Walter:	Manager, Rangers Football Club (16 April 1991 – 31 May 1998 and 10 January 2007 – 15 May 2011). Director, The Rangers Football Club plc (24 June 1992 – 12 August 1998). Non-Executive Director, Rangers International Football Club plc (7 December 2012 – 5 August 2013); Chairman, Rangers International Football

Name	Position/Role
	Club (30 May 2013 – 5 August 2013).
Somers, David:	Director and Chairman of Rangers International Football Club plc (7 November 2013 – 2 March 2015).
Stanton, Howard:	Director, The Rangers Football Club plc (21 February 1997 – 31 May 1999).
Stephen, James:	Binder, Dijke and Otte Joint Liquidator.
Stewart, Nicholas QC:	Part of Scottish Premier League Commission.
Stockbridge, Brian:	Director, The Rangers Football Club Limited (14 June 2012 – 24 January 2014) and Rangers International Football Club plc (4 December 2012 – 24 January 2014).
Summers, Alan QC:	Counsel for Rangers International Football Club plc in Imran Ahmad legal action.
Taylor, George:	One of 'The Three Bears.' Honk Kong-based Investment Banker.
Tudor Nash, Philip:	Director, Rangers International Football Club plc (25 July 2014 – 24 October 2014).
Thornhill, Andrew QC:	Murray International Holdings Limited advocate who defended The Rangers Football Club plc at the Her Majesty's Revenue and Customs First Tier Tax Tribunal.

Name	Position/Role
Wallace, Graham:	Director and Chief Executive Officer, Rangers International Football Club plc (20 November 2013 – 26 October 2014) and Director, The Rangers Football Club Limited (20 November 2013 – 26 October 2014).
Whitehouse, David:	Duff & Phelps Joint Administrator.
Whyte, Craig:	Principal shareholder, The Rangers Football Club plc (6 May 2011 – 13 May 2012).
Wilson, Alex:	Proposed Director to Rangers International Football Club plc.
Withey, Gary:	Partner at Collyer Bristow, the law firm who advised Craig Whyte on his acquisition of shares at The Rangers Football Club plc.

Glossary of Terms

Administration:	Company administration in Scotland is a court-sanctioned process allowing an insolvent company (one that cannot pay its debts) some breathing space to look at certain business rescue options. A moratorium is used to stop creditor pressure whilst the Administrator looks at how best to rescue the company.
Administrator:	A licenced insolvency practitioner.
Company Voluntary Arrangement:	A Company Voluntary Arrangement is an insolvency process that allows a company that cannot pay its debts to make a formal arrangement with its creditors to repay the debt over an agreed period of time.
Court of Session:	The Court of Session is Scotland's supreme civil court. It sits in Parliament House, Edinburgh and is presided over by the Lord President, Scotland's most senior judge. The second most senior judge is the Lord Justice Clerk, who can deputise for the Lord President.

Employee Benefit Trust: Introduced in the late 1980s. Used extensively by high-earning employees — ranging from IT specialists to Premier League footballers. They were used to minimise the income tax and national insurance charge on remuneration to employees and directors and to generate a claim for corporation tax deductions for payments into the trust (A Discounted Option Scheme is a more 'complicated' Employee Benefit Trust).

Floating Charge: A floating charge, also known as a floating lien, is a security interest or lien over a group of non-constant assets that may change in quantity and value. Companies will use floating charges as a means of securing a loan. Typically, a loan might be secured by fixed assets such as property or equipment. However, with a floating charge, the underlying assets are usually current assets or short-term assets that can change in value.

Fixed Charge: If a company fails to repay the loan or enters liquidation, the floating charge becomes crystallised or frozen into a fixed charge. With a fixed charge, the assets become fixed

	by the lender so the company cannot use the assets or sell them.
Liquidation:	Liquidation is a legal process which allows a company that is in financial difficulty to be closed by the directors or its creditors. Assets are sold to repay as much outstanding debt as possible to the creditors before the company's name is removed from the register at Companies House in Edinburgh.

Key Dates and Events

Date	Event
	27 August: Daniel Levvy (ENIC) resigned as Director of The Rangers Football Club plc. 1 September: David Murray returns as Chairman of The Rangers Football Club plc.
2006:	13 July: David Murray suggests that he may sell his shares in The Rangers Football Club plc in three years.
2007:	17 July: City of London Police 'raid' Ibrox over the transfer of Jean-Alain Boumsong (The Steven's Inquiry).
	Autumn: commencement of the Global Financial Crisis.
2009:	19 January: Lloyds TSB acquires HBOS to become Lloyds Banking Group.
	26 August: Alasdair Johnson takes over as Chairman of The Rangers Football Club plc from Sir David Murray.
	16 October: Donald Muir and Mike McGill appointed to Board of Directors of The Rangers Football Club plc.
	24 October: Rangers Football Club Manager, Walter Smith,

Date	Event

claims that Lloyds Bank Group is controlling Rangers Football Club spending.

2010:

6 March: Report on BBC Radio Scotland that a consortium headed by London-based property developer Andrew Ellis was preparing a takeover offer for The Rangers Football Club plc.

27 April: The Rangers Football Club plc confirm that they are under investigation by Her Majesty's Revenue and Customs over offshore payments to players from 2001.

October 2010: Craig Whyte travels to France to meet with Sir David Murray to discuss the possible sale of The Rangers Football Club plc.

18 November 2010: Craig Whyte publishes a statement to the London Stock Exchange confirming that he is considering making an offer for The Rangers Football Club plc and is in talks with Murray International Holdings Limited but that these are at an early stage and there can be no

Date	Event
	certainty that an offer will ultimately be made.
2011:	22 February: Ally McCoist confirmed as next Manager of Rangers Football Club.
	1 April: The Rangers Football Club plc mid-term accounts published. Alastair Johnston explains Discounted Option Schemes (The Small Tax Case) and Employee Benefit Trusts (The Big Tax Case). Alastair Johnston offers that it was a possibility that The Rangers Football Club plc could go 'bust' if The Big Tax Case was lost.
	6 May: It is announced that Craig Whyte had acquired the 85.3% shareholding in The Rangers Football Club plc from Murray International Holdings Limited for £1 after the Takeover Panel had ratified the deal.
	23 May: Chairman Alastair Johnston and Director Paul Murray are removed from Board of Directors of The Rangers Football Club plc. Martin Bain (Chief Executive Officer) and Donald McIntyre

Date	Event
	(Finance Director) are suspended and placed under internal investigation.
	3 August: Rangers Football Club eliminated from UEFA Champions League.
	25 August: Rangers Football Club eliminated from UEFA Europa League.
	27 September: In an interview with The Daily Telegraph, Craig Whyte says The Rangers Football Club plc will have to go into administration if they lose their tax case but he insists he will not allow the club to go bust.
	30 November: The Rangers Football Club plc confirms Craig Whyte was previously banned from company directorship for seven years in 2000.
2012:	9 January: The Rangers Football Club plc shares are suspended from trading on the PLUS Stock Exchange for its failure to submit audited accounts.

Date	Event
	13 February: In view of anticipated failure to meet future funding requirements of the The Rangers Football Club plc, Craig Whyte files a Notice of Intention to Appoint Administrators with Court of Session on 13 February 2012.

14 February: The Rangers Football Club plc formally enter administration after failing to pay £9M in PAYE tax and VAT. Paul Clark and David Whitehouse of Duff & Phelps are appointed as Joint Administrators.

18 January: Her Majesty's Revenue and Customs First Tier Tax Tribunal concludes in Edinburgh. |

Date	Event

A resultant chaos: 14 February 2012 – to 29 July 2012

17 February: Scottish Football Association launch inquiry into Rangers Football Club and Craig Whyte. Inquiry led by Lord Nimmo Smith.

8 March: Scottish Football Association's inquiry state that Rangers Football Club face Disciplinary Tribunal as they breached Articles of Association and that Craig Whyte was not 'fit and proper.'

5 April: After investigating the finances of The Rangers Football Club plc, the Joint Administrators reveal at least £55M is owed to various creditors as well as up to £79M in unpaid tax.

23 April: The Scottish Football Association fine Whyte £200 000 and ban him from Scottish football for life after finding him guilty of bringing the game into disrepute. They also fine Rangers Football Club £160 000 and impose a 12-month player registration embargo on them.

Date	Event

13 May: The Joint Administrators announce they have signed a contract to sell The Rangers Football Club plc to a consortium led by former Sheffield United Chief Executive Officer Charles Green for a deal reportedly worth £8.5M.

29 May: Lord Glennie at The Court of Session rules the Scottish Football Association's registration embargo on Rangers Football Club to be unlawful. The Joint Administrators also publish their Company Voluntary Agreement proposal to the plc's creditors.

12 June: Her Majesty's Revenue and Customs announce they will reject the Company Voluntary Agreement proposal and force The Rangers Football Club plc into liquidation.

14 June: The Company Voluntary Agreement proposal is formally rejected by Her Majesty's Revenue and Customs. The liquidation process of The Rangers Football Club plc commences.

Date	Event
	Charles Green's company Sevco Scotland Limited (subsequently renamed The Rangers Football Club Limited) acquires the football club, Ibrox Stadium and Auchenhowie, then known as Murray Park, for £5.5M.
	18 June: As a result of an investigation by law firm Harper McLeod, Scottish Premier League announce that there is a 'case to answer' over payments to players/dual contracts.
	4 July: Rangers Football Club is not allowed to join the Scottish Premier League.
	13 July: The Scottish Football League allows Rangers Football Club to enter the pyramid, beginning in what was then the Scottish Football League Third Division.

Date	Event

An emergence from chaos: 29 July 2012 – 6 March 2015

2012:

29 July: With a 'Conditional Scottish Football Association Membership,' Rangers Football Club play Brechin City Football Club in the Ramsdens Cup.

3 August: Full membership of Scottish Football Association is granted.

11 August: Rangers Football Club play Peterhead Football Club in first competitive match in Scottish Football League Third Division.

17 August: As a result of Harper McLeod investigation, the Scottish Premier League announce that an Independent Commission had been appointed to consider a case against The Rangers Football Club plc. The Commission was chaired by Lord Nimmo Smith with Charles Flint QC and Nicholas Stewart QC.

31 October: Creditors approve end of the Administration of The Rangers Football Club plc (now called RFC 2012 plc). Binder, Dijke and Otte

Date	Event
	appointed as Liquidator of The Rangers Football Club plc.
	20 November: Her Majesty's Revenue and Customs First Tier Tax Tribunal returns verdict which found in The Rangers Football Club plc's favour by 2:1.
	19 December: The entire share capital of The Rangers Football Club Limited was purchased in a share-for-share exchange, the date of the parent company's (Rangers International Football Club plc) IPO.
2013:	28 February: The Scottish Premier League Independent Commission give their verdict — the use of Employee Benefit Trusts conferred no sporting advantage. The Rangers Football Club plc was found to have not properly disclosed details of Employee Benefit Trusts loans to players. The club was only censured for these administrative omissions and given a £250 000 fine levied on The Rangers Football Club plc.

Date	Event
	30 March: Rangers Football Club win the Third Division title.
	15 April: The Board of Rangers International Football Club plc announce it is commissioning an independent examination (by Pinsent Mason and Roy Martin QC) and report relating to allegations made by Craig Whyte, the previous owner of The Rangers Football Club plc, concerning its former Chief Executive Officer (Charles Green) and former Commercial Director (Imran Ahmad).
	19 April: Following a backlash by supporters, Green steps down as Chief Executive Officer.
	29 May: Walter Smith is named as Chairman of Rangers International Football Club plc.
	30 May: Rangers International Football Club plc announce that the independent examination had been concluded on 17 May 2013. Rangers International Football Club plc found no evidence that Craig Whyte had any

Date	Event

involvement with The Rangers Football Club Limited.

9 July: Malcolm Murray steps down from the Board of Directors of Rangers International Football Club plc alongside Philip Cartmell. James Easdale is named as a Non-Executive Director.

12 July: Craig Mather is appointed as Chief Operating Officer and as Interim Chief Executive Officer of Rangers International Football Club plc.

1 August: A group of shareholders led by Paul Murray and Jim McColl launch a bid to remove Craig Mather, Finance Director Brian Stockbridge, and Director Bryan Smart.

2 August: Charles Green returns as a consultant of Rangers International Football Club plc.

5 August: Angered by Green's return to Ibrox, Walter Smith resigns as Chairman of Rangers International Football Club plc.

Date	Event
	20 August: Charles Green stands down permanently and sells his shares to Sandy Easdale, the brother of James.
	15 October: Paul Murray, Malcolm Murray, Scott Murdoch, and Alex Wilson win a Court of Session case to postpone the Rangers International Football Club plc Annual General Meeting and ensure they can stand for election to the Board of Directors.
	7 November: David Somers appointed as Acting Chairman of Rangers International Football Club plc. The Annual General Meeting is called for 19 December 2013.
	20 November: Former Manchester City Chief Operating Officer Graham Wallace is confirmed as the new Chief Executive Officer of Rangers International Football Club plc.
	21 November: The company's biggest shareholder, Laxey Partners Limited, confirm they will support the current plc

Board at the forthcoming
Annual General Meeting.

22 November: David Somers is
confirmed as Chairman of
Rangers International Football
Club plc on a permanent basis.

16 December: Ally McCoist
hands over his shares in
Rangers International Football
Club plc to supporters group
Calderwood Loyal Rangers
Supporters Club.

19 December: The Board of
Directors of Rangers
International Football Club plc
backed by shareholders at the
Annual General Meeting. Paul
Murray receives 31.7 per cent
of the votes.

2014:

24 January: Brian Stockbridge
resigns from Board of Rangers
International Football Club plc.

12 March: Rangers Football
Club win Scottish Football
League One title and are
promoted to Scottish
Professional Football League
Championship.

6 August: Rangers International
Football Club plc confirm to

Date	Event

the London Stock Exchange
that they are considering a
share issue to raise around
£8M.

3 September: It is revealed that
Newcastle United Football
Club owner Mike Ashley
bought the Ibrox naming rights
from Charles Green for just £1
in 2012.

2 October: Ashley buys more
than four million shares in
Rangers International Football
Club plc increasing his holding
to almost nine per cent.

27 October: Graham Wallace
resigns as Chief Executive
Officer.

14 December: Former
Newcastle Football Club
Managing Director Derek
Llambias is appointed as Chief
Executive Officer of Rangers
International Football Club plc.

21 December: Ally McCoist
leaves his position as Managers
of Rangers Football Club.
Kenny McDowall takes
temporary charge.

Date	Event

Date **Event**

22 December: The Rangers International Football Club plc Annual General Meeting once again votes to keep the current Board of Directors in place, but shareholders reject a proposal to issue a further 54M shares.

29 December: The Scottish Football Association reject Ashley's application to increase his shareholding in Rangers International Football Club plc to 29.9 per cent.

31 December: George Taylor, Douglas Park, and George Letham — known as 'The Three Bears' consortium — buy Laxey Partners Limited's entire 16.32 per cent shareholding in Rangers International Football Club plc.

2015:

2 January: New Oasis Investments Limited (a Company 100% owned by the Family Trust of Dave King) acquires 11,869,505 Ordinary Shares in Rangers International Football Club plc.

5 January: Barry Leach, a senior figure at Ashley's Sports Direct company, is appointed

Date	Event

as Finance Director at Rangers International Football Club plc.

16 January: Dave King requisitions an Extraordinary General Meeting of shareholders in an effort to have Chairman David Somers, Derek Llambias, Finance Director Barry Leach and James Easdale removed from the Board.

27 January: Mike Ashley loans Rangers International Football Club plc £10M secured against Rangers badges and Auchenhowie with a quarter of Rangers Retail Limited transferring to Sports Direct.

25 February: James Easdale resigns as Director of Rangers International Football Club plc.

2 March: David Somers resigns as Director of Rangers International Football Club plc.

6 March: Dave King, owner of 14.5 per cent of shares in Rangers International Football Club plc is appointed to the Board of Directors alongside Paul Murray and John Gilligan. Derek Llambias and Barry

Date	Event
	Leach are both voted off the Board of Directors.

Chapter One

Introduction

Chapter Contents:

1.1 Backdrop

On 14 February 2012, the Scottish company — The Rangers Football Club plc — and parent company to Rangers Football Club (hereafter known as Rangers FC) was placed in Administration. The principal activity of the company was the operation of a professional football club.[1]

In the (first) *Report to Creditors,* dated 5 April 2012, David Whitehouse (Duff & Phelps Joint Administrator) states (page 9):[2]

4 Background

4.3 The Football Club was founded in 1872 and incorporated as the Company in 1899. It is one of the most successful and renowned football clubs in the world. The club plays in the SPL and has been a member of the SPL since its formation.
4.4 The club has won 54 league titles, more top flight national titles than any other football club in the world. The club has also won the Scottish League Cup 27 times and the Scottish Cup 33 times.
4.5 The club has qualified for the UEFA Champions League 15 times since the inception of the competition in 1992. The club was runner up in the 2008 UEFA Cup Final and won the European Cup Winners Cup in 1972.
4.6 The club plays its home matches at Ibrox which is a 51,082 all-seater stadium in Glasgow and the playing staff train at Murray Park located in the outskirts of Glasgow.

Considering this history — and most significant football pedigree — one must wonder what happened when on Sunday 29 July 2012 the football club played Brechin City Football Club (FC) in the Ramsdens Challenge Cup and on 11 August 2012 played Peterhead FC in its first competitive match in the then Scottish Football League (SFL) Third Division. Arguably, this was the lowest point in the club's history at that time.

This book attempts to explain the events that led to this extraordinary situation. It also hopes to explain the recovery of

Rangers FC, and its parent companies, from 29 July 2012 to 6 March 2015 — the date of the so-called 'regime change.' Simply, it is a story of how 'corporate Rangers' (i.e. the companies that operated Rangers FC) contributed to a descent into chaos, how a resultant chaos ensued and the subsequent recovery from this most chaotic period in the history of Rangers FC.

A good starting point for the series of events is probably Friday 6 May 2011. On this day, it was confirmed that Sir David Murray had sold his controlling interest in The Rangers Football Club plc to Wavetower Limited (renamed as The Rangers FC Group Limited) — a company owned solely by Craig Whyte — for £1.[3] The Motherwell-born and London-based venture capitalist acquired Murray's 85.3% shareholding in The Rangers Football Club plc and, thus, became the majority shareholder of this Scottish company.[4] This acquisition was approved by the Takeover Panel [5] and concluded negotiations that had commenced some six months earlier in November 2010. In a statement to the London Stock Exchange, Wavetower Limited pointed out that — by buying Sir David's controlling interest for £1 — the Takeover Panel had given Wavetower Limited dispensation from making a cash offer to all other shareholders of the plc.

In parallel, the Independent Board Committee (IBC) — set up to examine Whyte's bid and consisting of the then plc Chairman Alastair Johnston, Chief Executive Officer (CEO) Martin Bain, former Chairman John McClelland, John Greig and Donald McIntyre — issued its own statement voicing its concerns. In detail, they were not convinced of Whyte's ability to meet any financial sanctions imposed by Her Majesty's Revenue and Customs (HMRC) over an outstanding tax investigation.[6] In addition, and although the IBC accepted that the decision on the sale of the majority shareholding in The Rangers Football Club plc ultimately rested with Murray International Holdings Limited, they went on to add via a statement on the official website of Rangers on 6 May 2011:

Although the IBC has no power to block the transaction, following its enquiries, the IBC and Wavetower have differing views on the future revenue generation and cash requirements of the club and the IBC is concerned about a lack of clarity on how future cash requirements would be met, particularly any liability arising from the outstanding HMRC case.

At the same time, Whyte expressed his delight with his acquisition in the following statement:[7]

As a keen Rangers supporter, I now look forward to helping the club secure its future as a leading force in Scottish and European football. I know the club has gone through some difficult spells in recent times, but it is my commitment to the manager, his backroom team, the players and, most importantly, the loyal supporters that I will do all I can to ensure further success in the weeks, months, and years to come.

Some nine months later, on Monday 13 February 2012 — and in distinct contrast to Whyte's statement — The Rangers Football Club plc filed legal papers at the Court of Session in Edinburgh giving 'notice of its intention' to enter Administration. The company owed substantial amounts of money to HMRC.[8]   In detail, it was revealed that it (The Rangers Football Club plc) had failed to pay £9M in PAYE and VAT from the current financial year (i.e. Financial Year 2011/2012). In a statement released on this day (13 February 2012), Whyte said:[9]

Since I took over the majority shareholding of the club in May last year, it was clear to me the club was facing massive financial challenges both in terms of its ongoing financial structure and performance and the potential consequences of the HMRC First Tier Tax Tribunal.

Whyte stated that the The Rangers Football Club plc was running a £10M annual deficit and that it was in the best interests of the company to cut costs significantly. Moreover — and in terms of the HMRC First Tier Tax Tribunal (FTTT) — he continued in the statement:[10]

4

There is no realistic or practical alternative to our approach because HMRC has made it plain to the club that should we be successful in the forthcoming tax tribunal decision they will appeal the decision. This would leave the club facing years of uncertainty and also having to pay immediately a range of liabilities to HMRC which will be due whatever the overall result of the tax tribunal. In blunt terms, if we waited until the outcome of the tax tribunal, the risk of Rangers being faced with an unacceptable financial burden and years of uncertainty is too great.

On the next day, Tuesday 14 February 2012, The Rangers Football Club plc entered administration. The London firm Duff & Phelps was appointed as administrators. This move followed an unsuccessful legal bid by HMRC at the Court of Session in Edinburgh to appoint its own administrator. It was initially thought that the company had 10 days (from 13 February 2012) to decide on whether to proceed (with administration) but the HMRC action on the Tuesday (14 February 2012) changed the dynamic of the situation. In a statement on the club's official website, Whyte said:[11]

> The club did not want nor anticipate having to take this course of action today but had no option. We had hoped that continued dialogue with HMRC would mean that a decision on administration would not have to be taken for 10 days while all other avenues were explored. Due to its cost structure, the club has been loss-making for many months. This situation has resulted in increasing liabilities and the club has been in discussion with HMRC regarding these liabilities. These liabilities combined with the threat of the outcome of the First-Tier Tax tribunal left the club no option but to formally restructure its financial affairs.

An HMRC statement — following on from the Tuesday morning's legal case — read:[12]

> We can't discuss specific cases for legal reasons but tax that has been deducted at source from the wages of players and support staff such as ground keepers and physios must be paid over to

5

HMRC. Any business that fails to meet that basic legal requirement puts the survival of the business at risk.

In tandem, Paul Clark (Duff & Phelps Joint Administrator) said:[13]

> HMRC have been working closely with the club in recent months to achieve a solution to the club's difficulties. However, this has not been possible due to ongoing losses and increased tax liabilities that cannot be sustained.

At this time, Whyte was thought to be the secured creditor of The Rangers Football Club plc via a floating charge over its assets. Thus, he would have to be paid first ahead of others such as HMRC. This would allow him to pursue other avenues to satisfy the debts which the company owed him if a Company Voluntary Arrangement (CVA) could not be secured. These avenues could involve transferring the assets of The Rangers Football Club plc out to another company (or companies). The new company would continue using the assets of the football club, while the old company — shorn of all its assets — carried the club's indebtedness into the corporate grave.

On 12 June 2012, after almost four months in administration, the major creditor HMRC — to which over 25% of the company's debts were due — made it clear that it would vote against a CVA. Their formal rejection of the proposed CVA on 14 June 2012 meant that The Rangers Football Club plc (the company) entered the liquidation process while the football club (Rangers FC) had to be relocated in a new company structure.[14] It is understood that the creditors' meeting lasted less than 10 minutes with HMRC's decision to reject the CVA having already ensured Charles Green (the preferred bidder) would not receive the 75% backing required. If this offer had been accepted, the company would have aimed to trade its way out of administration.[15]

Duff & Phelps then completed a sale of the business and assets of The Rangers Football Club plc to a new company, Sevco Scotland Limited, which later renamed itself The Rangers

Football Club Limited.[16, 17] Of note, Green completed his purchase of the said business and assets shortly after former manager Walter Smith announced an 11th-hour bid. The 'Smith bid' was in conjunction with Scottish businessmen such as Douglas Park and Jim McColl. The vast majority of Green's £5.5M payment to purchase the business and assets of The Rangers Football Club plc went to administrators Duff & Phelps and on legal costs. Green — who made no mention of Smith's bid — said:[18]

> Following the formal decision of the creditors' meeting at Ibrox Stadium today, the consortium I represent has fulfilled its agreement with the administrators and has completed the acquisition of the business and assets of The Rangers Football Club plc. The transfer of the business and assets to a new company structure has taken effect immediately and the new company is The Rangers Football Club. An application has already been made by the company to register with the Scottish Football Association and to participate in the SPL.

Green became CEO and Ayrshire-born pension fund manager Malcolm Murray — described as a 'Rangers supporter since a boy and a season-ticket holder' — was installed as Chairman. Green had plans for a dual governance structure with a football board and company board.[19] Duff & Phelps announced in October 2012 that creditors had approved an end to their administration and that they had applied to the Court of Session in Edinburgh for the professional services company Binder Dijker Otte (BDO) to be appointed as liquidator. Malcolm Cohen and James Stephen from BDO were appointed as Joint Liquidators. This appointment was legally approved on 31 October 2012.[20]

The new company — The Rangers Football Club Limited — failed to secure the transfer of the football club's previous place in the Scottish Premier League (SPL) but were instead later accepted into the Scottish Football League (SFL). As such, Rangers FC was awarded associate membership and placed in the lowest division, the Third, rather than the First Division as the Scottish Football Association (SFA) and then SPL had sought. This conditional offer allowed the Ramsdens Cup tie with Brechin City FC to go ahead on Sunday 29 July 2012. The eventual transfer of the SFA membership of Rangers FC — after lengthy, protracted and difficult negotiations — was agreed by the SFA upon acceptance of a number of conditions including a one-year transfer ban in time for the club to begin the 2012/13 football season.[21, 22, 23, 24, 25, 26, 27] A joint statement on behalf of the SFA, SPL, SFL and Sevco Scotland Limited (the company which operated Rangers FC) read:[28]

> Following the completion of all legal documentation, the Scottish Premier League will conduct the formal transfer of the league share between RFC (IA) and Dundee FC on no later than Friday 3 August 2012. At this point, the transfer of Scottish FA membership will be complete.

The key points of this joint statement were:[29]

- The SFA received all necessary information and documentation from Sevco Scotland Limited including details of the company structure, shareholders, financial projections, and business plan.
- Sevco Scotland Limited agreed to accept all conditions relating to previous charges of bringing the game into disrepute, namely the 12-month transfer embargo beginning at 0.01a.m on 1st September 2012 and payment of all outstanding fines and costs.
- Sevco Scotland Limited agreed to settle all outstanding football debts to other members of the SFA plus clubs under the jurisdiction of other football associations.
- The SPL and SFL reached agreement on the purchase of a package of broadcasting rights which allowed the former to include Rangers matches in contracts with broadcast partners.
- The SPL reserved its position in relation to the on-going investigation into employee benefits trusts.

8

The Rangers Football Club Limited CEO said that membership finally enabled the club to move forward. He offered:[30]

> The board has had to take some very difficult decisions to gain SFA membership, including accepting the delayed transfer ban and paying outstanding financial penalties.

This became known as The 5-Way Agreement, details of which has never been formally published. Full membership was granted on Friday 3 August 2012. Dundee FC replaced Rangers FC in the SPL after the SFL agreed to place Rangers FC in Division Three (the lowest division). From this date (i.e. the 2012/13 football season), although a 'recovery' commenced, there were a number of Board appointments including Non-Executive Directors and their subsequent resignations/terminations. This lack of stability, at Board-level, contributed to further turmoil.

On 6 March 2015, Dave King was approved by shareholders as Non-Executive Chairman.[31, 32] He bought a near 15% stake in The Rangers International Football Club plc by purchasing the shares held by institutional investors Artemis and Miton. The shares were purchased by New Oasis Investments Limited — a company wholly owned by King's family trust. Its transaction was completed two days after a group of three businessmen — George Letham, Douglas Park and George Taylor — purchased the 16% of shares held by Laxey Partners Limited, which was the single largest shareholder at this time. On the 6 March 2015, King said:[33]

> The club is pretty much broken. It's broken in many areas. Pretty much everything has to be looked at.

Since this date (6 March 2015), the parent companies and Rangers FC started a slow but deliberate renewal. This is a complex and complicated story.

1.2   Current Literature

There has been significant literature published in the print and broadcast media surrounding this story. To date, however, there have been limited books on this most extraordinary period in the history of Scottish and, indeed, British football. Of note, it is actually very difficult to find a book that describes this period in the history of Rangers between 2011 – 2015 in some detail.

At the time of writing, the following books are available:

- Franklin, W. S., Gow, J. D. C., Graham. C., & McKillop, A. (Eds.). (2013). *Follow We Will THE FALL AND RISE OF RANGERS*. Edinburgh: Luath Press Limited.
- Mac Giolla Bhain, P. (2012). *Downfall: How Rangers FC Self Destructed*. Edinburgh: Frontline Noir.
- Smith, P. (2012). For Richer For Poorer. *RANGERS: THE FIGHT FOR SURVIVAL*. Edinburgh: Mainstream Publishing Company Limited.

One may argue that *Follow We Will THE FALL AND RISE OF RANGERS* is written by established 'Rangers men' (for example, the Foreword is written by Walter Smith). In addition, *Downfall: How Rangers FC Self Destructed* is written by a well-known Rangers critic.

I suggest that such literature can be problematic — the outputs can be 'mired' by the authors' unique opinions and beliefs. For example, Mac Giolla Bhain's book is littered with most unhelpful comments (p103):

> Rangers are dead. I will not pretend that in writing that sentence did not give me great pleasure. It did. I am glad that they are dead.

In general, I offer that it is in our nature to preconceive before we understand or think we understand the full picture, thus not only inducing an increased level of bias into a research situation but also a tendency toward tarnishing and (perhaps) producing false results. Simply, for research — or knowledge generation as I call it — to be as bias-free as possible, the researcher (and

10

author) must attempt to remove themselves far enough so that previous experiences and cultural expectations will not have a detrimental or too influential an effect on subsequent outcomes and recommendations.[34]

The aforementioned books were published around the time of the company entering the liquidation process — a significant history has taken place since then. Moreover, and with regard to the Franklin et al (2013) book, I suggest that a 'Rise' had yet to take place. Smith has produced a most readable effort — at the time of publication, 'survival' was very much at stake. Of late, several other titles have appeared:

- O'Donnell, S. (2019). *Tangled Up in Blue: The Rise and Fall of Rangers FC.* Worthing: Pitch Publishing Limited.
- Whyte, C. (2020). *INTO THE BEAR PIT.* Edinburgh: Birlinn Limited.
- Cooper, M. (2021). *Rangers: The Lost Decade.* Self-published: Amazon.

O'Donnell's (2019) book is, however, another personal and subjective perspective. Like Mac Giolla Bhain's effort, there is a clear dislike of Rangers and the book is again littered with difficult and subjective comments. For example (pages 255 - 256):

> Whatever brave new world Murray and his cronies were anticipating, it failed to materialise and in the summer, just a few months after this piece was published, Rangers signed Ronald de Boer from Barcelona and started cheating the taxman.

Whyte's book is, of course, most readable — it is a personal and account of his time at Rangers. Cooper covers the period 2010 – 2020; however, there is limited coverage of the context in advance of Whyte's share purchase in The Rangers Football Club plc. These texts (O'Donnell and Whyte) again offer analysis up to and including the liquidation process of the parent company i.e. The Rangers Football Club plc. In addition, and consistent with the professional backgrounds of the authors, they tend to be somewhat descriptive and lack criticality i.e. they report what happened.

In respect of critical commentary, there is also limited, if any, academic research of Rangers during the period 2011 - 2015. Indeed, a search of the major academic databases from May 2011 to the present offers only two studies from my colleague Stephen Morrow:

- Morrow, S. (2012). *The financial collapse of Rangers: Lessons for the business of football.* Perspectives: Magazine of Scotland's Democratic Left (33), pp. 15-18.
- Morrow, S. (2015). *Power and logics in Scottish football: the financial collapse of Rangers FC.* Sport, Business and Management. 5(4): 325-343

In *The financial collapse of Rangers: Lessons for the business of football*, Morrow offers three elements to his analysis: what happened in terms of the club's activities, management and governance after Craig Whyte took over in May 2011; the management of the club prior to the takeover under the ownership of Sir David Murray; and the takeover deal and financial arrangements, which brought these two parties together. In *Power and logics in Scottish football: the financial collapse of Rangers FC*, Morrow details the implications of power imbalance and over-emphasis on commercial logic on the structure and governance of Scottish football; for example, an over-emphasis on a commercial logic led to power being concentrated in two clubs (Celtic and Rangers) and to other clubs (and, indeed, the league itself) becoming financially dependent on those clubs. The problems at/of Rangers, thus, threatened the stability of other clubs and the league.

At this juncture, I suggest, therefore, that a key point is that there is more to this Rangers FC story than Craig Whyte and the further descent into chaos. In this book, I will argue that there was 'organisational decline' in advance of Whyte's purchase, which was part of the overall descent into chaos. Moreover, the resultant chaos that followed Whyte's departure (for example the Spring/Summer of 2012) has received little attention (in book and academic study) too. As a business academic, I am also interested — like the case of The Royal Bank of Scotland — in organisational recovery and the subsequent emergence from chaos. In this respect, it is important, then, that a book tries to offer a critical and objective account detailing the period prior to Craig Whyte's purchase of The Ranges Football Club plc and to what the, then, Rangers International Football Club plc Chairman (Dave King) described as 'regime change' in 2015.

In summary, what we witnessed — in the period 1998 - 2015 — was an organisational descent into chaos, a resultant organisational chaos, and an emergence of an organisation from this chaos. This affected many people in, and beyond, football and Scotland. From an academic, practitioner and lay perspective, this was — and continues to be — a story of our time that demands significantly more objective and critical analysis and subsequent literature.

1.3   Method

I started thinking about writing this book in the spring of 2012. I have, for a considerable period of time, been interested in Keith Grint's ideas of wicked problems, their complexity, and the leadership of them.[35] In this regard, I recall thinking about the SFA's leadership of this complexity in the spring/summer of 2012 and how I may write about this. As this story, however, developed — and in understanding the various logics at play pre-Craig Whyte to Dave King's 'regime change' in March 2015 — it did occur to me that it would be difficult to understand this history and explain it via a simple linear narrative. Indeed, and in advance of writing this book, I met with several people to seek their advice. I recall Richard Wilson from BBC Scotland asking me how I would even start to 'unpack' this story.

But I did start with a linear narrative or chronological flow. I drew upon the literature that had been offered to date. At this stage, my method of enquiry was an in-depth analysis of secondary sources of literature to identify the key dates and themes. My general timeline is the period 1998 - 2015. This is shown at Figure 1.0.

1998	2000	2002	2006	2007	2008	2011	2012	2015
Dick Advocaat becomes Manager of Rangers FC.	Discounted Option Schemes are introduced.	Hugh Adam criticises the stewardship of The Rangers Football Club by David Murray.	It is suggested that David Murray may sell his shares in The Rangers Football Club plc.	City of London Police raid Ibrox over Boumsong (Steven's Inquiry).	Global Financial Crisis.

Lloyds TSB acquires HBOS.

HMRC tell The Rangers Football Club plc that they will have to pay £24M plus penalties for use of Employee Benefit Trusts. | Craig Whyte buys The Rangers Football Club plc for £1. | The Rangers Football Club plc formally enter administration after failing to pay £9M in PAYE and VAT since Whyte's takeover.

Paul Clark and David Whitehouse of Duff & Phelps are appointed as Joint Administrators.

Charles Green buys the history and assets of The Rangers Football Club plc.

Rangers FC commence play in SFL 3rd Division | Dave King, owner of 14.5 per cent of shares in the Rangers International Football Club plc, is appointed to the Board of the Rangers International Football Club plc alongside Paul Murray and John Gilligan.

Derek Llambias and Barry Leach are both voted off the Board of Rangers International Football Club plc |

Figure 1.0: General Timeline 1998 - 2015

From this linear narrative, several themes did emerge. For example: Sir David Murray's ownership, Discounted Option Schemes/EBTs, Craig Whyte, Charles Green, and the role (and interplay) of the SFA, SPL and the, then, SFL. But this became (and following on from my criticism of other authors' work) a descriptive approach. In addition, and early in the writing of this book, it seemed to me that there were three issues that had to be understood fully to explain this situation i.e. how a football club of this history and pedigree of Rangers FC ended up playing their football in the fourth tier of Scottish football. These issues were:

- The distinction between a company and a football club.
- Language and its use.
- Levels of analysis.

First, it is important to be clear about the distinction between the company and the football club. In detail, I now understand that the football club (Rangers FC) is operated by a company. At present — i.e. the year 2022 — the company is The Rangers Football Club Limited. Indeed, from *The Rangers Football Club plc Annual Report* of 31 May 1986, it states (page 3):

Business Review

The principal activity of the Group is the operation of a professional Football Club...[36]

This 'principal activity' is also echoed in *The Rangers Football Club Limited Annual Report* of 2013:

Principal activities

The principal activities of the Company comprise the operation of a professional football Club in Scotland, together with related commercial activities.[37]

Returning to Duff & Phelps (Joint Administrators), it is interesting that they too refer — throughout their five Reports — to both a company and a club. For example:

16

Interim Report to Creditors dated 10 July 2012.[38]

6. CVA Proposal and Meetings

CVA Proposal

6.1 As set out in the Proposals, a CVA would have enabled the corporate entity formed in 1899 in which the business and assets of the Club vest, to continue to trade.

10. Joint Administrators' Costs and Renumeration Charged

10.9 The history and spirit of the Club have been preserved by the sale which completed on 14 June 2012 and it is now the responsibility of the new owners to secure its future.

Administrator's Progress Report dated 24 August 2012.

Conclusion of the Administration Trading period

5.2: Following the sale of the business and assets of the Company on 14 June 2012, the responsibility for maintaining all trading operations passed to Newco which continues to operate Rangers Football Club.[39]

I do labour this point — it does help explain what happened to Rangers FC. For example, quoting Chris Graham: [40]

Lord Nimmo Smith stated:

> In common speech a Club is treated as a recognisable entity which is capable of being owned and operated, and which continues in existence despite its transfer to another owner or operator. It is the Club, not its owner and operator, which plays in the league.

Lord Glennie also made clear the distinction between club and company when he said:

> This is a petition for judicial review by the Rangers Football Club plc, a company presently in

administration. That company presently operates Rangers Football Club (to whom I shall refer as 'Rangers').

Second, I suggest that one of the problems in understanding exactly what happened to Rangers FC was that much of the literature concerning this story was, at times, casual and lazy. For example, it took me a period of time to be clear on Rangers FC (the football club) and the various corporate entities (i.e. the companies) that operated it. Such entities include: The Rangers Football Club plc (Company number SC 004276); RFC 2012 plc (Company number SC 004276); The Rangers FC Group Limited (Company number 07380537); Sevco 5088 Limited (Company number 08011390); Sevco Scotland Limited (Company number SC 425159); The Rangers Football Club Limited (Company number SC 425159); and Rangers International Football Club plc (Company number SC 437060). Such distinctions are important and, hopefully, will become clear as we progress through this book. At this stage, I provide two examples of this casual and lazy language:

- On 31 May 2013, it was reported that Walter Smith had become Chairman of Rangers. Actually, he became Chairman of Rangers International Football Club plc — the holding company of The Rangers Football Club Limited, which operated Rangers FC.[41]
- The Herald newspaper offered a headline on Wednesday 13 June 2012 which read: "Rangers Football Club Born 1872, died 2012." As well as being inaccurate, this is a most irresponsible headline from a so-called broadsheet.

Third, I consider that the level of analysis is important. For example, are we talking about the football club (i.e. Football Manager/Head Coach and players); the operation (Chief Executive/Managing Director and functional mangers) or the strategy-setting body i.e. Board of Directors? Let me explain — this 'levels' approach is used by the United Kingdom (UK) Ministry of Defence; for example, UK Defence Doctrine (2014) introduces the Levels of Warfare. Levels of Warfare provide a framework within which military activity is rationalised and categorised. This framework depicted at Figure 2.0 also clarifies the interrelationships between the various levels.

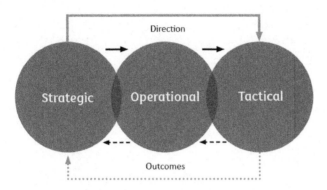

Figure 2.0: Relationships between the Levels of Warfare

The framework at Figure 2.0 — and based on the work of Baron de Jomini (2016) and Clausewitz (1832)[42] — of strategic, operational, and tactical levels does recognise the inevitable compression and blurring between them (levels) and reflects their dynamic interrelationship and non-linear interaction. Indeed, and similar to 'organisational life', the relationship between what is tactical, what is operational and what is strategic is both fluid and contextual. Tactical gains and losses may have far greater strategic effects than that which is immediately obvious (e.g. qualifying for UEFA competitions).

Returning to the organisational context, a brief and general description of each level is as follows:

- Strategic: at this level, we focus on how we develop and sustain competitive advantage?
- Operational: at this level, we 'operationalise' the strategy. In addition, we focus on the present i.e. how do we make work more effective and efficient.
- Tactical: at this level, this is *where the fighting takes place* or the *coal face* where work actually happens. In a football

19

context, the playing of the game takes place at the tactical level of analysis.

This approach to 'levels thinking' is brought together and is shown at Figure 3.0, which details the current structure of the companies (Rangers International Football Club plc and The Rangers Football Club Limited) and the football club (Rangers FC).

Level (UK Ministry of Defence)	General Work Functions	Level
Strategic	Chair, Board Director, Chief Executive Officer/Managing Director	Rangers International Football Club plc
Operational	Chief Executive Officer/ Managing Director and Functional Managers	The Rangers Football Club Limited
Tactical	Football Managers/Head Coach and Players	Rangers FC

Figure 3.0: General Work Functions and Level

Figure 4.0 details the companies involved in the operation of the football club i.e. Rangers FC.

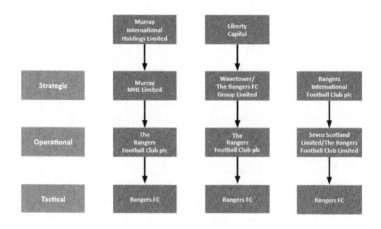

<u>Figure 4.0: Corporate Rangers and Rangers Football Club</u>

More generally, and as a business academic undertaking research, I follow a structured approach to knowledge generation. For example: establish a general research question; review the current literature relating to this general research question to identify 'gaps' in knowledge to establish a specific research question; offer a methodology as a means of 'surfacing' data; analyse and discuss the data; and conclude on this analysis to answer the specific research question. According to Barbara Czarniawaska — in her 2014 book *Social Science Research* — this structure may align with the following:[43]

a)   There is something strange going on in the world (Exordium).
b)   Has someone else explained it (Literature Review)?
c)   I had better go and learn a bit more about it. But how (Method)?

d)   Now I understand it, I will try and explain it to others (Narration).

e)   What does it remind me of — is there someone else who thinks similarly (Proof)?

f)   This is the end (and the point) of my story (Peroration).

Applying Czarniawaska's work to Rangers during the period 1998 – 2015, I suggest the following:

a)   There is something strange going on in the world (Exordium)? Indeed, there is. For example, from the Nexis Uni® data base, and using the keyword "Glasgow Rangers," there were 2826 articles written between 13 February 2012 and 31 July 2012.

b)   Has someone else explained it (Literature Review)? To an extent — some people have written about Rangers (see 1.2. Current Literature section), but I am not sure if they have explained the story fully especially the period 2011 – 2015.

c)   I had better go and learn a bit more about it. But how (Method)? My research strategy is a case study. In the social sciences, a case study is a research method involving an up-close, in-depth and detailed examination of a subject of study (the case) as well as its related contextual conditions. Case studies are a popular research method in business — they aim to analyse specific issues within the boundaries of a specific environment, situation, or organisation. According to their design, case studies in business research can be divided into three categories: explanatory, descriptive and exploratory. This is an explanatory case study — its aim is to answer 'how' or 'why' questions with little control on behalf of the researcher over occurrence of events. Simply, a case study is a way to apply the theoretical knowledge gained from the academic literature to real life situations.

d)   Now I understand it, I will try and explain it to others (Narration). I discussed my linear narrative (Figure 1.0) with Roger Hannah of The Scottish Sun. Roger offered that what we witnessed in the period 2011 – 2015 was a descent into chaos, a resultant chaos, and an emergence from chaos. As business academic, and drawing on Roger's views, I interpreted this as organisational (i.e. company) decline, organisational (i.e. company) retrenchment and organisational (i.e. company) recovery. More generally, however, I suggest that there was 'corporate decline' in advance of 2011.

The picture, then, stared to become clearer to me. In the business and management literature, we have models, theories, or frameworks to draw upon to help explain what happened. Without them, it can be hard to make sense of what is happening in the world around us. There are, of course, lots of models, theories, or frameworks to study Rangers (companies and club) in the period 1998 – 2015. To understand fully what happened, the following two academic frameworks are utilised to provide an in-depth analysis:

- McKiernan 's 6-stage Model of Organisational Decline and Renewal. McKiernan 's model offers the generic features and stages of organisational decline and renewal. The six-stages involved are: 1) organisational decline; 2) triggers for action; 3) diagnostics; 4) retrenchment; 5) recovery; and 6) renewal.[44]
- The Change Curve. The Change Curve has been utilised as a method in helping people understand their reactions to significant change or upheaval.[45] It is suggested that there are three distinct transitional stages: shock and denial; anger and depression; and acceptance and integration.

These are shown at Figures 5.0 and 6.0 respectively.

23

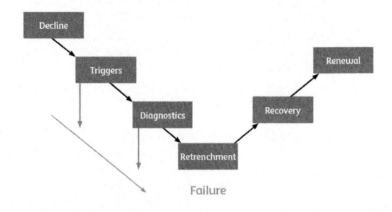

Figure 5.0:   McKiernan 's 6-stage Model of Organisational Decline and Renewal

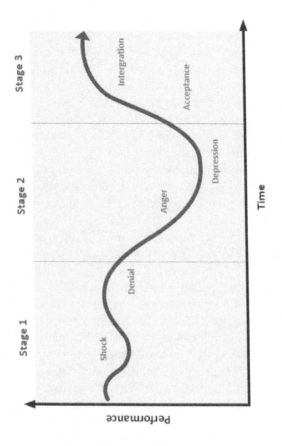

Figure 6.0: The Change Curve

Leavy & McKiernan 's 6-stage Model of Organisational Decline and Renewal helps us to understand, in detail, organisational decline (this framework can help explain the decline of, for example, the Royal Bank of Scotland). In addition, the period 1998 – 2015 involved many people — not just the Board of Directors of corporate Rangers. Many stakeholders were involved including, but not limited to, shareholders, players, leagues and federations, supporters, media, and national and local government. To understand how the supporters — and I suggest the 'Rangers-minded' media — reacted, I draw upon the Change Curve. This curve can help us understand their reactions (i.e. emotional response) to a significant change or upheaval.

Simply, and revisiting the title of this book, it was corporate Rangers (i.e. the many companies involved) that had a most significant effect on Rangers FC (the club) and its many stakeholders. I suggest that Murray International Holdings Limited was a factor in the **Decline** of The Rangers Football Club plc. In addition, the global financial crisis and the resultant relationship between Lloyds Banking Group (LBG) and Murray International Holdings Limited (**Triggers**) ultimately led to the sale of The Rangers Football Club plc. Whyte's ownership involved **Diagnostics** and ultimately **Retrenchment**. Green initiated a **Recovery** of both corporate Rangers and the football club from the **Retrenchment** period. And all of this (i.e. corporate activity) had a direct impact on stakeholders, which can be understood via the Change Curve. In this regard, I have located the story of Rangers within these frameworks. This is shown at Figure 7.0.

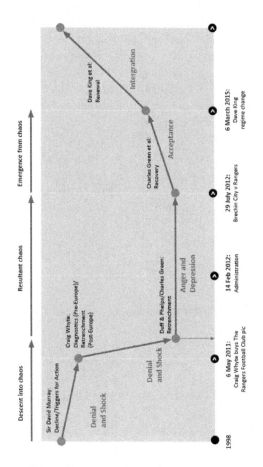

Figure 7.0: A Framework for The Story of Rangers

27

e).   What does it remind me of — Is there someone else who thinks similarly (Proof)? Other authors have commented on the organisational decline (for example: Franklin et al; Mac Giolla Bhain; Smith; and O'Donnell). But to date, I am not sure if this very intense period specifically 2011 — 2015 has been given detailed treatment.

f)   This is the end (and the point) of my story (Peroration): See the Purpose of Book below.

1.4   Structure of Book

This book has six chapters. These chapters are based on, and reflect, the Method described above:

•   Chapter One — Introduction

A descent into chaos: 1 June 1998 to 14 February 2012

•   Chapter Two — Corporate Decline: 1 June 1998 – 6 May 2011
•   Chapter Three — Craig Whyte and the Journey to Administration: 6 May 2011 – 14 February 2012

A resultant chaos: 14 February 2012 – to 29 July 2012

•   Chapter Four — Administration to Liquidation: 14 February 2012 – to 29 July 2012

An emergence from chaos: 29 July 2012 – 6 March 2015

•   Chapter Five — Brechin City FC and onwards: 29 July 2012 – 6 March 2015
•   Chapter Six — Conclusion/Personal Reflections

1.5   Purpose of Book

The purpose of this book is to attempt to explain the complexity of this story and to locate — in one volume — what happened to

Rangers FC from an objective viewpoint. The book will not seek to judge or blame or to make recommendations. It is also not an investigative piece of journalism. There is, I consider, an academic interpretation and I hope that I can explain it. The book will also contribute to several academic literatures: business strategy; Scottish society; Scottish history; and sport and football in general.

1.6   Audiences

This book will be of interest to several audiences:

- Fans and stakeholders of Rangers FC.
- Football fans in general but especially those who may want to understand the issues involved in a club's corporate parents' decline, retrenchment, and recovery. In this respect, I hope, therefore that Chapter Six (Reflection) may be applicable to other football clubs who are, or may be, in similar situations.
- Academics and practitioners who are interested in professional sport and elite professional football.

1.7   Chapter Summary

Backdrop

On Friday 6 May 2011, it was confirmed that Sir David Murray had sold his controlling interest in The Rangers Football Club plc to Wavetower Limited — a company owned solely by Craig Whyte for £1. Some nine months later, on Tuesday 14 February 2012, The Rangers Football Club plc entered administration. The London firm Duff & Phelps (a specialist restructuring practice) was appointed as Administrators. On 12 June 2012, after almost four months in administration, the major creditor HMRC (to which over 25% of the company's debts were due) made it clear that it would vote against a CVA. Their formal rejection of the proposed CVA on 14 June 2012 meant that The Rangers Football Club plc (the company) entered the liquidation process while the football club had to be relocated in a new company structure.

Duff & Phelps then completed a sale of the business and assets of The Rangers Football Club plc to a new company Sevco Scotland Limited, which later renamed itself The Rangers Football Club Limited. This new company failed to secure the transfer of the football club's previous place in the SPL but was instead later accepted into the SFL. Rangers FC was awarded associate membership and placed in the lowest division, the Third, rather than the First Division as the SFA and then SPL had sought. This conditional offer allowed the Ramsdens Cup tie with Brechin City FC to go ahead on Sunday 29 July 2012.

From this date (i.e. the 2012/13 football season), although a 'recovery' commenced_there were a number of Board appointments including Non-Executive Directors and their subsequent resignations/terminations. This lack of stability, at Board-level, contributed to further turmoil.

Dave King was approved by shareholders as Non-Executive Chairman on 6 March 2015. He bought a near 15% stake in The Rangers International Football Club by purchasing the shares held by institutional investors Artemis and Miton. Its transaction was completed two days after a group of three businessmen — George Letham, Douglas Park and George Taylor — purchased the 16% of shares held by Laxey Partners Limited, which was the single largest shareholder at this time. Since this date (6 March 2015), the company and football club have started a slow but deliberate renewal.

Current Literature

In this book, it will be argued that there was 'organisational decline' in advance of Whyte's purchase. Moreover, the resultant chaos that followed Whyte's departure (for example between 2012 – 2015) has received little attention too. In this respect, it is important that a book tries to offer a critical and objective account detailing the period prior to Craig Whyte's purchase of The Rangers Football Club plc to what the previous Rangers Chairman (Dave King) described as 'regime change' in 2015.

In summary, what we witnessed — in the period 1998 -2015 — was an organisational descent into chaos, a resultant organisational chaos, and an emergence of an organisation from this chaos. This affected many people in, and beyond, football and Scotland. From both an academic, practitioner and lay perspective, this was — and continues to be — a story of our time that demands significantly more objective and critical analysis.

Method

Two academic frameworks are used to help interpret what happened:

- McKiernan 's 6-stage Model of Organisational Decline and Renewal.
- The Change Curve.

31

1.8   Reflection

Once we understand the difference between a company and a club and the correct language, the 'Rangers story' is about the companies that operated the club being sold and bought at the strategic and operational levels of analysis. Simply put — and, indeed, a conclusion from the outset — I suggest that it was instability/distress in the companies (i.e. corporate Rangers) that operated Rangers FC that caused a significant effect on the club and its many stakeholders at the tactical level of analysis.

In this respect and echoing, therefore, the view of David Kinnon:[46]

> ...with liberal allegations of 'cheating' aimed at the club, although in fact it was the victim rather than the perpetrator of corporate wrongdoing.

A descent into chaos: 1 June 1998 to 14 February 2012

Chapter Two

Corporate Decline:
1 June 1998 – 6 May 2011

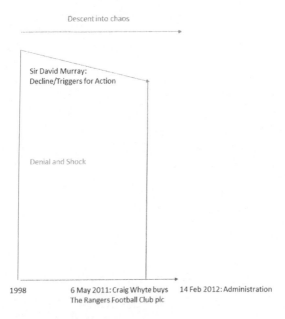

Descent into chaos

Sir David Murray:
Decline/Triggers for Action

Denial and Shock

1998   6 May 2011: Craig Whyte buys   14 Feb 2012: Administration
              The Rangers Football Club plc

Chapter Contents:

2.1   Introduction

> Unfortunately our fears were confirmed, not just about Craig
> Whyte but about the way the club had been run in the years
> before he took ownership. Nobody likes to be right when the
> outcome was as bad as it was for the club, but it turned out we
> were entitled to be worried.

Mark Dingwall[47]

I do not consider that it is fair to blame the descent into chaos
solely on Craig Whyte. Several writers, for example, suggest that
the decline started on 1 June 1998 when Dick Advocaat became
Rangers FC Manager.[48]   From the perspective of a casual
observer, there did seem to be some concern with the finances of
'Rangers'; for example, ex-Director Hugh Adam and journalist
Graham Spiers voiced significant concerns at the perilous state
of the finances of The Rangers Football Club plc early in this
millennium.   Moreover, it was reported that the departure of
Howard Stanton in 1999 was due to his (Stanton's) concerns with
the corporate finances.[49]   Indeed, in his Introduction, Smith
offers a summary of Sir David's time at The Rangers Football
Club plc:[50]

> Murray will always be revered as the chairman who delivered
> nine in a row, who broke down the barriers and who dared to
> dream. His was ambition with a capital 'A'. Realistically, he
> will also be remembered for allowing debt to spiral and for the
> painful end to his reign, with the decision to hand over to a man
> subsequently deemed 'not fit and proper.' His stay in the
> chairman's seat was far longer than those of his predecessor –
> but his departure was protracted too.

In this respect, it is not the purpose of this book to write about
the history of Rangers FC under Sir David Murray's ownership.
Several books are available in this regard.[51]   That being said, I
do consider that the ownership, governance and leadership of
The Rangers Football Club plc in the first decade of this century
was most significant and, of note, set the context for Craig
Whyte's purchase of the Rangers Football Club plc in May 2011.

More generally — and from a review of the available literature in addressing this 'decline' — this chapter has three sub-sections:

2.2   Finance: Annual Reports and Associated Commentary.
2.3   Employee Benefit Trusts.
2.4   Ownership, Governance and Leadership.

Each will be examined in turn. Simply put, during the period 1998 - 2011, I offer that there was:

- Financial excess; for example, the signing of Tore Andre Flo for £12M, which was the peak of Rangers FC transfer activity.
- The global financial crisis of 2007/2008 when banks became nervous about lending money (i.e. the 'credit crunch').
- Significant interest in The Rangers Football Club plc from HMRC.
- (Perhaps) a Chairman who became tired of owning and running Rangers.[52]

I also draw on the two academic frameworks (McKiernan 's 6-stage Model of Organisational Decline and Recovery and The Change Curve) to explain further this decline and the related emotional response of the many stakeholders that were involved. Consistent will other chapters, I will close by offering a Chapter Summary.

2.2   Finance: Annual Reports and Associated Commentary

In this sub-section, the key areas of finance from 1998 – 2011 will be examined. In doing so, I will draw primarily on key information that is contained within the Annual Reports of The Rangers Football Club plc and Murray International Holdings Limited. In effect, this analysis will provide a timeline of key events.

1998

On 9 May 1998, Celtic FC won the 1997 - 98 Scottish Premier Division and, thus, a new football era commenced i.e. the single-team dominance of Scottish football, by Rangers FC, ended. The 1997 - 98 Scottish Premier Division season was the last season of Scottish Football League Premier Division before the change to the Scottish Premier League, which began on 1 August 1998. On 1 June 1998, Dick Advocaat became the 10th Manager in history of Rangers FC.[53] On 25 September 1998 — in The Rangers Football Club plc Annual Report (to 31 May 1998) — David Murray comments:[54]

> Season 1997/98 will be seen by many as the end of a glorious era but in my view, we can now treat this year as the springboard for a great new future for the Club. Although we came very close, silverware eluded us, and no one can deny that this was a very disappointing outcome. We of course have not taken this set back lying down and have regarded it as a catalyst for significant restructuring both on and off the field of play. We have started the new season with a new coaching staff and almost a completely new team which we are hopeful will allow us to progress in both domestic and European competition.

Some two months later, on 23 November 1998, David Murray celebrated 10 years as owner of The Rangers Football Club plc.

1999

On 24 February 1999, The Bank of Scotland acquired the 'floating charge' over the income and assets of The Rangers Football Club plc — a security which would crystallise into a fixed charge should an insolvency event occur with the bank also taking a 7% stake in the club.[55] On 31 May 1999, Howard Stanton resigned as a Director of Rangers Football Club plc. Paul Smith suggests that this was because he (Stanton) and Murray were at: "loggerheads over spending plans that appeared, from the outside at least, to be unsustainable."[56,57]

On 17 November 1999, in *The Rangers Football Club plc Annual Report* (to 30 June 1999), David Murray comments:[58]

Financial Results

...additional player costs in building the new team, exacerbated by considerable injury problems which resulted in a higher number of players being retained resulted in a trading loss of £10.9m million (1998 - £4.7 million loss). The accounting policy in respect of transfer fees, noted below, required that player acquisition costs were capitalised and amortised to the Profit and Loss account over the period of the relevant contract. This resulted in a charge of £12.1 million producing an operating loss for the period of £23.1 million (1998 - £12.8 million loss). Many times I have said that, while losses of this size are not only unsustainable but totally unacceptable in the long term, they are necessary during a restructuring phase. I believe that this is now substantially complete and whilst we have had to incur a much higher level of debt in the short term, we are always looking at various areas of additional revenue and new methods of reducing operating overheads. Your Board firmly believe that we have now gone through a substantial restructuring and we can look forward to much greater financial stability. Indeed, after 5 months of this current financial year the signs are most encouraging.

General

During the year, Murray International Holdings Limited undertook a restructuring of its investment portfolio. This resulted in a demerger of the Club into a new holding company, Murray Sports Limited, which is controlled by exactly the same shareholders as Murray International Holdings Limited.

2000

This was a significant year for the plc in terms of finance. For example, Smith notes:[59]

As the millennium celebrations loomed, Rangers announced plans for a major share issue. The blueprint was designed to raise in the region of £40M and it was hoped the opportunity would entice big hitters from home and abroad. The timing of the share issue coincided with soaring debts, which had peaked at around £20M at that stage, a figure that the club had admitted was a concern.

On 30 March 2000, Dave King was appointed as a Director of The Rangers Football Club plc.[60] This formed part of a share issue that would see David Murray make an investment of £32.3M in new shares through Murray Sports Limited and its wholly owned subsidiary RFC Investment Holdings Limited. To quote Smith:[61]

> Shades of financial smoke and mirrors perhaps, but the headline-grabbing figure was a shot in the arm in the region of £53M.

The Guardian newspaper, commenting on further investment, is instructive in this regard. For example, in their 31 March 2000 article *Rangers to float as it chases global glory:*

> Rangers football club, on track for its 49th Scottish premier league title, announced plans yesterday to float the business on the stock market and disclosed that talks are under way with a number of potential media investors. The Glasgow club, listed on the unregulated Ofex market, also announced immediate plans to raise £53.1m through an issue of new shares, including a £20m cash injection from South Africa-based Scottish businessman Dave King who will become a director of the club. Mr King, a financial services tycoon who regularly caddies for golfer Gary Player, is a lifelong Rangers fan. The money from the rights issue will be used to eliminate debt running at £40m, buy new players and develop the Rangers academy for bringing on young footballers. Chairman David Murray, who owns 62% of the club, said further cash from the flotation would go into building Rangers as a global brand. The one for three rights issue will push out more than 15m new shares at 345p each. Mr Murray is taking up £9.3m worth. Turnover at the club in the last six months of 1999 increased by almost 40% to £29.8m while profits were £112,000.

In addition, the Financial Times reported as follows: [62]

Glasgow Rangers, the Ofex-listed football club, is to seek a full stock market listing in the near future. The club, which yesterday launched a 1-for-3 rights issue to raise 53.1 mln stg, said it had not considered a listing previously because of uncertainty about the potential of media rights and the impact of the Bosman ruling. The issue has not been underwritten, but Murray Sports, a company controlled by David Murray, the chairman of Rangers, is taking up its option, representing an investment of 23 mln stg. A further 20 mln stg is being invested by Ben Nevis Holdings, a company associated with Dave King, a Scottish businessman and lifelong Rangers fan who is based in South Africa.

Later in the year, on 4 September 2000, John McClelland was appointed as a Director of The Rangers Football Club plc[63] and on 30 September 2000 Hugh Adam resigned as Director of The Rangers Football Club plc.[64]

On 17 November 2000, in The Rangers Football Club plc Annual Report (to 30 June 2000), David Murray comments:[65]

Financial Results

Despite the effect of injuries which prevented us from reducing the playing squad to the extent which we had planned, we have significantly reduced the trading loss to £4.688 million (1999 - £10.974 million). After accounting for the amortisation of player acquisition costs, the operating loss for the year was £22 million (1999 - £23.1 million).

2001

On 4 May 2001, The Bank of Scotland merged with Halifax to form HBOS.[66] On 17 November 2001, in The Rangers Football Club plc Annual Report (to 30 June 2001), David Murray comments:[67]

This year, taking into account player acquisitions, contract extensions and the new training ground, has set our highest spend ever. Including recent player movements, our total investment exceeds over £40 million over the last 18 months.

However, poor financial results over three years confirm what has been emerging for some time: football in Scotland as we know it cannot sustain our present ambitions.

2002

On 2 February 2002, shortly after the publication of The Rangers Football Club plc Annual Report of 2001, former Director Hugh Adam published an article in The Scotsman newspaper entitled *Adam shakes Ibrox pillars with warning of bankruptcy*. They key text is as follows:

> There are licensed premises in Glasgow where the regular patrons will consider the recent deeds and utterances of the former Rangers director, Hugh Adam to be nothing less than acts of treason. This should be regarded as a natural, almost understandable, reaction from immovably devoted supporters of the Ibrox club to the decision by Adam to unload his 59,000 shares in Rangers on the basis that they were heading towards worthlessness, thanks to the unsatisfactory business methods of the chairman, David Murray. Almost certainly viewed as an even more heinous offence would be Adam's claim that Celtic are run much more competently and that investment in the Parkhead club would be a much sounder proposition for anyone wishing to purchase shares in a football institution. It would be tempting for many to dismiss Adam's action as merely a gratuitous attack on Murray by a disillusioned, 76-year-old ex-employee carrying a grudge. But Adam has been a candid critic of the way Rangers have operated for years, ever willing to voice his unease - indeed, his incomprehension - at losses he has always insisted were unsustainable.   Not given to sensationalism, this essentially conservative disciple of prudent forward planning and low-risk business principles did, however, cause something of a shock by observing almost matter-of-factly that, if Rangers continue on their present track, their ultimate destination will be bankruptcy.

> That's the logical conclusion to a strategy that incurs serious loss year on year, said Adam. In the past five years - and it's all there in the last annual report - Rangers have lost GBP 80million. Now, the banks are well

41

known for being a bit more tolerant of companies whose core business is a popular pursuit like football. But there is a limit to how far backwards they can bend to accommodate you. David Murray has always had an amazing persuasiveness when it comes to getting people to put money into his businesses, but the signs are that those sources have dried up. The GBP 40million worth of shares that ENIC (English National Investment Company) bought a few years ago are now worth about GBP 15million, with no evidence to suggest that they will recover. The money itself, that which was actually invested, was lost some time ago. Now the latest investor, Dave King from South Africa, will know that his GBP 20million shareholding is worth around half, or even less, of what it was when he bought. No proper businessman will want to buy into that kind of loss.

Adam sold 12,000 of his 59,000 shares last year and the balance of 47,000 just recently. For the latter, he got GBP 1.15 each; three years ago, they were valued at GBP 3.45.

But I'm 76 and haven't had a dividend in years, so what's the point of me keeping shares until they dwindle to nothing? And I'm certain the people at ENIC won't be too pleased with their investment.

On 5 July 2002, David Murray relinquished the Chairmanship of The Rangers Football Club plc. He was replaced, as Chairman, by John McClelland. David Murray remained the largest shareholder and owner and retained the title of Honorary Chairman.[68] Again, Hugh Adam offered further criticism of David Murray:[69]

Impresarios are for opera, theatre and the circus, where you do not have to confront your rivals head-to-head. One dimensional management is not for professional football clubs. Frankly, in future years, David might be remembered as actually having held Rangers back.

On 4 September 2002, in *The Rangers Football Club plc Annual Report* (to 30 June 2002),

Douglas Odam, Finance Director comments:[70]

> The operating loss for the year of £31.9m (2001 – £16.4m) includes the net charge for player registration of £12.8m (2001 - £8.5m) which includes amortisation cost and gain on sale. A new bank facility has been arranged with specific long term funding secured on the Club's assets. Rangers Development Fund have advised their intention to raise and donate sufficient funds over the long term to support and repay part of this borrowing facility.

2003

On 30 September 2003, in *The Rangers Football Club plc Annual Report* (to 30 June 2003), John McClelland states:[71]

> Last summer I explained that the Club, after many years of significant investment in our playing squad, and more recently on our state of the art facility at Murray Park, had embarked upon a three year business plan to stabilise and improve the club's finances. Our trading loss for last year of £11.2m reflects a £7.9m improvement versus the £19.1m loss for the previous year...
>
> Rangers Football Club's annual expenditure on football salaries has been amongst the highest in Britain. As with many other clubs, that expenditure will reduce. However, even at this reduced level, it will continue to be comparable to other successful European Clubs.

2004

On 6 February 2004, Alastair Johnston was appointed as a Director of The Rangers Football Club plc.[72] Some three months later, an article in the Observer newspaper detailed concerns about the significant debts at Murray International Holdings and, of note, Rangers 'location' and involvement in this group of companies.[73] For example, the article reads as follows:

> Analysis of Murray's business empire reveals little for Rangers supporters to cheer. The Ibrox club, marooned in the relatively

43

impecunious Scottish Premier League and eclipsed by arch-rival Celtic on the pitch, has been losing money. However, the stricken club is more deeply embedded in the MIH empire than it might at first appear. For a start, a number of other MIH subsidiaries have lucrative service contracts at Ibrox and are effectively dependent on Rangers. Charlotte Ventures made a quarter of its annual turnover providing financial advice to the club last year. Carnegie Information Systems billed it for more than £1.1m for IT services, and Azure Support Services a whopping £2.8m for catering - more than two-thirds of its total sales. These services probably double the football club's 'contribution' to MIH's overall performance. More to the point, however, is the money MIH is still owed from selling its stake in Rangers in 1999. The stake was transferred to Murray Sports, which still owes MIH £53m and has no obvious way of paying the money back. Rangers' shares, traded in limited numbers on Ofex, are worth 77.5p, which values Murray Sports' 65 per cent Rangers shareholding - its sole important asset - at £28m. The situation is already dragging MIH's bottom line south. In its last set of accounts, the company wrote down the value of Murray Sports' debt to it by £7.6m. It also knocked £4.2m off the estimated value of its own small stake in Murray Sports. Because of Rangers, then, nearly £12m was removed from the MIH profit and loss account last year - exceptional items, admittedly, but enough to put MIH in the red. This means several things. The good news for Rangers fans is that MIH could probably never contemplate letting the club go under, unless it were prepared to write a full £53m off its books. In this light, the £15m revolving credit facility MIH has extended to Rangers looks less like a paternalistic bail-out and more like the action of a concerned investor protecting its wider interests. But, by the same token, selling the club is almost impossible. Any rich sugar-daddy wanting control of one of Britain's most famous clubs would be asked to pay not the £28m that the Murray stake is worth, but £53m. Perhaps even more, if the deal jeopardised the contracts that Charlotte Ventures and other MIH companies have with Rangers. Even then, all the new owner would inherit is a club with mountainous debts of its own. Most of Rangers' £68m of borrowings are long-term, so there is no danger of a Leeds United-type meltdown. Equally, Rangers is unlikely to trade its way out of trouble soon. It made a loss of £30m last season and £35m the year before. Its numbers would look even worse if the club's bean-counters had not revalued the stadium and training ground last year, raising its 'tangible assets' from £93m to £130m. Unlike clubs in the English Premiership, Rangers derives little television income from its domestic league. Ibrox has embarked on a three-year plan to return to profitability, but that involves cutting the wage bill: expensive stars such as Barry Ferguson have already been offloaded. More will follow this season. Murray has spoken publicly of a rights issue to clear Rangers' debts - but that could cost him yet more tens of millions, and it is by no means clear that smaller shareholders such as Enic would play along. Either way, however, he seems to be stuck with the club. And – to the anguish of any fans dreaming of Russian oligarchs and billionaire benefactors – the club is stuck with him. The Ibrox 'convinced' can probably look forward to a long diet of bread and water.

On 27 August 2004, Daniel Levvy (ENIC) — and now Executive Chairman of Tottenham Hotspur Limited — resigned as Director of the plc. Some four days later, on 1 September 2004, David Murray returned as Chairman of the plc. This 'return' is reviewed in a Daily Mirror article:[74]

> Perhaps we did spend too much doing that, we all bought into it at the time, but I gave the supporters my word that when the situation had to be resolved I would do so, and that is what I have confirmed here. I think it was something that was never in doubt that we were going to do, it was just a timing issue. We felt collectively that it was time to attend to the problem and that time is now. We have a debt at the moment of just over pounds 70m and decided to issue pounds 57m of new shares at pounds 1 each of which Murray International, my holding company, will subscribe a minimum of pounds 50m if required, but that doesn't stop other people coming in as existing shareholders or even new ones to buy some of the equity. Murray is now hoping Rangers can move forward and revealed he is looking forward to resuming his hands-on involvement in the club.

Murray was unable to proceed with the share issue until he had bought out ENIC's shares, a development which gave him and his companies 86% of the club's stock.[75] This, however, added a further level of complexity. For example, Smith notes:[76]

> Delve into the detail and you soon come to realise that the club's affairs have been far from straightforward. Like the other companies under the Murray umbrella, Rangers was just one piece in a very large jigsaw.

On 12 November 2004, The Herald newspaper offered detailed analysis:[77]

> MIH is underwriting the Rangers rights issue to ensure that a minimum of £50m is raised after expenses.
>
> The Rangers prospectus this week revealed Bank of Scotland had committed borrowing facilities of £37m to the football club, comprising a £15m revolving credit facility to meet day-to-day working capital requirements and a £22m, 25-year term loan to refinance existing debt. The scale of this facility raised eyebrows, given Murray's pledge at last month's annual meeting of Rangers virtually to wipe out the club's debt in 12 months. However, Murray claimed it had been put in place because Rangers had to satisfy auditor Grant Thornton that it had sufficient funds for its rights issue business plan even "if everything went wrong", a worst-case scenario which might involve a swift exit from the UEFA Cup and even the unlikely event that Rangers failed to qualify for European football next time. A source familiar with Bank of Scotland said of the £37m facility:
>
>> (They) know Murray very well. This sort of thing is what (they) do. I think the comfort factor is extremely high.
>
> On MIH's overall debt level, Murray said:
>
>> If you actually look at the Murray group - out with the property positions we have and Rangers - we don't carry a lot of debt. The majority of our debt will be property.
>
> Murray emphasised that this debt was backed by both property assets and income from these. He has linked up with Bank of Scotland on several major property deals. The net debt of MIH

climbed by 21% to £230m in its last financial year to January 31. Emphasising the underwriting of the rights issue would be financed "from out our own (MIH) funds," Murray said:

> There is no pull back to Rangers. There is no way Rangers can be affected by Murray. There are no cross-guarantees.

The "bottom-line" result obscured a more complex picture, however. Operating profit from continuing operations actually fell from £12.5m to £9m. Murray was at pains to emphasise the need to pay down Rangers' debt and to spend only income which was coming in the door, believing this was far more important in the short term than results on the park. He said:

> Our wages target this year is going to be ... about 35% to 40% of turnover. This would be a big reduction from the 53% proportion for the year to June 2004.

Giving his key message to those shareholders being invited to put up funds in the rights issue, he told The Herald:

> You cannot raise money on the back of a prospectus if it is not your intention to run the club fiscally correct. That is what is very important.

In the BBC Documentary, *Rangers — the men who sold the jerseys*, Roger Isaacs states that Rangers owed the bank in excess of £70M.[78] Simply, £50M came from one of Murray Group companies who borrowed the money from bank. Rangers paid money back to the bank. So, the bank loaned with one hand and took back with other hand. Ultimately, the Murray International Holdings Limited debt increased. Of note, during the period 2003 – 2005, journalist Graham Spiers repeatedly used the term 'financial vandalism' when describing David Murray's stewardship of Rangers.[79, 80, 81, 82]

2005

On 31 August 2005, in *The Rangers Football Club plc Annual Report* (to 30 June 2005), David Murray comments:[83]

47

Success on the field was achieved by further improvements off the park. Our basic business strategy was laid out in the Rights Issue documentation of 9 November 2004. You have played a great part in maintaining the Club's financial stability with £51 430 995 being raised. I was delighted with the response with over 3000 shareholders subscribing to the issue and in many cases applying for additional shares.

In this respect, Smith notes:[84]

> In the final analysis, the 2004 issue pulled in £51.4 million – although £50.3 million of that had come from Murray International Holdings as underwriters of the scheme. The remaining £1.1m came from existing and new shareholders.

2006

On 10 March 2006, David Murray entered a deal with JJB Sports. A one-off payment of £18M was received in addition to £3M per year for 10 years. Rangers retail stores were closed and staff were made redundant.[85]

On 13 July 2006, David Murray suggested that he may sell the club in 3 years.[86]

2007

On 16 July 2007, The Rangers Football Club plc was 'raided' by the City of London Police in connection with The Stevens inquiry.[87, 88]

On 30 July 2007, in *The Rangers Football Club plc Annual Report* (to 30 June 2007), David Murray comments:[89,90]

> The operating loss for the year before exceptional items amounted to £5.1m against a profit of £4.4 million in the previous year due to the impact of the UEFA Champions League and higher amortisation charges on player registrations. The exceptional items include a 10million gain on the sale of player registrations and an additional provision of £10m in relation to

lease terminations. The trading loss coupled with working capital movements and investment in fixed assets and player registrations resulted in a closing net debt position of £16.5m.

In September 2007, the global financial crisis commenced.[91]

2008

On 16 September 2008, in *The Rangers Football Club plc Annual Report* (to 30 June 2008), David Murray comments:[92, 93]

> Net operating expenses increased as a consequence of improved turnover salary and related costs within the playing squad and costs associated with European competition. Amortisation of player registrations amounted to £7.0m as we added £18.0m to improve the composition of the playing squad. The gain on disposal of player registrations largely comprises the sale of Alan Hutton and resulted in profit before interest and tax of £8.3m, an improvement of £13.3m on the prior year and the best performance for a number of years. These operational movements together with an investment in our playing squad resulted in a cash outflow of £6.4m for the year and closing net debt of £21.6m.

On 17 September 2008, the BBC stated that the Lloyds TSB was set to take over HBOS in a £12B deal.[94] This, then, had significant implications for Sir David Murray and his group of companies (Murray International Holdings Limited).

More generally, in October of this year, a bank rescue package totaling some £500B was announced by the British Government as a response to the ongoing global financial crisis. After two unsteady weeks at the end of September 2008, the first week of October 2008 saw major falls in the stock market and severe worries about the stability of British banks. The plan aimed to restore market confidence and help stabilise the British banking system.[95] Questions regarding bank solvency, declines in credit availability and damaged investor confidence affected global stock markets where securities suffered large losses during 2008 and early 2009. Economies worldwide slowed during this period as credit tightened and international trade declined. Governments and central banks responded with unprecedented fiscal stimulus, monetary policy expansion, and institutional bailouts. Simply, banks stopped lending — this period of time became widely known as the 'credit crunch'.

In the wider *Murray International Holdings Limited Annual Report of 2008*, dated 12 November 2008, it states:[96]

> Over the last twelve months, the economic environment has undoubtedly changed for the worse and become more uncertain. No one foresaw that virtually all UK's banks would require substantial injections of capital to support their finances or the depth of the global financial crisis. Despite rights issues and government intervention, credit supply remains tight and the UK residential and commercial property markets continue to deteriorate. These developments, coupled with the onset of recession, make for a poor economic outlook.

Storm clouds were, indeed, coming....

2009

This was a very difficult year for Murray International Holdings Limited. Although outside the scope of this book, it is important — at this juncture — to focus on the finances of both Rangers plc and Murray International Holdings Limited in this year. A brief summary is as follows.

On 19 January 2009, HBOS was officially acquired by Lloyds TSB to create the Lloyds Banking Group (hereafter known as Lloyds).[97] In general, banks stopped lending. Lloyds inherited a level of debt of Murray International Holdings Limited at £942B.[98] Indeed, from early 2009, several writers highlighted that all was not well with Murray International Holdings Limited and The Rangers Football Club plc:[99]

> With Bank of Scotland and Rangers both struggling to retain their status as big-league players, it is tempting to believe the fate of one will determine the fortunes of the other. The troubled

50

bank, which came close to collapse last summer, is awaiting the verdict of its new Lloyds Bank owner and the knives are being sharpened for some deep cutbacks. Everybody knows that Rangers has been one of its biggest customers for years and with lending rules across the banking sector being tightened, logic suggests that the flow of funds into the Ibrox bank account will be turned off.

On 26 August 2009, Sir David Murray announced that he was to step down as the Chairman of The Rangers Football Club plc. Alastair Johnston was named as his successor.[100] On 31 August 2009, Sir David Murray resigned as Director of The Rangers Football Club plc. On 16 October 2009, Donald Muir and Mike McGill were appointed as Directors of The Rangers Football Club plc. Some eight days later, on 24 October 2009, Rangers FC Manager Walter Smith claimed Lloyds was controlling Rangers' spending following the appointment of one of their representatives, Donald Muir, to the board.[101, 102, 103] The Rangers Football Club plc issued a statement in which they also insisted they would not be forced to sell any players in the forthcoming January (2010) transfer window. But there was an absence of any commitment to invest money in improving a squad that had not seen a single player bought for more than a year. In this respect, Rangers FC said on their website (and quoted from the Belfast Telegraph (26 October 2009)):[104]

> For the avoidance of doubt, and due to recent media speculation, the club can confirm that while there have been tentative enquiries regarding the sale of the club, there are none that have realised an offer. As stated by Sir David Murray, it is not necessarily about price, but the new owner having the capability to take the club forward that remains essential. It is important to highlight the statement issued by Lloyds Banking Group to the press on Saturday evening that Lloyds Banking Group recognises the importance of Rangers Football Club to its supporters, shareholders and the wider football industry in Scotland. The bank continues to be very supportive of both the club and the board as they manage the business through the more difficult economic conditions currently prevailing. As such,

51

there is no need for the club to sell assets during the January transfer window.

In the said Belfast Telegraph article (and quoting Walter Smith):

> It's been up for sale for a while. I think we have been fairly honest about the situation. The players at the club have been up for sale since January and we haven't bought a player for what will be 18 months in this transfer window. The quicker that gets cleared up, the better it will be for Rangers.

In addition, on 31 October 2009, The Times newspaper offers:[105]

> Most Rangers fans must wonder how on earth their team, playing in front of home crowds of 51,000 and competing in the first group stage of the Champions League elite with its revenues of £12 million, can possibly be in financial trouble. The answer is that Rangers do have money worries, but they are small in comparison to those of the main owner, Sir David Murray's company – Murray International Holdings (MIH). And getting Rangers' difficulties sorted out quickly does look like a key part of saving MIH, on which not just Sir David's family fortunes depend, but also the jobs of 3,500 people. Indeed, the demands of keeping MIH going will be the key reason why Sir David stepped down from the Rangers chairmanship, for the problems at the family business vastly overshadow those of the football club. Up to 2008, when the present recession began, MIH's business looked reasonably healthy. It spanned a range of activities - buying and selling 330,000 tonnes of steel a year, running office and shopping complexes valued at £649 million, running call centres for other companies who paid MIH £50 million, and managing investment funds of £48 million. Altogether, these activities produced for Sir David's business an income of £542 million, of which Rangers' share was £52 million or slightly less than 10 per cent. The looming problem, however, was that this performance had been built on a massive pile of debt. By the beginning of 2008, MIH's net debt was a staggering £759.3 million, massively up from £468.3 million two years previously. However, recession means that the value of these assets has plummeted. The value of Sir David's property empire is likely to have fallen by nearly half since 2007. The value of his steel companies and their stocks will also have

dropped because construction work has shrivelled. So the assets may by now be worth less than the total debt. Sir David could solve a lot of these problems by selling bits of the business. That's where Rangers come in because, unlike most of the rest of the MIH business, football clubs have not lost as much of their value as have, say, office blocks. The first priority of Lloyds Bank, which has let most of MIH's borrowings, is to keep MIH going so that it can recover most, if not all, of its money. So selling Rangers, at the very minimum to recover £30 million of debt, is probably a top priority. So cutting costs, and players' wages are by far the biggest cost, is the top priority. Selling a player not only cuts the wage bill, but also has the handy bonus of bringing in transfer fees to cut the debt. The bank can force this to happen because it will have the security of MIH's and Sir David's shareholdings in the club. The unspoken threat, if Rangers do not cut costs and fail to make any debt repayments, is that the bank will seize the shares and Sir David will get nothing from any subsequent sale. Lloyds is not running Rangers, but Alastair Johnston, Sir David's successor as chairman, has little option but to do what the bank wants.

Continuing with this theme, on 1 November 2009, two articles appeared in The Sunday Times that offered further difficult reading for Rangers fans:

Rangers Empire Falling into Ruin. Rangers limp into two vital games crippled by debts that dictate a bleak financial future.[106]

The tactics for Dundee United this afternoon, or for Unirea Urziceni on Wednesday night, suddenly don't seem so important. The real strategy debate inside Rangers right now is how to deal with debt. The Murray Group, who own Rangers, cannot delay dealing with debt because they are under pressure from the Lloyds Banking Group who, in turn, are under scrutiny from the politicians and taxpayers who bailed them out last year. When Bank of Scotland became part of the Lloyds Banking Group as the institutions failed a year ago, levels of debt which had previously been permissible for Rangers suddenly became alarming figures for them. That is why Donald Muir, a freelance financial trouble shooter, has been parachuted into Rangers' board, to start removing it in large chunks. This would also make Rangers more attractive to potential buyers, who are not exactly knocking the door down just now. The wish of Alastair Johnston, the new chairman, that a sale could be achieved with dignity already seems a forlorn one. When manager Walter Smith confirmed suspicions that the club was no longer in control of its own affairs last Saturday night, he was mostly correct to say it was instead being run by the bank. It may not be direct control, as subsequent press releases from both Lloyds and the club were at pains to stress, but their debt dictates every move Rangers make, or don't make, just now.

Rangers' owner kicks accounts into long grass[107]

The owner of Rangers, Sir David Murray, has delayed making public the accounts of his steel and property companies until next March, avoiding further scrutiny of the club's financial health. The tycoon had been due to file the results of Murray International Holdings (MIH) - which owns a majority stake in Rangers - with Companies House this weekend. They would have shown the financial performance of his businesses for the 12 months to the end of January this year. However, a document issued to Companies House four weeks ago informed the government records body that MIH, along with a number of its subsidiaries, would change its financial year. Murray now has until the end of March next year before he has to file his next set of accounts, by which time he hopes to have found a buyer for the club. Last week it was reported that Dave King, a South African entrepreneur with a minority stake in Rangers, was among those who had expressed an interest in buying the club, which has debts of about £30m. Its last set of figures, for the year to the end of January last year, showed MIH had a net debt of £760m, of which £704m was in bank loans. Some £423m of these loans were due within a two-year period, which is likely to have come to an end now. The financial state of Murray's business empire has been under scrutiny in recent days after Walter Smith, the Rangers manager, claimed that the banks were running the club following the appointment of Donald Muir, a specialist in turning around ailing companies, to the board.

A spokesman for the tycoon said:

> I can confirm that we have changed the reporting period to June. By then [next March], we expect there to be a

lot less uncertainty around economic market conditions and more clarity around other issues, such as Rangers football club. It is the case that there is likely to have been an upturn in market conditions by then. The changes will also align the group's reporting period with that of Rangers.

Bryan Johnston, a divisional director at stockbroker Brewin Dolphin in Edinburgh, said he believed Murray - who was ranked Scotland's sixth richest man in this year's Sunday Times Rich List, with a personal fortune of around £500m - could be hoping to have found a buyer for the club before he has to publish the accounts.

> Private companies can do what they like and as long as they adhere to the rules and file reports in due course, they are perfectly entitled to change their reporting periods, said Johnston. The decision may well be to do with Rangers in the sense that he may want to be in a position to announce a sale and do that at the same time he is going to file the accounts. He should remember that bad news is bad news, whether he reports it in six months' time or now.

It is understood that the group's property arm, Premier Property Group - to which Muir, who was involved in the rescue of Northern Rock, has also been appointed as a board member - has been hit hard by the downturn. Lloyds Banking Group, Rangers' bankers, said that it supported a plan adopted by the club to "make the business sustainable".

As Lloyds was concerned with level of the Murray International Holdings Limited debt, it instigated a financial restructuring of Murray International Holdings Limited (this was known as Project Charlotte) prior to the financial statements being audited.[108] As such, the Murray International Holdings Limited accounting period was extended from 31 January 2009 to 30 June 2009 (and published on 28 April 2010). Murray International Holdings Limited also noted that Group net debt at the 2009 year-end had risen by £172.4m on the prior year to £954.8m.[109]

Therefore, in a 'credit crunch', and as banks stopped lending, I suggest that Sir David Murray was no longer in control of his own destiny. The media – with very few exceptions – did not question Murray's business model for Rangers pre-2009. It seems that the business model for Rangers/Murray International Holdings Limited was to borrow, speculate and gamble that the only direction for the economy was up. [110, 111]

On 12 November 2009, in *The Rangers Football Club plc Annual Report* (to 30 June 2009), Alastair Johnston comments: [112]

> In terms of financial performance, the Club has operated in the most challenging economic climate for many years. Turnover, due to the absence of European progression, reduced from a record high of last year of £64.5m to £34.7 m. The lack of European competition resulted in a decrease of £10.9 in commercial revenues whilst the 19 game reduction in the number of matches played in all competitions produced a £3m decline in ticketing, hospitality, events and catering income. Net operating expenses decreased by £8.6m to £48.2 m reflecting the reduced cost of non-progression in European competition including player incentives in comparison to last year. Clearly, costs at this level cannot be maintained without Champion's League income. Amortisation of player contracts amounted to £8.8 m following the £11.8m additions in the year. The gain on disposal of player registrations, primarily of Carlos Cuellar and Daniel Cousin of £6.2m represents a reduction of £1.5m on the prior year and resulted in a loss after tax of £12.7m. The cash outflow in relation to the operational activities of the Club, together with the net investment of the playing squad, resulted in a £9.6m increase in the net debt to £31.3m at 30th June 2009.

Sir David also said that Murray International Holdings Limited was also actively marketing its investment in Rangers for sale, adding:

> Stakeholders and supporters alike can be assured than the principal shareholder is completely committed to finding an appropriate investor to secure the future development and steward the progression of the club. [113]

At the trial of Craig Whyte in 2017, it was stated that by the end of 2009, the business empire of then Rangers owner, Sir David Murray, was left 'technically insolvent' after the global financial crisis. Sir David said he was simultaneously hit by, effectively, a triple whammy: the collapse of the global steel market; the collapse of the property market; and the collapse of the banking sector.[114] Murray International Holdings Limited Finance Director, Mike McGill, said that at the time that the Murray Group's liabilities were greater than its assets and that, if asked, would not have been able to pay its debts. A decision was, therefore, made to sell 'Rangers' as part of the Murray International Holdings Limited financial restructuring.[115]

It was later in this year (i.e. 2009) that a 'sale' of The Rangers Football Club plc was becoming a distinct possibility. In his book (INTO THE BEAR PIT), Whyte states that he was aware — in October 2009 — that Sir David Murray wanted to sell Rangers; for example, it was announced to the London Stock Exchange that Sir David Murray would consider selling his controlling interest. On Sunday 25 October 2009, it was also reported that although they had yet to receive a formal offer, Rangers were attracting 'tentative' sale enquiries as finance worries continued.[116]

At this time (i.e. 2009), the Aggregate Nominal Value of Issued Shares in The Rangers Football Club plc was 108 791 499.[117] Moreover, from The Rangers Football Club plc Annual Report of 2009, Murray MHL Limited owned 62 060 479 shares i.e. 55.09% of The Rangers Football Club plc. In addition, RFC Investment Holdings Limited — a subsidiary of Murray Sports Limited — owned 37 448 489 i.e. 34.45% of The Rangers Football Club plc.[118]

2010

On Saturday 6 March 2010, it was reported on *Sportsound* on BBC Radio Scotland and The Scotsman newspaper that a consortium headed by London-based property developer

Andrew Ellis was preparing a takeover offer.[119] Two days later, The Rangers Football Club plc confirmed that Sir David Murray was in takeover talks with 'certain interested parties', including Ellis, that may lead to an offer or offers for the entire issued share capital of the company.[120, 121, 122, 123]

The general outlook did, however, remain most bleak; for example, on 27 April 2010 The Rangers Football Club plc confirmed that they were under investigation by HMRC over offshore payments to players from 2001.[124, 125] This investigation would become 'The Big Tax Case.' Although there was ongoing and significant interest in the 'Rangers takeover,' this story (i.e. the HMRC investigation) appeared to slip under the radar.[126, 127, 128]

In addition, *PA Newswire: Sport News* reported some significant events in May and June of this year:[129]

3rd May 2010: Ellis reveals he is "optimistic" his proposed takeover will move closer to completion later in the month. Ellis claims that if his reported takeover bid of £33 million goes through, he will give Smith a new contract and offer the role of life President to Murray.

9th June 2010: Ellis' consortium, RFC Holdings (Guernsey) Limited announce to the Stock Exchange they are in "advanced negotiations" to buy a controlling interest in Rangers.

But on 15 June 2010, it was announced that Murray International Holdings Limited was no longer "actively marketing its controlling stake in the club for sale" after failing to receive a suitable offer.[130, 131] Although several questions were raised by the Rangers Supporters Trust, Murray Intentional Holdings Limited suggested that The Rangers Football Club plc would implement its business plan that was supported by Lloyds. At this time, two articles appeared in *The Scotsman* newspaper that offered insightful analysis:

16 June 2010: *David Murray rides out the storm as he takes Rangers off the market.*

Eight months after putting his controlling interest in the Scottish champions up for sale when the club's finances were ailing and external investment was required, Murray announced he has not received any offer for the club which he regards as acceptable. It brings to an end any prospect of London property developer Andrew Ellis acquiring Rangers. The former Northampton Town chairman, through a specifically formed company RFC Holdings (Guernsey) Ltd, had declared his interest in buying out Murray's stake in the Ibrox club back in March. Ellis entered a period of due diligence with a view to his £33 million purchase of the Murray Group's shares in Rangers but his bid, which was constantly the object of widespread scepticism, was killed stone dead by the current owner's dramatic move last night. Murray released a statement to the London Stock Exchange just before close of business last night which read:

> On 26 October 2009, the principal shareholder of The Rangers Football Club plc (the "Club"), Murray International Holdings Limited ("MIH"), advised the board of directors of the Club that it was considering options regarding the controlling shareholding in the Club held by its subsidiary Murray MHL Limited. MIH also advised that this may or may not lead to it disposing of some or all of its majority stake in the Club to a third party. MIH has received interest in its controlling stake from a number of parties. At this time, however, the board of MIH has not been able to secure an offer which it considers to be in the best interests of the Club, its shareholders and its fans. Following on from the success of winning the 2009/10 SPL title and thereby securing participation in the group stages of the Champions League during 2010/11, the Club recently announced that the football management team had signed new contracts. At the same time the board of directors of the Club announced improvements in its financial position compared to the previous year stating. We believe the outcome of our recent positive discussions with the bank gives us a real platform for operational stability at the Club and we thank Lloyds for their support. We have a

clear business plan in place and will continue to maximise efficiencies and endeavour to increase our non-playing income. The board of directors of MIH therefore considers that the interests of stakeholders are presently best served by providing the football management team and board of directors with an opportunity to implement its business plan which is supported by Lloyds Banking Group. In these circumstances, MIH hereby announces that it is no longer actively marketing its controlling stake in the Club for sale.

Rangers, whose most recent annual accounts recorded a debt of £31million, had not purchased a player in the transfer market since August 2008 as they were forced to operate under strict restrictions imposed by Lloyds. However, recent negotiations with Lloyds, which involved manager Walter Smith and chief executive Martin Bain, reached an agreement which saw funds released to strengthen the squad for the start of the following season. The talks persuaded Smith to commit himself to a final year in charge of the team, after which his assistant Ally McCoist would succeed him as manager.

16 June 2010: *Long-term player David Murray in no hurry to offload prized asset so close to his heart.*

It's clear Murray did mean to sell Rangers. But, as he emphasised again and again, both in private and in public, there was no-one out there rushing to take the form of a white knight, no Dubai property magnates willing to plough millions into the club. And even had there been, Murray had outlined from the start that he had to be assured such characters had Rangers' best interests at heart. In reality, the only ones showing interest were limping like mangy dogs towards Ibrox. The sniffing around had to stop eventually. Murray put an end to it last night, although, again, the wording has to be acknowledged. MIH, the statement said, is no longer "actively marketing its controlling stake in the club for sale", but Murray will remain open to offers. In effect, little has changed, except for Ellis' removal from the equation. While, for some, the announcement made to the Stock Exchange last week on behalf of Ellis' company RFC Holdings - saying only that the company was in "advanced negotiations" to buy a controlling interest in Rangers - offered an impression of something about to happen in terms of a buy-out, others were right to interpret it as little more than a death rattle on the part of the London-based property dealer. There is a difference between being diligent and being dilatory. Ellis, as the announcement made clear last week, was not even at the stage of making a formal offer, after months of apparent courtship. Had he been trying to buy a house he would have been kicked into touch long ago by the frustrated selling party.

2011

In this year, The Rangers Football Club plc did not publish an Annual Report. However, in the Murray International Holdings Limited Annual Report to 30 June 2010 — published on 1 April 2011 — it says:[132,133]

> Given the greater operational and financial stability of the club, largely reflecting participation in the Champions League in successive years, the Group considers that the interests of the club were best served by providing the football management team and board of directors with an opportunity to implement its sustainable business plan, supported by Lloyds Banking Group. Despite speculation and comment on the contrary, stakeholders and supporters should be assured that the Group and I, as respective principal shareholders, are committed to finding a long term investor capable of developing the Club going forward.

Moreover, on this date (1 April 2011), Alastair Johnston stated that it was a possibility that Rangers could go 'bust' if The Big Tax Case was lost. To many Rangers fans, the existence of a life-threating tax case was news indeed.[134] The existence of this potential liability may have been increased Murray's attempt to sell Rangers Football Club plc and, of note, may have put off any potential purchaser.[135]

2.3   Employee Benefit Trusts

In this sub-section, analysis on EBTs will be offered. First, EBTs will be described. Second, the 'Rangers EBT' will be explained. Third, when and why they were used by The Rangers Football Club plc will be suggested. Finally, thoughts on the outcome of the EBT will be offered: namely, the perception of wrongdoing by Rangers FC and the potential HMRC liability making The Rangers Football Club plc difficult to sell.

2.3.1   What are Employee Benefit Trusts?

According to Real Business Recue,[136] EBTs were in existence for several decades (since the late 1980s) and were used to provide benefits to former and existing company employees and their families. Such Trusts were originally intended to act as an incentive for employees to encourage greater loyalty towards a company and to reward members of staff at the appropriate time. In setting up these Trusts, companies were able to attract highly qualified staff likely to remain with them for the long-term. Laingrose Trust Management states that they were used extensively by high-earning employees ranging from IT specialists to Premier League footballers.[137] In detail, and of note, they were used to minimise the income tax (PAYE) and National Insurance charge on remuneration to employees and Directors and also to generate a claim for corporation tax deductions for payments into the said Trust.[138]

Simply, an EBT was a Trust set up by a company to provide benefits for some or all of its employees. The company would pay money into the Trust and the Trustees would pay it out later to the employees. In the meantime they (Trustees) would invest the money. As a 'discretionary trust' with offshore Trustees, it was designed to act as a 'money box' for those high-earning employees who did not need immediate access to their full remuneration package. In other words, EBTs were often used to pay deferred bonuses to high-earning employees. Thus, companies and personnel could minimise their liability for tax (PAYE) and National Insurance. As such, an EBT affected the way these contractors and other Trust beneficiaries were paid.

Rather than receive all money as traditional 'earned income', they (employees) were instead paid a minimal salary and then the remainder of their remuneration by way of low interest loans routed via a sub-Trust set up by their company, which limited significantly the associated burden of tax (PAYE) and National Insurance.[139]

In recent years, EBTs were targeted by HMRC who claimed they were a form of a disguised remuneration scheme. The UK Government believed that, in many cases, the overriding motivation for setting up an EBT was tax avoidance and so introduced legislation to deter their use via the Finance Act of 2011.[140] In this respect, the BBC's Douglas Fraser suggests that the tax authorities had not gone after 'Rangers' because HMRC had much interest in Scottish football; rather, it was because it (HMRC) had been told to step up its pursuit of those who avoided tax — this was in context of the global and UK financial crisis of 2007/2008. [141] EBTs were used by around 5000 British companies of all sizes. The potential 'tax take' for the UK Government was, therefore, most significant. Many of these offshore EBTs have now been closed with HMRC citing the reason as follows: [142]

> EBTs have increasingly been used for avoidance purposes, with the aim of providing employees and directors with benefits in ways that aim to defer, minimise or avoid liability to income tax (and PAYE) and employers' National Insurance Contributions (NICs).

The idea was that there was no employee tax charge until the Trustees distributed benefits, which could be many years after those benefits had been earned. The tax charge might be theoretical rather than real and the employee or ex-employee could have moved to a low tax jurisdiction or tax haven.

2.3.2   The Rangers EBT

In the book, *Follow We Will THE FALL AND RISE OF RANGERS,* Kinnon states:[143]

The Trust was established in the year 2000 for senior executives of the Murray Group. In the year 2001, it was extended to Rangers for payment of senior executives and football players.

This 'Trust' is evident in *The Rangers Football Club plc Annual Report* of 2001 (In the Full Group Accounts (to 30 June 2001)). At the Notes to the Accounts, Note 5 Staff Costs, it states:

> The Rangers Employee Benefit Trust was established to provide incentives to certain employees. Payments to the Trust are charged to the Group Profit and Loss Account in the year incurred.

In this year (2001), £1 010 000 was paid into the Trust. Further details (i.e. payments by year from 2001 - 2010) are shown in Table 1.0.

Year	Notes to the Accounts (5. Staff Costs)	Contribution to Employee Trusts (£)
2001	The Rangers Employee Benefit Trust was established to provide incentives to certain employees. Payments to the Trust are charged to the Group Profit and Loss Account in the year incurred.	1 010 000
2002	The Rangers Employee Benefit Trust and Murray Group Management Ltd. Remuneration Trust were established to provide incentives to certain employees. Payments to the Trust are charged to the Group Profit and Loss Account in the year incurred.	5 176 000
2003	The Rangers Employee Benefit Trust and Murray Group Management Ltd. Remuneration Trust were established to provide incentives to certain employees. Payments to the Trust are charged to the Group Profit and Loss Account in the year incurred.	6 791 000
2004	The Rangers Employee Benefit Trust and Murray Group Management Ltd. Remuneration Trust were established to provide incentives to certain employees. Payments to the Trust are charged to the Group Profit and Loss Account in the year incurred.	7 252 000
2005	The Rangers Employee Benefit Trust and Murray Group Management Ltd. Remuneration Trust were established to provide incentives to certain employees. Payments to the Trust are charged to the Group Profit and Loss Account in the year incurred.	7 241 000
2006	The Rangers Employee Benefit Trust and Murray Group Management Ltd. Remuneration Trust were established to provide incentives to certain employees and other service providers. Payments to the Trust are charged to the Group Profit and Loss Account in the year incurred.	9 192 000
2007	The Rangers Employee Benefit Trust and Murray Group Management Ltd. Remuneration Trust were established to provide incentives to certain employees. Payments to the Trust are charged to the Group Profit and Loss Account in the year incurred.	4 988 000
2008	The Rangers Employee Benefit Trust and Murray Group Management Ltd. Remuneration Trust were established to provide incentives to certain employees. Payments to the Trust are charged to the Group Profit and Loss Account in the year incurred.	2 291 000
2009	The Rangers Employee Benefit Trust and Murray Group Management Ltd. Remuneration Trust were established to provide incentives to certain employees. Payments to the Trust are charged to the Group Profit and Loss Account in the year incurred.	2 360 000
2010	The Rangers Employee Benefit Trust and Murray Group Management Ltd. Remuneration Trust were established to provide incentives to certain employees. Payments to the Trust are charged to the Group Profit and Loss Account in the year incurred. On the basis of expert tax advice, the Club is defending a query raised by HMRC into this Trust which is part of an ongoing tax enquiry scheduled to be heard by a tax tribunal before the end of the year.	1 358 000
		47 659 000

Table 1.0: Payments to The Rangers Employee Benefit Trust
(2001 – 2010)

In total, and from the Annual Reports of The Rangers Football Club plc 2001 - 2010 (Notes to the Accounts, Note 5/6 Staff Costs), £47 659 000 was paid into these Trusts. All payments made under these Trust arrangements were disclosed fully within the relevant financial statements by The Rangers Football Club plc. This was echoed by the then plc Chairman, Alastair Johnston who said that the major accounting firms were content with the use of the Rangers EBT.[144]

The Rangers EBT was relatively straightforward. Simply, it is understood that the employer (The Rangers Football Club plc/Murray International Holdings Limited) paid money into an offshore Trust (Murray Group Management Limited Remuneration Trust (MGMRT)). In addition to his fully disclosed salary, a player or other employee would be able to take out loans from his individual sub-Trust of which he was the nominated 'protector' to an amount that was already agreed and stipulated in a 'side letter.'

Kinnon offers that the mechanism of the Rangers EBT was set out at paragraph 103 of the Judgement, which is subject to appeal by HMRC:[145]

- Payments were made into a main Trust. Sub-Trusts were created for each individual.
- As part of contractual agreements, players entered into a contract and the club gave a letter of undertaking to recommend the payer for inclusion within the Trust arrangements. The letter of undertaking became despairingly known as a 'side-letter'.
- Money paid into the main trust was allocated to the relevant sub-Trust.
- Under a 'Letter of Wishes', the player named the beneficiaries of the sub-trust, such as his wife and family members. The player was not the ultimate beneficiary – these nominated by him were.

Loans could be deferred until he (the player) died at which point the amount owed could be written off against inheritance tax. The player was entitled to borrow from the sub-Trust.[146]

Theoretically, as they were loans, they were not subject to PAYE and National Insurance contributions. Of note, what the EBT could not be used for was paying normal contractual obligations to an employee — like wages and bonuses. This is what HMRC allege that The Rangers Football Club plc used the MGRT for over a ten-year period: pretending that players were getting loans from the Trust when it was in fact money due to them as part of their salary was, in the opinion of HMRC, tax avoidance.[147]

In 2010, it became apparent that HMRC had become interested in these EBTs.[148] For example, in The Rangers Football Club plc Annual Report of 2010 (In the Full Group Accounts (to 30 June 2010)), Notes to the Accounts (Note 5 Staff Costs), it states:

> The Rangers Employee Benefit Trust and Murray Group Management Ltd. Remuneration Trust were established to provide incentives to certain employees. Payments to the Trust are charged to the Group Profit and Loss Account in the year incurred. On the basis of expert tax advice, the Club is defending a query raised by HMRC into this Trust which is part of an ongoing tax enquiry scheduled to be heard by a tax tribunal before the end of the year.

In the BBC Documentary, *Rangers — the men who sold the jerseys*, it is stated that a total of 111 sub-trusts were set up between 2001-2010 for Rangers Directors, players and other staff — along with employees of Murray International Holdings Limited and its subsidiary companies. In detail, a total of 53 Rangers players and staff received side 'contracts' giving undertakings to fund their sub-trusts with cash.

In April 2011, a further tax liability of £2.8M was revealed stemming from the use of a Discounted Option Scheme (DOS) — which some players were part of — between 1999 -2003. This Small Tax Case arose from an historic dispute between The Rangers Football Club plc/Murray International Holdings Limited and HMRC regarding the use of a DOS by The Rangers Football Club plc for former players De Boer and Flo between 2000 - 2003. In early 2011, HMRC issued The Rangers Football

Club plc with a bill for £4M for outstanding amounts owed from the DOS. The Rangers Football Club plc accepted the assessment and it did not go into the tribunal system.

These EBT schemes were subject to extensive dispute starting with the FTTT and the SPL Commission chaired by Lord Nimmo Smith. Many writers — particularly the print and broadcast media — have offered extensive analysis on these (EBT) schemes. Simply, The Rangers Football Club plc/Murray International Holdings Limited were in dispute with HMRC as it was considered that payments from an EBT should not — as was alleged — be made on a contractual basis. If they were, this would make them part of an employee's salary and, therefore, subject to PAYE and National Insurance. HMRC claimed that Rangers EBT scheme was a 'tax scam' as it was non-discretionary and contractual, which formed the basis of the so-called Big Tax Case.

2.3.3   When and Why?

Perhaps the real issue is why EBTs were used by The Rangers Football Club plc/Murray International Holdings Limited. But let's start with when they were used. Kinnon offers that before such Trusts, discretionary bonuses were paid by The Rangers Football Club plc to players.[149] In the BBC Documentary, *Rangers — the men who sold the jerseys*, Daily offers that it was Paul Baxendale-Walker who first suggested that the use of EBTs might provide a convenient way of mitigating the considerable tax burden that a squad of well-paid footballers was starting to place on the plc. On 30 August 2000, Rangers FC signed Ronald de Boer for £4.5M. In November of the same year, they signed Tore André Flo from Chelsea. It is understood that de Boer and Flo agreed to receive some of their pay through a DOS, which required part of the player's salary to be promised through 'side letters' in addition to the formal contract. Simply, by 'reducing' the player's wages in his official contract, this would result in reduced PAYE and National Insurance contributions. The rest of his promised wage would be paid with little or nothing deducted for tax. These letters — guaranteeing tax free income — would later alert HMRC in what became colloquially as The Small Tax Case (i.e. DOS). HMRC eventually asked The Rangers Football Club plc for £2.8M in overdue tax and penalties on these contracts (i.e. the £4M stated above), an amount which would ultimately remain unpaid despite the club admitting liability for the claim.

It is understood that over the next few years, Murray International Holdings Limited switched to a simpler form of EBT arrangement. Over the next few years, the use of EBTs developed with 40% of all players eventually enrolling in the scheme.[150] Therefore, a lower tax bill would relieve some of the mounting pressure on the overall costs to The Ranges Football Club plc suggesting that Rangers FC could continue to sign better, more expensive players and afford to pay wages that these top players demanded. Perhaps it allowed the club to acquire players who they would otherwise not been able to afford. In this way, Rangers FC could see off the threat from a rejuvenated Celtic FC.

The Celtic angle is especially important in this analysis. By the turn of the century, Celtic plc had finally got their 'ducks in a row' off the field and it seemed — to many observers — to be the better-placed of the two football clubs.[151] Perhaps, then, and faced with a resurgent and share issue-funded Celtic plc, it was suggested that The Rangers Football Club plc started to seek an edge by lowering the taxes it had to pay on players' wages. Moreover, and as Franklin, Gow, Graham and McKillop state:[152]

> ...under Advocaat, the pursuit of European success became all-consuming once the thrill of dominating Scottish football diminished towards the end of the 1990s. For example, Flo was by no means a bad player but the outlay — in the context of Scottish Football at that time — underlined both a loss of perspective and financial gambling.

2.3.4   Outcome

69

I consider that there were four main outcomes of the Rangers EBT for both the football club and the plc.

For Rangers FC:

- Although legal until they were outlawed under new legislation passed in 2010 (and implemented in 2011), they would play a critical role in the public perception of wrongdoing at Rangers FC.
- The scale of the potential liability led then-chairman Alistair Johnston to admit in 2011 that the 'club' could go out of business. This was a most significant shock for all Rangers FC stakeholders.

For The Rangers Football Club plc:

- Irrespective of the rights and wrongs of EBTs, the potential liability to HMRC was a major hurdle in the sale of The Rangers Football Club plc. Of note, with such a significant potential liability, it made the club unsellable to any serious buyer. Perhaps only an insolvency expert like Craig Whyte would have an interest in the Club.
- Uncertainty: at the initial Duff & Phelps Press Conference on Thursday 16 February 2012, Paul Clarke stated that the ongoing tax tribunal and potential outcome caused a great deal of uncertainty. In many respects, "this uncertainty was the club's biggest enemy."[153]   This uncertainty was also echoed by Craig Whyte:[154]

> I made it clear the problem remained with HMRC, whose reluctance to compromise had left us facing a bill that could top £75 million unless we took drastic action.

2.4   Ownership, Governance and Leadership

In this sub-section, the ownership, governance, and leadership of The Rangers Football Club plc in the period 1998 – 2011 will be examined. First, I will draw on key information that is contained within the Annual Returns and Annual Reports of The Rangers

Football Club plc during this period to understand the ownership of the plc and, ultimately, Rangers FC. Second, key personnel — charged with 'running' the plc and Rangers FC during this period — will also be detailed. Third, I will attempt to understand the leadership of both the plc and the club during this period to determine who was 'pulling the levers.' Finally, I will offer my summary thoughts on these corporate themes in this period.

2.4.1 Ownership

Paul Smith offers key analysis on the history of ownership of Ranges FC.[155] Summary details are as follows:

- On 27 May 1899, Rangers Football Club incorporated forming The Rangers Football Club Limited.
- No single shareholding exceeded 50% of The Rangers Football Club Limited until 1985 when the Lawrence Group increased its shareholding to a 52% majority, following a deal with then club Vice-chairman Jack Gillespie.
- On 31 March 1982, The Rangers Football Club Limited re-registered as a private company – The Rangers Football Club plc.[156]
- On 22 November 1988, the Head of John Lawrence (Glasgow), Lawrence Marlborough sold his shares to David Murray for £6M (with associated and debts and overdraft reported to be £8M).[157]

Table 2.0 details the Issued Shares and Key Shareholders from 1998.

71

Year	Annual Return	Annual Report/Key Shareholders	Notes to Annual Report
1998	14 January 1998: Number of shares issued: 46 141 522	25 September 1998: David Murray: 28 058 367 (= 60.8%) Albany Inc.../ENIC plc 11 581 522 (= 25.1%)	
1999	27 January 1999: Number of shares issued: 46 141 522	17 November 1999: David Murray/Murray Sports Limited: 28 058 367 (~ 60.8%) Albany Inc.../ENIC plc 11 581 522 (~ 25.1%)	In Annual Report of 1999, David Murray states that Murray International Holdings Limited undertook a restructuring of its investment portfolio. This resulted in a demerger of the Club into a new holding company, Murray Sports Limited, which was controlled by exactly the same shareholders as Murray International Holdings Limited.
2000	31 January 2000: Number of shares issued: 46 141 522	17 November 2000: David Murray/Murray Sports Limited: 37 448 489 (~ 65.38%) D C King/Murray Sports Limited: 3 064 627 (= 5.35%) Albany Inc.../ENIC plc 11 581 522 (~ 20.22%)	In the Full Group Accounts (to 30 June 2000), David Murray comments (17 November 2000, page 2): Our significant investment in players in recent years has caused our borrowing levels to rise. Your board wished to reduce the Club's short term borrowings and on 30th March we raised £38 million by way of a 1 for 3 rights issue principally subscribed by Murray Sports Ltd (£32.3 million) but also supported by 3552 smaller shareholders; my sincere thanks to all who contributed at that time. On 3 March 2000, in conjunction with the Rights issue referred to above, Dave King — a Scottish-born businessman based in South Africa — was invited to join the Board of The Rangers Football Club plc as a Non-Executive Director.

Year	Annual Return	Annual Report/Key Shareholders	Notes to Annual Report
2001	12 January 2001: Number of shares issued: 57 277 310	17 November 2001: David Murray/Murray Sports Limited: 37 448 489 (~ 65.38%) D C King/Murray Sports Limited: 3 064 627 (~ 5.35%) Albany Inc., /ENIC plc 11 581 522 (= 20.2%)	
2004	27 January 2004: Number of shares issued: 57 277 310		In the Full Group Accounts (to 30 June 2004), David Murray comments (14 September 2004): On 1st September 2004, I announced my decision to return to Rangers as Executive Chairman. At the same time, the Board of the Club announced its intention to raise up to £57million by way of a rights issue, which my trading group (Murray International Holdings Ltd) will underwrite up to a level of £50million. It was, however, apparent that a solution would eventually be required to resolve the Club's historic current debt position and the Board has been giving consideration options for restructuring our finances for some time. At the same time, I have consistently confirmed my willingness to play a leading part in whatever type of long term financial solution was deemed to be appropriate. While trading performance has improved significantly in recent years, the reduction of historic debt eliminates negative media attention, removes the significant interest burden and enhances the Clubs net asset position. Although the fundraising will not alter our basic business strategy, which is to maintain a balanced approach on and off field activity, it will enable us to re-invest which would have otherwise gone to service debt. On 27 August 2004, ENIC Group sold 11 581 522 shares to Murray MHL Limited.

2005	7 January 2005: Number of additional shares issued: 51 430 995. Number of shares issued: 108 707 499	31 August 2005: David Murray/ Murray MHL Limited: 62 060 479 (~57.45%) David Murray/RFC Investment Holdings Limited – a subsidiary of Murray Sports Limited: 37 448 489 (~34.425%) D C King/Murray Sports Limited: 3 064 627 (~5.35%)	
2006	27 January 2006: Number of shares issued: 108 707 499	31 August 2006: David Murray/ Murray MHL Limited: 62 060 479 (~57.45%) David Murray/RFC Investment Holdings Limited – a subsidiary of Murray Sports Limited: 37 448 489 (~34.425%) D C King/Murray Sports Limited: 3 064 627 (~5.35%)	

Table 2.0: Issued Shares and Key Shareholders (1998-2011)

On 22 September 2010, the Murray International Holdings Limited shareholding in The Rangers Football Club plc is shown at Table 3.0 (taken from The Rangers Football Club plc Annual Report (page 10)):

Registered Holder	Ordinary Shares	Percentage of Issued Share Capital
Murray MHL Limited	62 060 479	57.45 %
RFC Investment Holdings Limited	37 448 489	34.42%

Table 3.0: Shareholding in The Rangers Football Club plc as of 22 September 2010

In the Notes to the Financial Statements of Murray Sports Limited, for the year ended 30 June 2011, it states (Note 5. Investments):[158]

> On 31 January 2011 the Company acquired the entire equity shareholding in the Rangers Football Club plc which had been held by RFC Investment Holdings Limited, a subsidiary of the Company. On 2 February 2011 the Company then sold its entire equity shareholding in The Rangers Football Club plc to Murray MHL Limited, its immediate parent company...

To 31 January 2011, I offer a 'visual representation' of the Murray International Holdings Limited ownership of Rangers FC. This is shown at Figure 8.0.

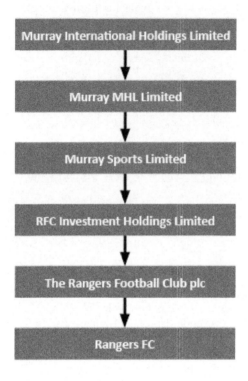

Figure 8.0: A Visual Representation of the Ownership of Rangers Football Club

On 6 May 2011, Murray MHL Limited transferred 92 842 388 shares to The Rangers FC Group Limited.[159] It seems that, at this stage, all of Sir David Murray's shares in The Rangers Football Club plc were transferred by Murray MHL Limited – via a Share Purchase Agreement – to The Rangers FC Group Limited. This is detailed at Table 4.0.

Year	Annual Return	Annual Report/Key Shareholders	Notes to Annual Report
2011	27 January 2011: Number of shares issued: 108 791 499	No Annual Report	On Page 2 of the Murray MHL Limited Annual Report for the year ended 30 June 2011 it says:[160] MHL Limited acquired 37 448 489 shares in The Rangers Football Club plc for £11 905 121 from Murray Sports Limited. The company's entire shareholding in The Rangers Football Club plc was then sold to a third party for a consideration of £1 creating a loss on disposal of £54. 493. 923.

Table 4.0: Shareholding in The Rangers Football Club plc of Murray MHL Limited

Figure 9.0, thus, offers details of the share transfer in The Rangers Football Club plc from Murray MHL Limited to Wavetower/The Rangers FC Group Limited. Simply, Wavetower bought the shares in The Rangers Football Club plc from Murray MHL Limited via a Share Purchase Agreement.

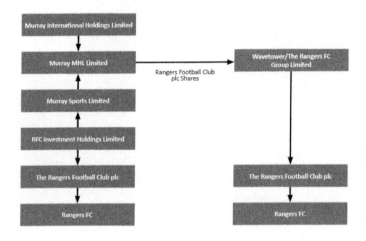

Figure 9.0: The Share Transfer (in The Rangers Football Club plc) from Murray MHL Limited to Wavetower/The Rangers FC Group Limited.

2.4.2   Governance

In a (football) publicly owned company, the Board of Directors is appointed to oversee the corporate operations of the company that owns the club with the Chairman being considered as the most senior and high-profile corporate figure. The Chairman has generally been the prominent executive on the Board although this has begun to change with the appointment of Chief Executives, which led to some Chairpersons being appointed in a non-executive capacity.[160]

In the period 1998 – 2011, the Governance of The Rangers Football Club plc was as follows:

	Chairman	Deputy Chairman	Chief Executive Officer	Finance Director	Secretary	Directors
1998	David E Murray	Donald R Findlay	Robert Brannan		R Campbell Ogilvie	R Campbell Ogilvie, Ian B Skelly, Hugh R W Adam, Howard B Stanton, Daniel P Levy, James MacDonald
1999	David E Murray	Donald R Findlay	Robert Brannan		R Campbell Ogilvie	R Campbell Ogilvie, Ian B Skelly, Hugh R W Adam, Howard B Stanton, Daniel P Levy, James MacDonald
2000	David E Murray	John F McClelland		Douglas J Odam	R Campbell Ogilvie	R Campbell Ogilvie, Ian B Skelly, Hugh R W Adam, Daniel P Levy, James MacDonald; David C King, James D G Wilson
2001	David E Murray	John F McClelland		Douglas J Odam	R Campbell Ogilvie	R Campbell Ogilvie, Ian B Skelly, Hugh R W Adam, Daniel P Levy, James MacDonald; David C King, James D G Wilson
2002	John F McClelland			Douglas J Odam	R Campbell Ogilvie	R Campbell Ogilvie, Martin Bain, Ian B Skelly, Daniel P Levy, David C King, James D G Wilson, Nick Peel
2003	John F McClelland			David Joliffe	R Campbell Ogilvie	R Campbell Ogilvie, Martin Bain, Daniel P Levy, David C King, James D G Wilson, Nick Peel
2004	David E Murray	John F McClelland		David Joliffe	R Campbell Ogilvie	R Campbell Ogilvie, Martin Bain, Daniel P Levy, David C King, James D G Wilson, Nick Peel, A J Johnston, J Greig
2005	David E Murray	John F McClelland	Martin Bain	David Joliffe	R Campbell Ogilvie	Martin Bain, David C King, James D G Wilson, A J Johnston, J Greig
2006	David E Murray	John F McClelland	Martin Bain	Donald C McIntyre		Martin Bain, David C King, James D G Wilson, A J Johnston, J Greig
2007	David E Murray	John F McClelland	Martin Bain	Donald C McIntyre		Martin Bain, David C King, James D G Wilson, A J Johnston, J Greig
2008	David E Murray	John F McClelland	Martin Bain	Donald C McIntyre		Martin Bain, David C King, James D G Wilson, A J Johnston, J Greig, P Murray
2009	Alastair Johnston	John F McClelland	Martin Bain	Donald C McIntyre		Martin Bain, David C King, A J Johnston, J Greig, P Murray, D W Muir, M S McGill
2010	Alastair Johnston	John F McClelland	Martin Bain	Donald C McIntyre		Martin Bain, David C King, A J Johnston, J Greig, P Murray, D W Muir, M S McGill
2011					Gary M Withey	Craig T Whyte, Philip J Betts

2.4.3   Leadership

In his book Leadership in Organizations, Gary Yukl suggests that
— at the level of organisation (i.e. Board of Directors) —
leadership involves strategy and change management.[161]   The
leadership function is to develop and sustain competitive
advantage. In terms of the strategic leadership of The Rangers
Football Club plc and Sir David Murray, the available literature
points to his (Murray's) leadership of 'finance'. Roger Isaacs,
for example, in the BBC Documentary, *Rangers — the men who
sold the jerseys* details the rapid expansion of Murray
International Holdings Limited from 1999 onwards. In detail, it
appears that Murray International Holdings Limited borrowed to
acquire property and assets. In this respect, Isaacs asks the
question: when does responsible risk taking become reckless
gambling? The borrowing of Murray International Holdings
Limited was, therefore, described as a high risk strategy.

This concern of Murray's leadership of finance was echoed
elsewhere; for example Hugh Adam and Graham Spiers (see
pages 35, 47). Moreover, David Edgar says that the Rangers
Supporter Trust (between 2005 – 2010) issued many warnings
about the parlous state of the Club's (I suggest plc's) finances
and the direction that it (the plc) was taking.[162]   Paul Smith
suggests that Howard Stanton (from ENIC) was critical of
Murray's leadership of finances too.[163]   Although Walter Smith
praises Murray's leadership there were other detractors.[164]   Of
note, Alastair Johnston suggested that Celtic provided his role
model for leadership.[165]   In addition, and in criticising Murray's
leadership of finance, Wade (commenting on Donald Muir's
appointment) states: [166]

> A successful turnaround needs external leadership turnaround
> [and] rigorous focus on internal operations and finance.

Murray's leadership was also a cause of significant concern for
Hugh Adam:[167]

One dimensional management is not for professional football clubs.

Celtic also opined:[168]

> That was parodied last week by followers of the Parkhead club, who have been assuring their rivals that "for every fiver we borrow, you'll borrow a tenner". The irresponsible financial dealings have left Rangers with debt said to be £30m, but the true figure has yet to be revealed. The poverty at Ibrox, however, finally gave John Reid, chairman of a financially buoyant Celtic, the opportunity to retaliate. At his club's annual meeting on Friday, he told shareholders and the listening media: "It's not an act of character, courage or leadership to get into debt - it's an act of moral cowardice."

More generally, and towards the end of his (Murray's) chairmanship at The Rangers Football Club plc, Jordan wrote in the Evening Times: [169]

> Murray now finds himself mired in the biggest crisis of his tenure at the club - just a couple of months after he celebrated his 20th anniversary at the helm. The Gers owner blasted the supporters seeking to express disapproval of the club's leadership, telling disgruntled fans to get used to "reality".

Echoing this view, Paul Smith offers that Murray increasingly became tired towards the end of his Rangers reign.[170] Mac Giolla Bhain — a critic of both Murray and Rangers FC — offers that Sir David was not a team player and meetings were rare.[171] Indeed, he quotes Hugh Adam who described Sir David as a one-party state.[172] Elsewhere, David Edgar suggests that Sir David Murray lost interest in Rangers sometime around 2002.[173] Ross Hendry is, however, more critical:

> With hindsight, the motivation for Murray to enter into partnership with JJB was clear; up-front cash injection, yet again outsourcing the assets of the club. Once again, we were served up evidence of how disastrous the second half of the Murray regime was for the club; short-term, low value thinking.[174]

In addition, Roddy Forsyth states:[175]

> Anyway, what does bother Rangers fans is the visible rundown of assets, from the almost unused stadium TV screens to the overused playing squad.

Although Ross Hendry comments on Sir David's long drawn-out exit from the Club,[176] the last word should be left with Richard Wilson: [177]

> ...Murray changed the very nature of the Club, its psyche. Rangers became brash, arrogant even, and began to take glory for granted, as well as presenting a kind of conceited disdain for others.
>
> Murray had not encouraged that kind of relationship between the fans and their team. The fans were, essentially, disengaged.

2.5   Academic Frameworks

2.5.1. Organisational: Six Stages of Organisational Decline and Renewal

For the purpose of this chapter, I will consider the first two stages of Organisational Decline and Renewal, namely: Decline and Triggers for Action.

2.5.1.1 Decline.

It is instructive to start by looking at what happens when an organisation goes into decline. Kiernan offers that we can observe the process of decline by examining its symptoms and the causes of the symptoms.[178]

a.   Symptoms of Decline

Symptoms are different from causes. Symptoms are a sign or an indication of the existence of a problem. Common symptoms of organisational decline are presented below in Table 5.0. These symptoms are not exhaustive but representative and can be either public or private

Physical	Managerial	Behavioural	Financial
Old plant and equipment	Managerial paralysis	Culture of cynicism and failure	Decreasing: profit, sales, liquidity, dividends
Problematic access to raw materials	High turnover of good employees	Increase in red tape	Window-dressing of accounting information
Repeated failure of product launches	High absenteeism	Retreat internally	Increase debts
Obsolete or hopeless products	Employees withdraw from communal activities	Problems ignored	Deteriorating gearing (i.e. relationship or ratio of company's debt-to-equity), shareholder value
Lack of investment in new technology	High levels of managerial stress	Reasons for problems blamed on others	Public refinancing
Worsening terms of trade	Embarrassing loss of CEO	No sense of urgency	Financial restructuring plans
Major disaster	Emergency board meetings/loss of credibility of senior staff	Lack of strategy	Worsening terms of trade
	Emergency board meetings	Fear	Litigation
	Board conflict	Declining levels of service	
	Lack of leadership		

Table 5.0: Common Symptoms of Organisational Decline (From Page 247 to Leavy, B., & Leavy & McKiernan, P. (2009). Strategic Leadership. Governance and Renewal. Basingstoke: Palgrave Macmillan).

Leavy and McKiernan also offer that public symptoms relate to mainly financial resources and are easy to measure and observe in the public domain; for example, a company's Annual Report. In this respect, I offer analysis of the accounts of The Rangers Football Club plc (1998 – 2010) in terms of:

- Profit.
- Liquidity.
- Increasing debt.
- Deteriorating gearing i.e. ratio of debt/equity.

In the period 1997 – 2010. The Rangers Football Club plc was seldom in profit. This is shown at Table 6.0.

Table 6.0: Total Annual Profit/Loss

In terms of liquidity (i.e. the ability to meet short-term financial obligations), although many organisations operate within 'tight' industry norms, the downward trend of The Rangers Football Club plc is noticeable.[179,180] This is shown at Table 7.0.

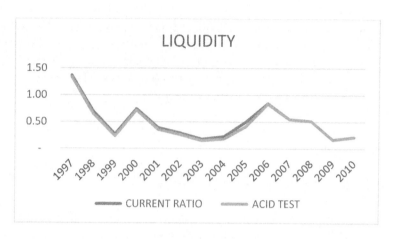

Table 7.0: Liquidity (i.e. how easily assets can be converted into cash)

In terms of what 'return' the business is giving its investors, we see that in most years (1998 – 2010), the return on equity in Table 8.0 below. [181]

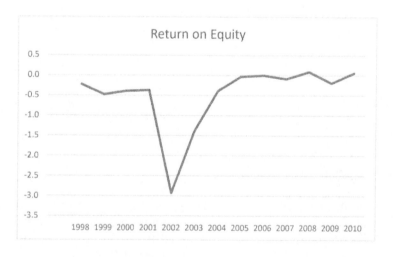

Table 8.0: Return on Equity

Gearing is a ratio of Debt/Equity. This ratio is associated with financial risk. High gearing is associated with high financial risk. Simply, there is a higher risk of insolvency. If a company fails to repay its debtors, they (the debtors) can, under insolvency law, have a legal right to 'go to court' to recover the debt.[182] This is shown at Table 9.0.

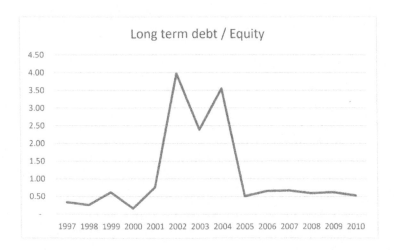

Table 9.0: Long Term Debt to Equity

In summary, there were — I suggest — significant symptoms of corporate decline:

- Decreasing: profit and liquidity.
- Increasing debts.
- Deteriorating gearing i.e. higher financial risk.

Moreover, and in line with other financial symptoms, we also observed financial restructuring plans. In this regard, Smith notes:[183]

> Rangers had tried everything from debentures to share issues and from sponsorship deals to licensing arrangements, but, eventually, old-fashioned loans and overdrafts proved to be the

lifeline that kept the club functioning while a permanent solution to the ownership conundrum was sought.

Private symptoms of decline pertain mainly to the other two resource categories in Table 5.0 — managerial and behavioural. They are more difficult to measure and are more likely to be part of the internal reporting systems thus giving top management some discretion on their dissemination. As such, they are not easy to identify or confirm by external observers. We may, however, suggest:

- Physical (old plant and equipment i.e. visible rundown of assets)
- Managerial (Board conflict (see Chapter Three)/lack of leadership)
- Behavioural (lack of strategy).

b.   Causes of Decline

Leavy & McKiernan also offer that the main causes of decline are poor management and poor financial control. These can be termed secondary causes and can be distinguished from their underlying primary causes, which are due to dysfunctions in the corporate learning system.

Secondary causes of decline.

The main secondary causes of decline are outlined in Table 6.0.

Financial	Managerial
Poor financial control	Poor management
Acquisitions	Management unresponsive to change
Poor financial policy	Management problems
Big projects fail	Poor strategy formulation
Overtrading	Poor strategy implementation
Poor accounting information	Strategic oscillation
Poor gearing	Strike activity
High cost structure	
Excess plant capacity	
R&D overspend	
Poor working capital management	

Table 10.0: The Main Secondary Causes of Decline

In terms of secondary causes, I also suggest that there was evidence of:

- Financial (control, policy, gearing)
- Managerial (strategy formulation).

2. Primary causes of decline.

It is not the purpose of this book to examine dysfunctions in the corporate learning system. However, organisational learning (i.e. the process by which an organisation improves itself over time through gaining experience and using that experience to create knowledge) plays a central role in distinguishing failing from surviving companies and underpins superior performance.[184] Learning becomes important when conditions begin to change.[185]   Hence, companies with good learning routines will be expected to survive and some to prosper. Companies with defective routines are more likely to drift down the spiral of decline.

The main defective routines at the organisational level of analysis are the 'rigidity' of mindsets. As the mindset becomes more rigid, learning can become an obsolete activity thereby preparing the organisation for ossification.[186]   I suggest that this is related directly to organisational leadership and in, particular, the leadership of Sir David and Murray International Holdings Limited, which ultimately 'controlled' The Rangers Football Club plc.[187]   An example of this organisational leadership is offered by Alasdair McKillop:[188]

> ...during the Murray era, the Rangers Supporter's Trust (RST) 'We Deserve Better' campaign sought to draw attention to the various financial failings, the lack of strategic vision at boardroom level and a tendency to treat:
>
>> Rangers fans with disdain as 'customers' instead of valuing and working with them as 'supporters' and part of the Rangers family.

Moreover, Adam also opines:[189]

> Perhaps because he was afforded such impunity he often had little interest in balance sheets, preferring to splash out recklessly because this appealed to his sense of showmanship. Long-term effects were not considered...
>
> This, though, should not exempt him from criticism – something he cannot handle.

2.5.1.2 Triggers for Action

In organisational decline, powerful routines that control behaviour can prevent early action taking place. When crisis looms, managers may (naturally) hold on to what is familiar and their existing routines act as a comfort zone, artificially and temporarily protecting them from change.

McKiernan states that to achieve change against a strongly held belief system frequently requires significant external or internal jolts. Something happens that triggers the action. Externally, outside stakeholders can exert influential pressure. In the case of The Rangers Football Club plc, I suggest that such external jolts and outside stakeholders included the global financial crisis and the relationship between Lloyds and Murray International Holdings Limited. In the process of decline, organisations are faced with a search for solutions. First, the search for solutions is sought at the operating-level via cost cutting and tighter controls (for example) and then to the strategic-level. But, in the case of Murray International Holdings Limited (and, thus, The Rangers Football Club plc), I advance that the template had to be dismantled by an internal reorganisation initiated by Lloyds i.e. Project Charlotte.

2.5.2 Stakeholder: The Change Curve.

For the purpose of this chapter, I will consider the first two stages of The Change Curve, namely Denial and Shock.

In the case of The Rangers Football Club plc — and in terms of denial — although some commentators (e.g. Hugh Adam/Graham Spiers) were critical of the finances of The Rangers Football Club plc/Rangers FC, many (perhaps most) did not appreciate or understand the scale of the developing debt at Murray International Holdings Limited i.e. that it had become almost £1B. In this respect, Paul Smith notes:[190]

The irony was that few had voiced concerns years earlier, when the expensive new faces had begun to sap resources and — admittedly unbeknown to most — the deficit crept up to record levels. While the silverware staked up and star players rolled in, there was no reason to question running of the club. What fan would?

There was shock when The Big Tax Case liability was reported in the News of the World newspaper in April 2010 and The Rangers Football Club plc Annual Report of that year too.

The initial shock — while usually short-lived — is often due to a lack of information and a fear of the unknown.[191] After the initial shock has passed, it is common for individuals (in this case stakeholders) to again experience denial. At this point, the focus tends to remain in the past. Common emotions can include: fear of failure; being comfortable with the status quo; and feeling threatened. Individuals who have not been affected by change before can be particularly affected by this first stage. Indeed, it is common for people to convince themselves that change is not going to happen or if it does, it will not affect them.

I suggest, however, that there was ongoing denial; for example, any problem (i.e. a tax liability) would be 'resolved/dealt with' by Sir David Murray/Murray International Holdings Limited. Indeed, Graham Spiers offered that Sir David Murray may have a moral obligation to do so and Alastair Johnston opined that it (tax liability) was an issue for Murray International Holdings Limited.

The emotions of denial and shock are evident in the newspaper reports detailed below:

1. *Ibrox faithful face worrying summer*
Aberdeen Press and Journal

> If reports are to be believed the club has been hit with a tax bill in the region of £24million from Her Majesty's Revenue and Customs. HMRC has been taking a close look at the tax

arrangements of major British clubs. I do not understand how this has come as a surprise to Rangers, but, if the worst case scenario comes true, they will have major problems. The champions are already £30million in debt, their management team is out of contract and leading players are being sold or are moving on.

2. *Deal? No deal*
The Herald
March 19, 2010

Throughout all this the pawns go about their duties. Smith, Ally McCoist and Kenny McDowall work without contracts. Kris Boyd, Nacho Novo, Kirk Broadfoot and DaMarcus Beasley see their deals wind down to their final weeks. None of them knows where he'll be next season. The football department should matter more than anything, but in all this it seems small and vulnerable. They go about their shift in a state of denial, hardly daring to think what it will mean for Rangers if Ellis says what he's expected to in the next few days.

3. *TAXMAN COULD KILL GERS!; Chairman's doomsday warning Whyte gets 48 hours or takeover's off*
Scottish Star
April 2, 2011

Yesterday it emerged the club had been hit by a shock NEW tax demand from HMRC for £2.8m which Johnston claimed "came right out of left-field". But it's the outstanding tax wrangle over payment of players during the Dick Advocaat era - a bill which could run into tens of millions - which threatens Rangers' long-term future. And it's the potential for that case - which Rangers are vigorously defending - to land the club with a bill they can't pay. An outcome may not be known until October or November but Johnston said: "It's like a gorilla in the room and you don't know what its appetite is." Asked if Rangers could go bust, Johnston nodded and replied: "The reality is there is a possibility that there could be a judgment that the club can't pay. I will say that Rangers can't afford much.

4. *Rangers say tax battle no risk to club*
The Herald
April 2, 2011

> RANGERS yesterday took the unusual step of denying that it could go bust as talks about a takeover were nearing conclusion. The Ibrox club released a stock market statement refuting a BBC report that they could go out of business if they lost their battle with the HMRC over their players trust s tax liability.

Further shock was not too far away....

2.6. Chapter Summary

2.6.1 Finance

In 2000, Rangers announced plans for a major share issue. The timing of the share issue coincided with soaring debts, which had peaked at around £20M at this stage — a figure that the club had admitted was a concern. On 30 March 2000, Dave King was appointed as a Director. This formed part of a share issue that would see Sir David Murray make an investment of £32.3M in new shares through Murray Sports and its wholly owned subsidiary RFC Investment Holdings Limited. On 30 September 2000, Hugh Adam resigned as Director of The Rangers Football Club plc.

On 4 May 2001, The Bank of Scotland merged with Halifax to form HBOS, which would later be purchased by Lloyds TSB a result of the global financial crisis of 2008/9.

On 5 July 2002, Sir David Murray relinquished the Chairmanship of The Rangers Football Club plc. He was replaced, as Chairman, by John McClelland.

On 27 August 2004, Daniel Levvy resigned as Director of the plc. ENIC shares were sold to Murray MHL Limited. Some four days later, on 1 September 2004, David Murray returned as Chairman of the plc. A further share issues took place underwritten by Murray International Holdings Limited.

On 13 July 2006, David Murray suggested that he may sell the club in 3 years.

In September 2007, the global financial crisis commenced. Simply, banks stopped lending. This became known as the 'credit crunch'.

In spring 2010, the outlook for Rangers was bleak. On 27 April 2010, The Rangers Football Club plc confirmed that they were under investigation by HMRC over offshore payments to players from 2001.

2.6.2 Employee Benefit Trusts

EBTs had been in existence since the late 1980s. In setting up these Trusts, companies were able to attract highly qualified staff likely to remain with them for the long-term. The Rangers EBT was established in 2000 for senior executives of the Murray International Holdings Limited. In the year 2001, it was extended to The Rangers Football Club plc for payment of senior executives and football players.

The Rangers EBT was relatively straightforward. Simply, the employer (The Rangers Football Club plc/Murray International Holdings Limited) paid money into an offshore Trust. In addition to his fully disclosed salary, a player or other employee would be able to take out loans from his individual sub-Trust of which he was the nominated 'protector' to an amount that was already agreed and stipulated in a 'side letter'. Simply, by 'reducing' the player's wages in his official contract, this would result in reduced PAYE and National Insurance contributions. Therefore, a lower tax bill would relieve some of the mounting pressure on the overall costs meaning that Rangers FC could continue to sign better (more expensive) players and afford to pay wages that these top players demanded. Perhaps it allowed them to acquire players who they would otherwise not have been able to afford. In this way, Rangers FC could (perhaps) see off the threat from a rejuvenated Celtic FC. The resulting tax liability became known as The Big Tax Case.

In April 2011, a further tax liability of £2.8M was revealed stemming from the use of a Discounted Option Scheme — which some players were part of — between 1999 - 2003. This became known as The Small Tax Case.

There were significant (negative) outcomes of the Rangers EBT for both the Football Club and the plc.

2.6.3   Ownership, Governance and Leadership

Rangers FC was operated by The Rangers Football Club plc. Shares in this plc were owned by, ultimately, Murray International Holdings, via Murray Sports Limited and Murray MHL Limited.

2.6.4   Leadership

In terms of the strategic leadership of The Rangers Football Club plc, the available literature points to Murray's leadership of 'finance'. There was rapid expansion of Murray International Holdings Limited from 1999 onwards. Indeed, Murray International Holdings Limited borrowed to acquire property and assets. The borrowing of Murray International Holdings Limited was described as a high-risk strategy.

There was concern of the leadership of finance by many: Hugh Adam and Graham Spiers; The Rangers Supporter Trust; Howard Stanton; and Alastair Johnston.

2.6.5 Academic Frameworks

There was organisational decline at The Rangers Football Club plc in the first decade of this century. The global financial crisis and Lloyds 'triggered' significant change at Murray International Holdings Limited. Many stakeholders did not appreciate or understand the scale of the developing debt at Murray International Holdings Limited i.e. it had become almost £1B.

There was shock when The Big Tax Case liability was reported in the News of the World newspaper in April 2010 and The Rangers Football Club plc Annual Report of that year too. There was ongoing denial; for example, any problem (i.e. a tax liability) would be 'resolved/dealt with' by Sir David Murray/Murray International Holdings Limited.

Chapter Three

Craig Whyte and the Journey to Administration: 6 May 2011 – 14 February 2012

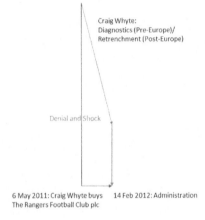

Descent into chaos

Craig Whyte:
Diagnostics (Pre-Europe)/
Retrenchment (Post-Europe)

Denial and Shock

6 May 2011: Craig Whyte buys   14 Feb 2012: Administration
The Rangers Football Club plc

Chapter Contents

98

3.1   Introduction

If I move on from Rangers I will leave it in the hands of people who I think have the best interests of the club.

Sir David Murray (2006)[192]

The recession in early 1990s hit hard in Scotland. Then a major customer reneged on an outstanding bill... ...I took advice from a practitioner. He took me through the process. I set up a new company and put the old one into liquidation. Not one person lost their job. They all came with me to the new company. However, the pain of seeing a company go bust stung me. For a long time I didn't tell anyone, but in some ways that period defined my whole career. It was eye opening. I saw how things could be done and how ailing businesses could be restructured. The lesson was not to get too attached to one legal entity. You can restructure these things and keep going.

Craig Whyte (2020)[193]

Due to its cost structure, the club has been loss making for many months. This situation has resulted in increasing liabilities and the club has been in discussion with HMRC regarding these liabilities. These liabilities combined with the threat of the outcome of the first-tier tax tribunal left the club no option but to formally restructure its financial affairs.

The Daily Telegraph (2012)[194]

In this chapter I aim to explain the key issues leading from the purchase of The Rangers Football Club plc by Craig Whyte on 6 May 2011 to its administration on 14 February 2012. In addition, I will focus on Craig Whyte's (suggested) diagnostics of the company's financial situation and the subsequent retrenchment that was required as a result of no additional revenue from European football post July/August 2011. This loss of key income led, arguably, to administration in February 2012.[195] Therefore, I aim to detail:

- The general (and increasingly desperate) history of Rangers FC — leading to the administration of The Rangers Football Club plc — based on a timeline of 2010 to 14 February 2012.
- The 'finance deal' that enabled Craig Whyte to purchase the 85.3% shareholding in The Rangers Football Club plc from Sir David Murray on 6 May 2011.

3.2 History of Rangers Football Club: 2010 to 14 February 2012

2008 was, I suggest, a very important year in the history of Rangers FC. In his book, *INTO THE BEAR PIT,* Craig Whyte explains that around 2008, he acquired financial services companies and tried to make them work. He bought (via his British Virgin Islands-based holding company Liberty Capital) several stockbroker and asset management companies under the umbrella of the Merchant House Group plc.[196]

In 2010 — and as part of his work with the Merchant House Group plc — Craig Whyte states that he met George Cadbury in June who, with a colleague, was working on a venture for Merchant Capital — a subsidiary of the Merchant House Group. Cadbury and colleague were trying to finance a deal (from the Middle East) to take over a Scottish football club. Craig Whyte states that in the summer of 2010, there was a desperation — by Sir David Murray — to sell The Rangers Football Club plc. Indeed, anyone with money could meet Sir David. The asking price, at this time, was £33M. Cadbury invited Craig Whyte to meet Andrew Ellis. Whyte offers that the deal was 'done' but he (Andrew Ellis) had no money.[197,198]

Whyte states further that, at this time, he saw it (Rangers) — and I suggest naively — as another company that he could buy, put a management team in to 'sort out' the issues and, if need be, take it through an administration process. The Rangers Football Club plc had assets worth £100M and he (Whyte) was looking for money on the back of those assets to buy it. Indeed, and at this time, he was thinking of mortgaging the stadium or training ground — a typical method of financing the purchase of a business.[199]

In terms of the actual finance, Whyte states that his colleague Phil Betts had a 'city contact' called Nigel Farr.[200] In turn, Farr had a contact at Octopus Investments — an investment company and fund managers that owned Ticketus LLP, a London-based Limited Liability Partnership. The relevant contact was Ron Bryan — he administered two funds for Octopus (Ticketus and Ticketus 2). Of note, Octopus was already involved with Rangers — The Rangers Football Club plc had disclosed that to Andrew Ellis and David Gilmore. Through Octopus, Ticketus had provided The Rangers Football Club plc with working capital in exchange for future season ticket sales. Indeed, Rangers FC season tickets had been sold to them (£5-6M) over the previous 2-3 seasons.

The 'Ticketus arrangement' is generally straightforward. For example, football clubs generate money in the summer (specifically via season ticket sales). Once a football season starts, there can be minimal additional revenue over and above cup runs or European football. Therefore, by the time the following January comes there can be limited money left. So, football clubs sell future season tickets for money and this money is paid back to the lender. Craig Whyte viewed this Ticketus arrangement as similar to invoice financing i.e. borrowing money against a/the sales ledger. At this time, Ticketus had verbally committed finance of £20M for the proposed Craig Whyte deal. Whyte also wanted to pursue other asset finance options to cover the balance. Craig Whyte does state that he did not want to use his own money for the purchase.[201] There was also an equity element of £5M to buy the shares, which was later reduced to £1.[202] Once Craig Whyte received a Letter from Ticketus confirming the availability of funds, he told the solicitors of Andrew Ellis that he had money; ergo, he had proof of funds and capability to talk to the vendor (Sir David Murray) to strike a deal.

101

Further analysis of this finance arrangement is contained in the Duff & Phelps (first) *Report to Creditors.*[203] In detail, they state that Ticketus advanced £20.3M to the Collyer Bristow client account (around May 2011) in name of RFC Group Limited in consideration of future season ticket revenue of £25.4M (to be repaid over three football seasons: 2011/12; 2012/13; and 2013/4).

This is shown in Figure 11.0

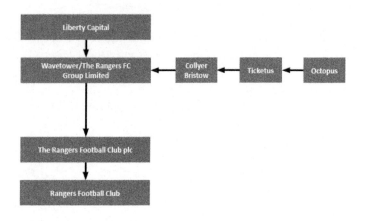

Figure 11.0: Ticketus, Collyer Bristow and The Rangers FC Group Limited

Whyte states further that if he could find a way to break even, without relying on Europe, he could make the Rangers purchase a success.[204] In October 2010, Whyte went to France to meet with Sir David Murray to discuss the possible sale. In advance of this meeting, Whyte was advised by Donald Muir that the 'Bank' had a bigger say in Rangers but Craig Whyte should tell Sir David Murray what he (Sir David) wanted to hear. [205] Sometime after this meeting in France, it was suggested by Craig Whyte that Sir David 'leaked' Whyte's interest in The Rangers Football Club plc to The Daily Record, The Sun and The Herald newspapers. As such, Whyte sought Public Relations advice from Jack Irvine (founder of Media House International Limited). Irvine advised Whyte to contact another PR agency, Hay McKerron. Whyte, thus, put out a statement to the London Stock Exchange. The statement released to the Stock Exchange on 18 November 2010 read: [206]

> Craig Whyte notes the articles in today's press regarding discussions between him and Murray International Holdings Limited with a view to him acquiring MIH's majority shareholding in Rangers Football Club Plc. Mr Whyte confirms that he is considering making an offer for RFC and is in talks with MIH but that these are at an early stage and there can be no certainty that an offer will ultimately be made. Mr Whyte has not yet approached the board of RFC. A further statement will be made in due course.

On 3 December 2010, PA Newswire: Sport News reported that Whyte had reached an "agreement in principle" with Murray and had met Alastair Johnston for the first time.

At this juncture, we should ask why Sir David Murray wanted to sell:

- Sir David himself — perhaps he was 'bored' with Rangers dating back to his original decision to sell in 2006.
- The EBT tax case carried a significant liability for The Rangers Football Club plc.
- The Lloyds restructure of Murray International Holdings Limited (Project Charlotte):

  - ➢ There was an incentive to keep his 'metals business.' [207] Whyte offers that a deadline was set by Lloyds so that Sir David could buy back his metals business.[208] Certainly, it appeared that

Lloyds applied some pressure. The, then, Chairman of The Rangers Football Club plc, Alistair Johnston — in the BBC documentary (*Craig Whyte Uncovered: Rangers Thousandaire & His Dodgy Past*) — stated that Lloyds thought that the IBC was being obstructive. Unless they 'did a deal', Lloyds would withdraw its credit line to The Rangers Football Club plc.

In respect of the incentives to sell Rangers, in 2017 — and during the Craig Whyte trial — it was reported that no due diligence was undertaken on Craig Whyte.[209] In detail:

Nothing spent on Craig Whyte checks:

When asked how much was spent investigating Craig Whyte and his business ahead of the Rangers takeover deal, a key adviser to Sir David Murray admitted it had not been a lot. In referring to the amount spent on due diligence into Craig Whyte, David Horne told the trial: "Not very much at all. I don't know. Possibly nothing."

Bank role:

Senior Lloyds Banking Group manager Ian Shanks told the trial that it had played a strong role in the Whyte takeover. Lloyds inherited Rangers' multi-million pound debt after it took over the club's long time bank, Bank of Scotland. Mr Shanks said Lloyds was keen that the Whyte deal was seen through. He said Lloyds wanted its money back and wanted to get out of the football sector in general. Mr Shanks said Lloyds had no involvement in running Rangers. However, the Murray group appointed two members to the Rangers board, who were described as having a good working relationship with the bank.[210]

Finish line:

Gary Withey, Whyte's lawyer, told the court that Sir David Murray's advisers were "desperate" to get the takeover "over the line" and "did not seem to care" how Whyte was financing any deal. Mr Withey told the court: "This was the only deal I have been involved in where the vendor was pushing more than the purchaser."

Moreover, at the said trial — and although Sir David did not accept that he failed to carry out due diligence on Craig Whyte — Whyte's defence lawyer Donald Findlay QC told the jury the Murray Group "just didn't care. The deal was all that mattered." [211]

Equally, it is important to consider why Craig Whyte wanted to buy?

- He was a Rangers fan.
- Ego/vanity considerations?
- By his own admission, perhaps he was undergoing a 'mid-life crisis.'
- Could he make it work after all? To him, was this just another business?
- His motivation — he was a venture capitalist with a history of asset stripping. As Smith notes:

> It sounded very much as though Whyte was going into the Rangers project with his eyes open; it was an organisation being prepared for major restructuring, one way or another." [212, 213]

Analysis, in this regard, is offered by The Daily Telegraph: [214]

> Whyte has openly considered the prospect of administration since he took over at Ibrox, notably in an interview with The Daily Telegraph last September, and statements released last night suggested the latest move is part of a negotiation with HMRC. In normal circumstances HMRC would be first in the queue for repayment of outstanding debtors, but in administration the taxman has no protection, and will have to join the line behind Whyte and the players to get its money back. If administration is successfully negotiated, Whyte could emerge in control of the club, albeit through a new holding

company, with any potentially crippling tax liability drastically reduced.

From the BBC documentary (*Craig Whyte Uncovered: Rangers Thousandaire & His Dodgy Past...*), Daily — and quoting from Kevin Sykes — states that Whyte would buy a stake in a failing UK business and that he (Sykes) would help Whyte restructure the business to be able to leave the unsecured creditors behind. In this regard, and in this documentary, Daily offers that Whyte had two options for Rangers (post-restructure):

- He could call in the administrators and assets would have to be sold. Whyte would be first in line to be paid — he was the only secured creditor as he cleared the £18M bank loan. If he walked away, he would lose nothing.
- If he stayed, it could be a clever strategy to leave company debt free with creditors, including HMRC, empty handed.

This is a key area of debate. As such, I invite my colleague, Dr Mathew Bonnett, to offer further insight.

Whyte became a secured creditor in The Rangers Football Club plc (hereafter known as company) when his company Wavetower/The Rangers FC Group Limited paid the £18M owed to Lloyds Banking Group and inherited Lloyds' floating charge over all the assets in the company. The debt was owed by the company to Lloyds Banking Group, and so when it was settled by Wavetower, the company became indebted to Wavetower and its ultimate owner Craig Whyte.

A charge is a clause in a debt contract which gives the lender protection in case the borrower defaults on the debt. The charge gives the lender ownership of an asset, or pool of assets, in the case of default by the borrower. The terminology used is that the debt is secured against these assets. The lender of a debt that contains this clause is called a secured creditor. Should the lender default, delay or just doesn't honour the contractual terms of repayment then the charge comes into force and the lender would have the right to take ownership of the secured assets and recover the amount they were due to be paid. A fixed charge is where the clause relates to a specific asset and a simple example is a traditional mortgage, which is usually secured against the property the loan relates to. For example, if you take out a mortgage to buy a house and then default on the repayments the bank will take ownership of your house. This is done via a fixed charge over the property. By selling the ceased asset and collecting the proceeds the lender receives the money they were due under the debt contract. A floating charge meanwhile is secured not on a specific asset but over a pool of assets. The charge is for a specific amount of money and should the borrower default, the lender can cease assets in that pool up to the value of the floating charge. The floating charge allows assets to be bought and sold within the pool so long as the value of the pool of assets remains about the value of the charge.

Whyte had a floating charge over key assets of the company. In the event that the company later fell into insolvency, creditors of the company would be paid in order according to the rank of their claims. Whyte's floating charge would rank him at the front of the queue for receiving a pay-out as a secured creditor. Generally, secured creditors are paid first before any unsecured creditors and any owners of preference or ordinary shares.

The payment of £18M to Lloyds Banking Group was a condition of the share transfer between Sir David Murray and Wavetower which saw Craig Whyte acquire 85.3% of the ordinary shares in The Rangers Football Club plc for the nominal payment of £1.

In corporate takeovers, the item being traded is the ordinary shares of the company as these confer the effective ownership via voting rights attached to the shares. With over 85% of the ordinary shares, Whyte now controlled the company as no-one could outvote him in any vote of the shareholders. Examples of shareholder votes include voting Directors onto the Board meaning Whyte now controlled the composition of the Board of Directors and could elect his own people to control the company.

There is one point in time when the ownership of a company does not reside with its equity holders and that is in times of insolvency. When a company cannot pay its debts, it is left for administrators to try and get as much value out of the company as possible and transfer this to the creditors who are owed monies by the insolvent company. This is effectively a transfer from the old shareholders, who often are left with nothing, to the creditors who may well not get all they are owed, but at least they get paid first, before the equity holders. Alternatively, the administrators may try to sell the company as a 'going concern' and keep the business alive. If they can find someone willing to run the company, then this often saves the most value. But the existing shareholders would lose their ownership in favour of the new buyer.

Whyte, therefore, was both in position as an equity holder via his 85% ownership of the ordinary shares and simultaneously as a key debt holder via this floating charge on the debt now owed from the company to Wavetower.

If the company did not become insolvent, Whyte owned it. If it did fall into insolvency, he owned a priority claim on its assets.

Returning to the general timeline, early in 2011 there was a change in share ownership in The Ranges Football Club plc. In the Financial Statements for the year ended 30 June 2011 for Murray MHL Limited, it says on Page 2, Activities:

> On 2 February 2011, the current year the company acquired 37, 448, 489 shares in the Rangers Football Club plc, for a consideration of £11, 905, 121, from Murray Sports Limited, a company in which the Company has a participating interest. The company's entire shareholding in The Rangers Football Club plc was then sold to a third party for a consideration of £1 creating a loss on disposal of £54, 493, 923.

Murray MHL Limited then owned 92 842 388 shares in The Rangers Football Club plc. It was this amount (i.e. 85.3%) that Craig Whyte bought from Sir David Murray on 6th May 2011.[215]

This is shown at Figure 12.0.

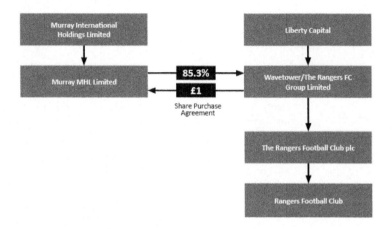

Figure 12.0: Murray MHL Limited to Wavetower/The Rangers
FC Group Limited

On 22 February 2011, it was confirmed that Ally McCoist would
be the next Manager of Rangers FC.[216] At around this time —
and reported in the (first) *Report to Creditors* — the Joint
Administrators (JAs) state that MCR Business Consulting (MCR
BC) (that subsequently became part of Duff & Phelps) was
engaged by Liberty Capital Limited to assist with negotiations
with Lloyds as part of Liberty Capital's intended acquisition of
the shareholding in The Rangers Football Club plc from Murray
International Holdings Limited. [217] An agreement was reached
in principle with Lloyds in April 2011 in respect of the debt that
Lloyds required to be settled upon completion of the sale.

PA Newswire: Sport News of 6 May 2011 details some
significant events during March and April of this year:

6th March 2011: Release of Rangers mid-term accounts was delayed.

18th March 2011: Whyte meets Smith and Chief Executive Martin Bain to hear their spending recommendations for the playing squad.[218]

28th March 2011: Lloyds Banking Group deny claims they had demanded a £1million 'exit fee' from Whyte, who officially completes his due diligence.

30th March 2011: Whyte and Lloyds appear to reach agreement over the debt repayment.

31st March 2011: Whyte meets members of the IBC to outline his plans for the Club.[219,220]

31 March 2011 was also the deadline for a license — provided by the SFA — to play European football for Season 2011/2012. To obtain such licenses, it was important that 'applying clubs' must not owe tax. O'Donnell states that the club's application for a European license was approved by SFA.[221] On 1 April 2011, The Rangers Football Club plc produced the delayed mid-term accounts and admitted openly for first time that two separate tax cases were hanging over the company i.e. The Small Tax Case and The Big Tax Case. In these accounts, a £11.9M profit for the last six months of 2010 was announced but £2.8M was 'wiped off' for a one-off tax payment over an issue relating to 1999-2003 (DOS/Small Tax Case). Moreover, Alistair Johnston admitted the other ongoing tax probe (The Big Tax Case) could leave the company with a bill they could not afford to pay.

At this stage, analysis by Chick Young — in the BBC article *Rangers chairman admits club could go out of business* — is instructive:[222]

> The reality is that, if the decision is bad and the club can't pay, there would be a decision to be made," said Johnston, who expects a decision on the purchase of the club in the next couple of days:
>
> > It's not clear where the liability lies. It could be October or November before we find out. The situation is not holding up the sale, but it does inhibit new financing and

new investment. I have no idea of the sum for which we may be liable, but Rangers cannot afford much.

However, Rangers later released a statement to say:

> Further to some press comment today following the release of our Interim Results, we would like to clarify that our Chairman did not state that the club could go out of business. Moreover, we would refer interested parties to the section in the Interim Results (paragraph 7) that covers the current position with the HMRC enquiry and importantly to the fact that the Club continues to vigorously contest HMRC's challenge and in doing so continues to receive reassuring opinion from tax, accounting and legal specialists. The directors of The Rangers Football Club plc accept responsibility for this announcement.

The real concern for Rangers was the judgement they awaited from Her Majesty's Revenue and Customs over a tax issue relating to offshore payments to players and the Murray Group Management Limited Remuneration Trust. Johnston admitted that "but for the HMRC verdict, life would be a lot easier" and he acknowledged in his statement to the Stock Exchange the investigation relating to offshore payments to players and the Murray Group Management Limited Remuneration Trust.

> I would emphasise that no allegations have been made to suggest any illegal activity and tax vehicles of this type have been used by a number of companies throughout the country.

The club's financial position had also been hit by a separate charge from the HMRC for £2.8m for activities in a player compensation scheme between 1999 and 2003. All this was happening as Rangers were deep in talks with Whyte, who was hoping to take over ownership from Sir David Murray.

> This is a two-way street said Johnston. He is still enthusiastically addressing the issue and we are looking at his credentials. I want a forcing mechanism to force him to do what he says he is going to do in terms of future

investment in the club. His agreement with the bank and with David Murray has nothing to do with Rangers. I want assurances of his ability to fund what he says he is going to do. Craig has to understand the club's position and the expectation level of the fans. It is very easy to talk about £25m investment, but there must be a forcing mechanism. We must get it into any purchase agreement. I admit this is very unusual.

Rangers' Chairman had criticised the club's banker in his statement to the Stock Exchange for making Smith's job more difficult than necessary.

While we appreciate the support of the Lloyds Banking Group through the Bank of Scotland in extending our credit arrangement and recognising the progress that has been made in developing a template for collaboration, certain provisions imposed on the club continue to compromise, in our opinion, management's ability to conduct its role with maximum efficiency.

Continuing with this theme of the role of the banks, Roddy Forsyth offers further analysis:[223]

Asked how Lloyds had 'compromised' Rangers, Johnston said:

The bank looks on us as a short-term project to the extent that at every opportunity they're not willing to concede that there isn't an occasion or a transaction where they might want to participate. If we sell players, do we have any certainty that we will get all the money, 90 per cent of it, 80 per cent of it, whatever? It makes it tough for our management to understand and to plan for selling players when we don't know how much of the money we're getting to keep. The management team is reluctant to sell players because they don't know if they'll get enough money to replace them. So when I say they compromise us, I mean they compromise our ability to plan three-year cycles. They [Lloyds] have been fairly assiduous at saying, 'While we are willing to look at this on a case-by-case basis, we're never going to give you carte blanche to think it's all your money — if you get into the Champions

League we'll want part of it'. Therefore our management team is wary of doing certain things that in the long run might come back and haunt them.

But wasn't the purpose of having Muir on the Ibrox board to ease communications between the directors and the bank?

Let's be very clear on the situation with Donald Muir - it's a condition of our credit facility agreement that Donald Muir is the representative of the bank on the board. It's very tough to engage in conversations at board level about strategies with the bank when we know that the bank guy is sitting there," said Johnston who, when asked why it had been denied previously that Muir was Lloyd's man, had a sharp retort. "I think it was Donald that denied that. It's been denied by a lot of people, but I'm telling you what the issue is right now. I decided that I might as well," said Johnston.

What happened when I got here was that the banker that was involved with us refused to talk to our chief executive or to our chief financial officer. It was one of the most stupid aberrations that I've ever come across and I said that to the bank. He had never met our chief financial officer. He had never met Martin Bain [Rangers' chief executive], so all the communications had to go through Donald Muir and Mike McGill, the other director, although essentially it was more through Donald than it was Mike. So a lot of stuff got lost in translation.

Would it be better for Rangers, therefore, if Muir - who is understood to have left the Murray Group on Thursday - also departed the club? "No question that his presence compromises things," said Johnston, although he added: "I've always got on well with Donald Muir but I deal within the context of who he is." Johnston revealed that there were two HMRC issues, the latest - and much the smaller - being a claim by the tax authority for £2.8 million. "It relates to more than two or three players, but it relates to an issue 10 or 11 years ago - I don't know the context of doing it," said the Chairman. "I don't think it is a deal breaker. It wasn't in any plan, it wasn't in our budgets or anything that we have been trying to do. We have a very disciplined approach and I didn't like that appearing over the horizon suddenly."

As for the Whyte bid, it is understood that Murray had set a deadline of March 31 for completion but that other delays - including slow delivery of the bank's authorisation for the bid to go through - required an extension.

> The club is the commodity - we don't have a seat at the deal. We have to shove ourselves into the room. Our mission has been to represent the hundreds of thousands of supporters. We have no legal right to request it - but we have a moral right to request it.

And if the deal fails and the HMRC judgment goes against Rangers in a few weeks? "There's a 10,000lb gorilla in the room and you don't know what its appetite is," Johnston replied. "Even accessing all the resources we have access to, we couldn't pay the bill."

From which the only conclusion is that, if there is no Whyte knight and if faced with an adverse judgment in the main HMRC case – which could amount to as much as a £30 million liability – Rangers would go bust after 139 years of existence. Johnston's silent nod of assent when asked that question was even more eloquent than any of the scalding words he had just uttered.

> Even accessing all the resources we have access to, we couldn't pay the bill.

"The club is the commodity - we don't have a seat at the deal" is also most instructive. The 'deal' involved Lloyds, Murray International Holdings Limited and Craig Whyte. In this respect, the club (i.e. Rangers FC) was a commodity to be sold and bought.

On 19 April 2011, Johnston casted doubt on Whyte's ability to immediately transform the club's fortunes and revealed an Ibrox Director had proposed an alternative £25M investment.[224] This 'rival plan' was also reported in The Daily Telegraph:[225,226]

The seemingly interminable saga of the attempt by Craig Whyte - the London-based Scottish entrepreneur - to assume control of Rangers took yet another twist yesterday when the Chairman, Alastair Johnston, revealed that an Ibrox director had proposed an alternative funding plan to Whyte's bid.

Johnston's statement raised more questions than it answered, although The Daily Telegraph understands that the director involved is Dave King, who is based in South Africa and who has been the subject of a case involving the tax authorities there. King, who is a non-executive director of Rangers, invested £20 million in the club in 2000 and has the backing of Paul Murray, an accountant and board member since 2007. Johnston's statement yesterday expressed doubt about Whyte's ability to deliver his promises, which include a £25million transfer spending pot for Ally McCoist, who will succeed Walter Smith as Rangers manager at the end of this season. Johnston said:

> Based on the documents we have only been able to review within the last week, we are disappointed that they ultimately did not reflect the investment in the club that we were led to believe for the last few months would be a commitment in the purchase agreement. Given the requirement to repay the bank in full under the proposed transaction, there appears to be only a relatively modest amount of money available that would positively impact the club's operations, especially as it relates to an urgent requirement to replenish and upgrade the playing squad.

Johnston added:

> The board has had an approach from one of its directors, who wishes the board to consider an alternative funding option. This would involve a fresh issue of new capital to raise £25million to be invested directly into the club. The board believes that it has a responsibility to examine this proposal whilst continuing its review of the Craig Whyte transaction. After six months of limited engagement in the process, the board believes that is not in the best interests of its stakeholders for it to be pressed into an unrealistic timescale.

In response, a source speaking on behalf of Whyte said that the move made "no sense at all" and declared that the financier's patience would soon run out. He added:

> The deal Craig Whyte is putting forward is worth £52.5million, more than double the amount apparently to be raised by this unnamed Rangers director. Further, the Craig Whyte investment in the club would begin on day one of a deal being completed. Most importantly, it would mean that the debt owed to the Lloyds Banking Group would be cleared - which has been one of the key demands of the entire deal.

The source added that proof of funds had been given to Murray International Holdings and Lloyds by Whyte, who is looking to buy 75 per cent of David Murray's shareholding, with the rest going to partner Andrew Ellis. "This means that not only will debt be repaid immediately, but that £10million will go into Rangers' bank account on the first day as working capital," the source added. "Any contrary suggestion about funding is not only untrue but also defamatory."

Continuing with the 'concern' with Whyte, and from *16 things we learned from the Craig Whyte fraud trial*:[227]

> Two weeks before Craig Whyte took over Rangers, Dave King, then a director at the club, warned of a possible future police investigation into the Whyte takeover. His warning came in a letter in April 2011 to the statutory takeover panel, set up in relation to the deal. Mr King wrote of concerns about the source of Mr Whyte's funds to buy the club. Mr King said he was excluded from involvement in the takeover deal. Sir David Murray said this was not true.

In this respect, in the BBC documentary (*Craig Whyte Uncovered: Rangers Thousandaire & His Dodgy Past)*, Alistair Johnston stated that he offered an Independent Dossier to the IBC that had been prepared by a Private Investigator. Of note, Johnston was concerned that Craig Whyte did not have the money to pay the bills.

On 22 April 2011, Roddy Forsyth, in The Daily Telegraph, also commented on the ongoing takeover saga:[228,229]

> The rival camps who are bidding for Rangers have bedded in for the Easter holidays as the saga looks increasingly likely to grind on past the point where supporters must make up their minds whether or not to buy season tickets for the campaign that begins in late July. It was anticipated that Craig Whyte, the London-based Scottish financier, would have completed his attempt to purchase the controlling interest in the Ibrox club from Sir David Murray earlier this week, after five months of due diligence. Instead, two Ibrox directors, Paul Murray and Dave King, announced that they were in a position to put together a consortium of like-minded businessmen to make an alternative offer. Interest by the second group, which also includes the car and bus tycoon, Douglas Park, began in late 2009, but only re-emerged this week when Alastair Johnston, the Rangers chairman, issued a statement to the effect that the Ibrox board's vetting committee - which also includes the chief executive, Martin Bain, former captain and manager, John Greig, former chairman, John McClelland, and another director, John McIntyre - were not satisfied that Whyte could deliver the investment he had promised would be put towards the purchase of players during the summer transfer window. The Whyte camp believes that Johnston's statement was a sign of panic by the rival group because the final agreement between Sir David Murray and their man was at hand. A source close to the Whyte bid insists that their offer would have paid off the bank and made £10 million working capital available from day one of his ownership. They also believe that Johnston's statement, which appeared first on Rangers' website, was posted before the Stock Exchange was informed, in violation of the rules governing takeovers. However, the Stock Exchange is now closed until Tuesday morning and even were Sir David Murray to agree final terms with Whyte over the weekend, nothing could happen officially until the markets re-open.

It would appear that significant politics were at 'play' at this stage. In his book *INTO THE BEAR PIT,* Whyte suggests that the IBC was more aligned to Paul Murray and Dave King and that the IBC was trying to block Whyte's takeover. In addition,

Whyte suggests that a clear split in the Boardroom was evident — it seems that Mike McGill and Donald Muir were clearly working with Murray International Holdings Limited and Lloyds who wanted the sale to go through. Moreover, Craig Whyte suggests that majority of Rangers Board wanted Sir David Murray out. There seemed to be a Muir & McGill (representing Murray International Holdings Limited/Lloyds) versus 'the others.' Whyte suggests that the others (especially Paul Murray and Dave King) wanted to tip it (the plc) into insolvency and buy it back i.e. they did not want Whyte to buy and scupper their plans.[230]

Whyte's team included financial advisors at MCR BC — a corporate restructuring and turnaround firm that focused on insolvency administration. The key 'actors' were David Grier, Paul Clark and David Whitehouse. Pill Betts had introduced Craig Whyte to David Grier at MCR BC. Grier was a specialist in rescuing failing businesses. Whyte — like the previous Board — had considered putting The Rangers Football Club plc into administration. As such, all the problems would have sat with the old management at time of takeover. In addition, the debt would have gone. The significant problem was the outcome of the big tax case — the hearing of the FTTT was due in April 2011 but delayed to May 2011. If The Rangers Football Club plc 'won' the tax case, this would not have looked good for Mr Whyte.

Looking specifically at the 'finance deal' that enabled Craig Whyte to purchase the 85.3% shareholding in The Rangers Football Club plc from Sir David Murray on 6 May 2011, in April 2011 Whyte states that he was told about The Small Tax Case /DoS liability of £2.8M and that £1.75M would be required to be spent on the stadium (Public Address System and catering) to ensure that it was ready to open in Season 2011/2012. As such, the previous £5M that was demanded for equity (shares) was reduced to £1. The 'deal' was effectively, then, about debt financing.[231]

On Friday 6 May 2011, it was announced that Craig Whyte had acquired the 85.3% shareholding in The Rangers Football Club plc from Murray International Limited for £1 after the Takeover Panel had ratified the deal. Whyte states that Wavetower was an 'acquisition vehicle' for the takeover of The Rangers Football Club plc.[232] Wavetower and Liberty Capital gave a guarantee to Ticketus.[233] Craig Whyte and Phil Betts were Executive Directors and had full authority. In addition, the securities that Lloyds bank held over The Rangers Football Club plc's principal tangible assets were assigned to Whyte's companies. [234]

At this juncture — and in simple terms — I suggest that Figure 13.0 represents the acquisition.

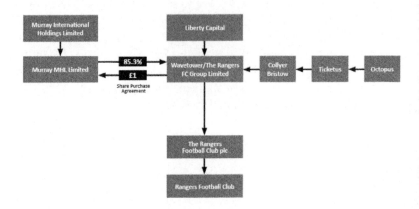

Figure: 13.0: Whyte's Acquisition of The Rangers Football Club plc

The key points from Figure 13.0 are as follows:

- 85.3% of shares in The Ranges Football Club plc were held by Murray MHL Limited.
- These shares were sold — for £1 — by Murray MHL Limited to Wavetower.
- A Share Purchase Agreement was in place.
- The liability from The Ranges Football Club to Lloyds was paid by Wavetower. The Liability of the Rangers Football Club plc was now with Wavetower, which renamed itself as the Rangers FC Group Limited on 12 May 2012.[235, 236]
- Wavetower received funds to pay Lloyds — from Ticketus.
- These funds (i.e. monies from future season tickets) would be repaid to Ticketus.

On purchase, Whyte stated that the plc's revenue was £35M but costs were at £45M. Clearly, he needed the additional revenue

120

from European football — especially the Champions' League income. It is also understood that the Share Purchase Agreement (for £1) was as follows:

- £5M would be invested in the playing squad and a further £20M invested in the team by 2016.
- Provision of a further £5M in working capital would be provided to the to the club to provide capital expenditure to bring catering facilities and the public address system at Ibrox up to date.
- A confirmed agreement to cover the £2.8M liability owed from DOS (plus charges/penalties = £4M).

In advance of the purchase, 'Letters of Support' and 'Proof of Funds' were received from John Newlands and the MHG. In detail, in *16 things we learned from the Craig Whyte fraud trial,* [237] London financier John Newlands said that he had seen documents relating to Whyte's Liberty Capital company and, in March 2011, Mr Newlands wrote a letter to Murray International Holdings Limited stating Whyte could "comfortably underwrite" a possible £10M "rights issue". In addition, in the BBC documentary *Rangers – the men who sold the jerseys,* Daily suggests that the UK financial institution MHG stated that Liberty Capital had £33M for purchase of Rangers. [238] Of note, Whyte says that he owned 30% of MHG. [239] In addition, it is suggested that an additional £4M came from Merchant Turnaround plc (£1M) [240] and Jerome Group Pension Fund (£3M). [241] The Daily Telegraph reported the purchase as thus: [242]

> Businessman Craig Whyte has completed his takeover of Rangers after acquiring an 85.3 per cent stake, his Wavetower company said last night. The takeover panel has granted Whyte a dispensation from making a cash offer to all other shareholders in Rangers, who lead the Scottish Premier League by one point from Celtic. Whyte bought the stake for £1 from Murray International Holdings and replaces former Rangers chairman David Murray as majority shareholder. "Craig is a lifelong Rangers supporter and is very much looking forward to guiding and assisting Rangers in its development over the coming

121

years," said a statement from Wavetower issued on behalf of the 40 year-old. Whyte arrived in Edinburgh on Thursday for talks with Murray and members of the club's board but technical issues delayed the completion of the takeover which has rumbled on since November.

The firm that financed Rangers with £24M stressed that it bought the club's season tickets and did not lend the money. Indeed, Octopus Investments clarified its arrangement with the stricken club, through its Ticketus arm, after the administrators of The Rangers Football Club plc revealed the money could not be traced in the Club (The Rangers Football Club plc) accounts. A statement on the investment company's website read:

> Octopus Investments would like to clarify the position of Ticketus with regard to the current Glasgow Rangers coverage. Ticketus is one of the many entities into which Octopus Protected EIS invests. Ticketus has purchased tickets for Glasgow Rangers games for a number of seasons in advance, as it has done for a number of years previously with the club. Ticketus does not lend money; Ticketus is the owner of assets - the tickets. Octopus is continuing to work with the administrators and Glasgow Rangers on this matter.

Returning to the 'timeline', on 24 May 2011 changes were made in the Boardroom of The Rangers Football Club plc. For example, Martin Bain, the company's CEO and Director Donald McIntyre were suspended and placed under internal investigation.[243] Alistair Johnston and Director Paul Murray were removed from the plc Board having refused to resign their posts.[244] On 20 June 2011, it was reported that Martin Bain commenced legal action against the plc. Four days later, he resigned. In addition, Alistair Johnston warned supporters to 'police' Craig Whyte. He stated that Craig Whyte needs to 'walk the walk'.[245]

On 27 May 2011, Phil Betts was confirmed as a Director. Gary Withey replaced Donald McIntyre as Company Secretary and Andrew Ellis was a Director of the Rangers FC Group Limited but not on the Rangers Football Club plc Board. On 1 June 2011

— and stated in their *Statement of Administrators Proposals* — Duff &Phelps offer that MCR BC was engaged by Liberty Capital to give advice to the management team on short-term cash flow, organisational structures and liaising with HMRC in respect of the Small Tax Case.[246] Moreover, in the said *Statement of Administrators Proposals, Duff* & Phelps state that on 13 June 2011:[247]

> MCR BC provided HMRC with a formal update, which included an overview of the Company's projected working capital shortfall in the following 3 months (as identified by the short-term cash flow forecast review), an overview of company's financial position and an assessment that the Company would be unable to trade in the medium term without an introduction of third party funds or shareholder support. Given this position, an offer of an immediate payment on account of £200 000 was proposed to HMRC and request made for time to formulate a proposal to HMRC relating to the balance of the Company's Small Tax Case liability.

On reflection, I suggest that this is actually astonishing. It seems to me that — within 3 weeks of the purchase of The Rangers Football Club plc — concerns were raised (by MCR BC) about a working capital shortfall and an assessment that the company would be unable to trade without an introduction of third-party funds or shareholder support. Moreover, it would seem that, at this time, there were concerns if The Small Tax Case liability could be paid. Of note, it was understood that this liability would be paid at the takeover time and from his (Whyte's) Letter to Shareholders.[248]

At this stage, perhaps the only available money to Whyte was the £20.3M from Ticketus (that repaid Lloyds) and £4M [from Merchant Turnaround (£1M) and Jerome Group Pension Fund (£3M)]. This also chimes with the comments by James Traynor who said on the BBC Scotland Newsnight programme that Whyte had a flawed business plan — simply, Whyte did not have enough money. In other words, why would he buy a club (that

123

no one else wanted to 'touch' due to the potential EBT liability) and not have enough money to run it?[249]

Moreover, Duff & Phelps state that in June 2011, the first £3M of the liabilities due to Ticketus was paid by The Rangers FC Group Limited, followed by an additional payment of £5M in September 2011.[250] In addition, Duff & Phelps state that MCR BC was engaged by Liberty Capital to conduct review of long-term forecasts and to assess options (i.e. capital raising and restructuring options).[251] MCR BC was also tasked to assist in further discussions with Liberty Capital, The Rangers Football Club plc and HMRC following submission of the initial proposal to HMRC (of £200 000).

Of worry — and causing some embarrassment — on 11 August 2011, Sheriff Officers 'raided' Rangers FC over an ongoing tax bill dispute with HMRC (The Small Tax Case). It was understood that Craig Whyte had promised to pay this amount.[252] In this regard, The Herald newspaper offered analysis:

> RANGERS dispute with Her Majesty s Revenue and Customs escalated yesterday after sheriff officers presented the club with a list of scenarios for recovery of debt if a repayment agreement is breached. In a move leading tax experts describe as highly significant and a step away from a winding up order, two sheriff officers served papers on the club over an outstanding tax liability of £2.8 million, including details on potential recovery. The Ibrox club has insisted the sheriff officers were not there to carry out an asset evaluation, which would list assets it could seize if the bill is not paid, and said it believed they had been instructed by HMRC for dramatic effect. A Rangers spokesman said the club had held several meetings with HMRC representatives this week and that it had reached an outline agreement with the tax office on repayment. Club sources, though, said they did not recognise the reported figure of £1.4m that the club would have to pay on top of the £2.8m as a penalty payment. They also insisted the two officers were there as a formality, delivering paperwork that must be put in place should negotiations prove to be unsuccessful and that the visit lasted

five minutes. But a leading taxation expert, who asked not to be named, said:

> This is quite a significant development and an extreme measure for HMRC to send sheriff officers. It's always the stage before taking court proceedings and seeking a winding up order for outstanding debts. It's not something that happens to HMRC clients every day to have sheriff officers at the door and is a clear indication of the seriousness with which HMRC is taking the matter. They are not there to negotiate. They arrive to tell you how monies will be collected and their use today suggests a breakdown in communication between the parties involved.

Another expert said sheriff officers were used to be a frightening thing as much as anything, adding:

> When a third party is dispatched it will always come with a warning of what follows if the debts are unpaid but there is still scope for a resolution.

The £2.8m bill stems from liabilities run up on deals done during the high-spending reign of Dick Advocaat but was only identified in the later stages of the process which led to the takeover of Rangers by Craig Whyte in May. Last night, Rangers sources told The Herald there was no question of the agreement on the bill not being adhered to and there were continuing concerns of how the club dealings with HMRC were being made public. A Rangers spokesman said:

> RFC has been in detailed discussions with HMRC over a tax liability that was revealed during due diligence prior to the takeover of the club by a new majority shareholder earlier this year. The Sherriff officers visited Ibrox to warn of consequences should the club fail to pay an outstanding charge. Meetings have been held with representatives from HMRC this week and are ongoing and we have reached outline agreement with HMRC. Discussions today dealt with formalities. We are utterly dismayed that there are people who have been involved in this process who think it right to conduct normally confidential business

discussions in public. They clearly would not do that with other businesses but think it all right with Rangers.

During late July and August of that year, results in Europe were, I suggest, most significant in the history of Rangers FC. At this stage, I consider that Whyte was 'banking' on the revenue from such European football. Indeed, he said so much in his dealings with the IBC i.e. Europa League football was a minimum.

Date	Round	Ground	Opponent	Score
26 July 2011	QR3	Home	Malmö FF	0 - 1
3 August 2011	QR3	Away	Malmö FF	1 - 1

Union of European Football Associations (UEFA) Champions League

Date	Round	Ground	Opponent	Score
18 August 2011	POR	Away	Maribor	1 – 2
25 August 2011	POR	Home	Maribor	1 - 1

UEFA Europa League

Of note, there was no additional revenue into The Ranges Football Club plc. I consider that things started to 'snowball' from here.[253] 'Retrenchment' also started — Whyte notes that failure to reach the Champions' League meant that The Rangers Football Club plc was deprived of additional revenue of £15-20M. This loss of revenue was also echoed by Donald Findlay QC who commented:[254]

> During his closing argument, Mr Findlay also referred to Rangers' early Champions' League exit against Swedish side Malmo after Mr Whyte took the helm at Ibrox in 2011. He told the court:

126

If Rangers had made the league section of the Champions League, do we actually think we would be here today? The probability is no.

In domestic cup competitions things became somewhat difficult too, which further reduced additional income. A third-round defeat to First Division side Falkirk FC in the League Cup and a fifth round exit at home at the hands of Dundee United FC contributed further to the significant lack of revenue.[255] Of note, The Rangers Football Club plc did not have a credit line and the Malmö FF 'debacle' was a significant factor that scuppered a most limited business pan. In parallel, Whyte suggests that there were lots of leaks and 'whispering' which significantly undermined his ability to do business. For example, he states that Martin Bain claimed that Rangers were on the brink of insolvency, which was embarrassing and damaging.[256] At this time, he, again, considered the 'need to go into administration' i.e. step back before stepping forward.

In respect of The Rangers Football Club plc running out of money, it is also interesting that the JAs state that Ticketus advanced a further £5M to the Collyer Bristow client account in the name of The Rangers FC Group in consideration of future season ticket revenue of £9.3M (to be repaid over seasons 13/14 and 14/15).[257] The JAs also state that the company continued to incur arrears with HMRC in relation to PAYE and VAT.[258] Moreover, and in terms of business analysis and succession planning, a further (and significant) operational problem was caused by the previous Board of Directors leaving all at once during a turbulent financial period for company. Key experience and insight were lost — this, to me, was important.

On 3 September 2011, and contributing further to a poor public perception, The Herald newspaper reported that The Rangers Football Club plc had £2.8M seized after an Arrest Order was issued over an unpaid tax bill. In addition, and on 10 September 2011, The Rangers Football Club plc was forced to pay costs of £10 000 to Levy & McRae (a specialist litigation law firm) by Lord Hodge who had represented them in their dealing with

127

UEFA against sectarian signing by their fans in two Europa League games against PSV Eindhoven in the previous season.[259] And, on 14 September 2011, Martin Bain secured a court order to 'freeze' £480 000 as Lord Hodge said that there was a real and substantial risk of insolvency.[260, 261]

Although the focus during this period was on Craig Whyte, Roddy Forsyth suggested that Rangers were paying a heavy price for damage done by Murray:[262]

> The tax tribunal that could tip Rangers into insolvency is the legacy of an era of such profligacy that it makes the eyes water to consider how money was once lavished on the club in a vain - and the word is employed here in both its meanings - attempt to conquer Europe. No manager of a Scottish club has ever come close to Dick Advocaat's spending on players and, as matters stand, none ever will. Advocaat laid out £80million on players who made no impact whatsoever in European competition. Even worse, their brief period of domestic domination came to a crunching end when Martin O'Neill arrived at Celtic in 2000. Sir David Murray's tenure at Ibrox is encapsulated in his boast that if Celtic spent £5, he would outlay £10 and - as was pointed out in these pages when Craig Whyte assumed control of the club - Murray's cash did bring in almost exactly twice as many trophies as Celtic over the period of his ownership. The fatal flaw in the calculation is that the honours were all domestic, a native Scottish currency that was rapidly declining in value compared to the prestige and riches to be acquired from success in the Premier League and Champions League. However, Celtic - deeply scarred by the events of 1994 when they came within minutes of bankruptcy - did learn a traumatic lesson. Although their trophy cabinet was replenished much less frequently than its Ibrox equivalent, they can bring another perspective to bear on Murray's now notorious pronouncement. For every £1 of Celtic debt, Rangers have run up £25 - and that is not counting the worst case scenario of an adverse verdict in the HMRC tax tribunal, which could take the Old Firm debt ratio up to 1:120. As for Whyte, nobody knows how he has made his money - because he is remarkably secretive about its provenance - or how much he is worth or what his business plan promises, other than the reduction of salaries and

an increased dependence on the notoriously unreliable commodity of young players. Perhaps he will have Rangers declared insolvent - when we spoke on Monday he did not refute the suggestion that the notion must have its attractions - and, if so, it is very likely that the club will endure a welter of recriminations that will make the current publicity look like a favourable advertisement. If it does come to that, though - and whatever responsibility or culpability falls upon Whyte - the serious damage was done back in the days of Advocaat, when the manager and the owner of Rangers revelled in their ability to outspend their local rivals.

On 26 September 2011, the same author (Forsyth) suggests that it might be in the owner's best interest to declare the club insolvent ahead of the HMRC hearing (the FTTT). Continuing with this theme, and in an interview with The Daily Telegraph, Whyte believes that they would win the tax case but administration was the likeliest outcome if the tax tribunal — scheduled for November 2011 — went against them.[263]

> Her Majesty's Revenue and Customs is seeking £49million in back-taxes, interest and penalties from Rangers, a claim that could see one of the great institutions of British and European football become the game's highest profile financial failure.

> Speaking exclusively to The Daily Telegraph, Whyte said he would actively seek to leave the SPL to secure Rangers' financial future and suggested the club could even consider running two teams, one each side of the border once the case and its implications have been dealt with. Whyte also confirmed that while he believes Rangers will win the case, administration is the likeliest outcome if the tax tribunal, scheduled for November, goes against them. Asked if administration would follow, Whyte said:

>> It is one of the possibilities we have looked at, yes. The choice, in terms of an adverse finding, is pretty obvious really.

> Administration would bring an immediate 10-point penalty and the possibility of more sanctions, depending on the club's exit

strategy. But Whyte is adamant that there is no threat to Rangers' long term future:

> Whatever happens Rangers will be moving forward. I will not allow the club to go bust. I can control the debt process absolutely, and whatever happens Rangers is going to be there playing in the SPL at Ibrox.

The threat to Rangers stems from a claim for £35million in back-tax and interest and £14 million in fines relating to the Murray regime's use of a tax-avoidance device called Employee Benefit Trusts. HMRC claims Rangers wrongly used EBTs for a decade, effectively to reclassify regular salaries as loans that avoided income tax and National Insurance. Rangers' own advice when the schemes were established was that they were legal, and HMRC made no complaint until last year, when it changed its guidance on EBTs. It has now targeted Rangers among 5,000 companies it believes misused EBTs. Whyte believes the club have been singled out as a test case and accuses HMRC of leaking information. Whyte acknowledges the risk, but insists the club's long-term future is secure. He has repaid the £18 million to Lloyds, a fact confirmed by the bank, and transferred the debt to Rangers' holding company, which is ultimately owned by his Liberty Capital Limited, a company registered in the British Virgin Islands. Whyte has committed to writing off the debt if the club avoids administration. This structure means Whyte is the largest secured creditor and has control of any administration.

> Nothing is out of my hands because I control the club, I am the only secured creditor, or rather Rangers FC Group is. So on any decision, while HMRC might push, the group company controls the debt.

The JAs state that in September 2011, HMRC arrested £2.9M held in company's accounts with the Bank of Scotland in respect of tax arrears.[264] To compound matters further, on 10 October 2011, Donald McIntyre resigned as Finance Director. It was reported in the Daily Telegraph of 11 October that he, too, was considering taking legal advice against Rangers. The JAs state that an Arrestment Order of £375 000 was served by McIntyre in

October 2011. Such arrestment orders froze funds which would have been otherwise available to the company.[265]

On 18 October 2011 — and of great emotional significance — John Greig (and former chairman John McClelland) resigned from the Board of Directors of The Rangers Football Club plc. On 20 October 2011, the BBC aired its documentary *Craig Whyte Uncovered: Rangers Thousandaire & His Dodgy Past.* As a result, it was reported in The Daily Telegraph on 21 October that Whyte was ready to sue over this television programme.[266] In this newspaper article, it is interesting that Whyte mentions the word 'restructuring'. This is what he has been doing for most of his professional career.

> Meanwhile, Whyte insists he is doing everything in his power to prevent the club from going into administration. Rangers are involved in two separate disputes with HM Revenue and Customs, relating to payments before Whyte's takeover. The larger of those cases could leave Rangers facing an estimated tax bill of £49million. Whyte has always maintained he is confident of winning the case but did address the issue of administration in the interview with STV. He said:
>
>> It's certainly not something we want to see happen and we are actively doing all we can to avoid it. There is no chance of Rangers going out of business, no chance whatsoever.
>
> If Rangers do succeed with the dispute, Whyte has vowed to write off the club's £18 million debt, which is currently on the books of his holding company.
>
>> It's not going to be converted to equity which would dilute the other shareholders of Rangers," he said. "We've got 26,000 shareholders who are very important to us, they are all fans of the club, and I want to make sure they are not diluted in any way. The debt is effectively going to be written off. I own a fantastic asset and a business that, once it has been restructured, I think is going to be very valuable so it's certainly not an act of charity. I see it as a sound business decision.

Asked about plans to appeal if Rangers lose the tax case, Whyte said:

> That's a decision that we can make at the time. What I will say is that I think it would be impossible for any business to operate with that level of scrutiny, with that tax debt hanging over it and tribunals going on for potentially months and years to come. I think it's better for everybody, better for Rangers and everybody involved at Rangers, that a conclusion is reached as quickly as possible.

Whyte acknowledges that the Ibrox club face a difficult chapter but is adamant he is the right man to steer Rangers through tough times. He said:

> There were many times when I could have walked away from it but I decided to persevere. Somebody had to do this, somebody had to take up the challenge and I think I can do that. There are days when there are challenges and it's tough but it's a privilege to be in this position, a privilege to own Rangers and be chairman of Rangers. There is a big job to do here and somebody has to sort it out and I'm the guy to do that.

In his book (*INTO THE BEAR PIT*), Whyte does, however, offer his concerns of events at this time (i.e. October/November 2011):[267]

> The dam was bursting. We had legal action from Martin Bain and Donald McIntyre, we had HMRC freezing the bank accounts for money that was due. The money we'd taken from season ticket sales in the summer – around £12million to £15 million – was being used to pay the bills, but these funds were dwindling and due to run out in March.

Whyte writes that that he attempted to 'sort out' the problem with HMRC.[268] He also states that — after the meeting with HMRC — that there was a high probability that administration was likely.[269] Indeed, he discussed a solvent restructure with the SFA/Harper McLeod in October 2011 in case the FTTT was lost.

In addition, he states that administration may have been a good thing — the tax debt would be gone, all 'Sir David contracts' would go and he would lose players too.[270]

On 7 November 2011, the FTTT reconvened. However, on 16 November 2011, it was postponed to January (16 -18) 2012. This did cause further uncertainty. Whyte reflects that he should have 'gone for administration' in October 2011.[271] Moreover, and later in this month, The Rangers Football Club plc confirmed to the PLUS Stock Exchange that Whyte had previously been disqualified as a Director. This was reported widely. For example, in the Daily Telegraph of 1 December 2011:

> Rangers released their figures to the PLUS Stock Exchange and also issued a statement to the London-based market confirming Whyte had previously been disqualified as a director. The statement read:
>
> > Craig Whyte was disqualified to act as a director of Vital UK Limited in 2000 for a period of seven years.
>
> The revelation had been contained in a documentary screened on BBC Scotland in October, a programme which prompted Whyte to take legal action against the broadcaster.

In addition, it was reported on the 2 December 2011 — again in the same newspaper (Daily Telegraph) —:

> The Scottish Football Association is preparing to investigate Rangers chairman Craig Whyte to discern whether or not sanctions should be taken against the Clydesdale Bank Premier League champions. Whyte may fall foul of the SFA's Articles of Association, specifically 10.2, which specifies instances in which a director may not be considered a fit and proper person to hold office. In his case, it is section 10.2 (g) - where individuals would not be allowed to be appointed to a club's board if "he has been disqualified as a director pursuant to the Company Directors' Disqualification Act 1986 within the previous five years" which appears to have set alarm bells ringing. On Wednesday, when Rangers posted their figures for the financial year until June 2011 (which were filed at the last

133

possible minute and, unusually, not signed off by the club's accountants, Grant Thornton), he announced to the Stock Exchange that he had been banned from being a company director by the UK Insolvency Service in June 2000, a complete disqualification which lasted until 2007. That prompted a statement from the SFA's chief executive, Stewart Regan, last night:

> The Scottish FA has noted the Rangers FC statement to the stock exchange regarding the club's owner Craig Whyte. We have been in dialogue with the club on this matter and in light of today's developments have requested clarification by return. We await disclosure of key information before we can make any further comment.

Under 10.4 of their Articles of Association, any club which fails to disclose relevant information about a registered official "shall be liable to a fine, suspension or both or such other penalty, condition or sanction as the Judicial Panel considers appropriate". The 40 year-old also failed to disclose his previous suspension from directorships to the PLUS Exchange, where Rangers shares are traded, when he bought the club from Sir David Murray for just £1 in May. Under the exchange's rules, directors are compelled to inform them of any "official public incrimination or sanction" they have received. Whyte's failure to do so could result in him being penalised by PLUS. Responding to the comments from the SFA, a spokesman for Rangers said:

> At no stage did the club believe there had been a breach of SFA regulations. The club will be happy to provide the SFA with all the relevant information and discuss the matter with them fully.

On 9 December 2011, it was reported in The Daily Telegraph that Whyte put the Rangers AGM on hold until the New Year.

> Rangers chairman Craig Whyte will put off the club's AGM until the new year in a bid to ensure a more positive meeting. The AGM had been expected this month but Rangers will first seek to make progress on their dispute with Her Majesty's

Revenue and Customs. A tax tribunal was recently postponed from November until January and Whyte hopes to face shareholders with the outlook more favourable as the club's lawyers work to avoid a bill of up to £49million. Rangers last week published annual figures showing their debt had almost halved to £14million during the year to June 30, but the accounts were not signed off by an independent auditor. Whyte told The Scottish Sun:

> We'd still hope to have our accounts signed off before the end of the year. It will not be logistically possible to have the AGM in what remains of 2011, though. We will have it in the first quarter of 2012 when we'll have a better indication of how the tax case will play out. I'd like to face that AGM with more certainty and positive news on the way ahead for Rangers.

Throughout December 2011 and January 2012, Duff & Phelps was requested by The Rangers Football Club plc to recommence discussions with HMRC in respect of The Small Tax Case liability and arrears in PAYE/National Insurance and VAT that had accrued since August 2011.

2012

The new year did not start well. For example, on 9 January 2012, The Rangers Football Club plc shares were suspended from trading on the PLUS Stock Exchange for its failure to submit audited accounts. This was reported in The Daily Telegraph on 10 January 2012:[272]

> Rangers suffered another financial blow yesterday when trading on their shares was suspended because of their failure to submit audited accounts. Rangers published their annual financial figures on November 30 but they were not signed off by an independent auditor and the club subsequently failed to meet the six-month deadline from the end of their financial year. Rangers chairman Craig Whyte quickly responded to the PLUS Stock Exchange's suspension by downplaying the merits of being listed on the market.

In this respect, Whyte offers that with 85% of shares owned by a single company there was little tangible benefit for the club to be a listed company.[273] Continuing with this theme of financial difficulties, Grahame — in The Daily Telegraph of 11 January 2012 — offers excellent analysis:[274]

Rangers will need to contend with their own localised version of the credit crunch for the next few months until the verdict in Her Majesty's Revenue and Customs case against them is finally announced.

The Top Tier Tribunal meets in Edinburgh from Jan 16-18 in order to decide whether, as HMRC argue, the club is guilty of tax evasion through the use of Employee Benefit Trusts from 2000-2010. Should the verdict, which is expected in either March or early April, go against Rangers then the club could face a bill of £49million in unpaid tax, interest and penalties. On Monday the PLUS stock exchange suspended trading in Rangers shares as a result of the club failing to abide by the Companies Act (2006) by not publishing audited accounts or holding their AGM on time. They could also face a fine of £100,000 from PLUS, who wish to know why owner Craig Whyte failed to disclose to them until Nov 30 that he had been disqualified from becoming a company director for seven years by the UK Insolvency Service in 2000. Whyte concedes that the tax case represents "a dark cloud" over Rangers, who could not possibly pay such a bill. He is not alone in thinking that way. Former finance director Donald McIntyre had £300,000 of the club's assets frozen last year while he sued for alleged breach of contract, a case which was settled out of court in December. Former chief executive Martin Bain, who is seeking £1.3million from Rangers, has frozen £480,000 of their assets due - his solicitors claim - to the risk of insolvency. HMRC themselves have already frozen £2.3 million over a separate tax bill of £2.8million (plus an added £1.4million in penalties) dating from nine months ago. In November, Capita Trustee Services, which had taken legal action in pursuit of alleged unpaid fees, also agreed an out-of-court settlement. Celtic took the unprecedented step of demanding cash up front before handing over tickets for away fans for the Old Firm match at Parkhead. Independent financial analyst David Low, who helped engineer Fergus McCann's takeover of Celtic in 1994, believes that

136

Rangers will now be forced to pay in full for everything they need for the next few months.

Until the tax case is clarified, one way or another, then it will be impossible for Rangers to plan for the future. That involves having the trading of shares restored, it involves having qualified accounts signed off and spending money on both the team and the club. As things stand, there are an increasing number of third parties who are unwilling to lend them any credit at all because they know Rangers' financial position.

Of course, it is possible that venture capitalist Whyte, as secured creditor, could potentially stand to profit from the club going bust, by then taking them out of administration, debt-free, after buying the club 10 months ago from Sir David Murray for just £1. The chairman confessed in October that the club faces a credibility crisis.

It affects us commercially. How can anyone enter into, say, a five-year deal with Rangers in the midst of this uncertainty?

The SFA have confirmed yesterday's Daily Telegraph report that Rangers have until March 31 to publish audited accounts and prove that they do not owe money to the tax authorities if they are to be granted a licence to enter European competition next season. Stewart Regan, the SFA's chief executive, had publicly demanded clarification from Rangers in November concerning Whyte's previous ban on becoming a company director. The governing body confirmed yesterday that the club has responded to that request but that Regan would not be commenting on the substance of that reply.

On 13 January 2012, Phil Betts resigned from The Rangers FC Group Limited. On 16 January 2012, the FTTT began in Edinburgh — it concluded on 18 January 2012. On 20 January 2012, Phil Betts resigned as a Director of the Board of Rangers Football Club plc. He was replaced by Andrew Ellis on the Rangers Football Club plc Board on 20 January 2012.

On 31 January 2012, Whyte offered that — due to the precarious position of the finances of The Rangers Football Club plc — Nikica Jelavić was sold to Everton FC. Duff & Phelps state that Jelavic was sold for £5M plus VAT — half of which was received in the main bank account on 2 February 2012.[275] It became apparent, however, that in the absence of significant working capital or an agreement with HMRC, the company would be unable to meet its liabilities as they fell due and the company could not avoid formal insolvency proceedings. Moreover, and on 31 January 2012, The Daily Record newspaper revealed the Ticketus deal. As such, and on the 1 February 2012, The Rangers Supporters Trust urged Whyte to clarify the situation involving Ticketus and their relationship with Rangers.[276] This was also reported in The Daily Telegraph: 1 February 2012:[277]

> Rangers chairman Craig Whyte has denied using supporters' money from season ticket sales to fund his takeover of the club from Sir David Murray. Whyte bought Murray's stake for £1 in May last year but also agreed to pay Lloyds their debt of around £18million while investing in the playing squad. In an open letter published on the club's official website, Whyte said:
>
>> I can categorically assure supporters that when I launched a takeover bid for the club it was funded entirely from one of my companies and that was demonstrated clearly to the satisfaction of the previous owner, Lloyds Banking Group and professional advisers.

3 February 2012:[278]

> The purchase of a season ticket is an act of faith that the money will be invested in renewed ambition. Whyte has hawked four years' worth of such dreams along with the team's top scorer at a time when the SPL championship still hangs in the balance - if only just so. Some Rangers supporters now take the view that they should not renew season tickets until he parades signings that would make it worth their while. And if revenue from season tickets is withheld, how does Whyte pay off the debt he has incurred using them as security, never mind recruit fresh talent? Nobody can get the figures to square apart - perhaps -

from Whyte himself and he is in no hurry to present them for scrutiny, even by his own fellow shareholders. In the Murray/Advocaat era it was the chasm between earnings and spending that created Rangers' current troubles. In Whyte's case the difference between the facts he is prepared to share and those that are dragged into the public domain against his will is becoming a chasm of credibility. In more prosperous times the Ibrox support might have yearned for the club to be hauled back from the brink by a white knight. These days, who'd thank you for one of those?

Things got worse for Whyte. On 9 February 2012, it was reported in The Guardian newspaper that former plc Chairman Alastair Johnston asked the Intelligence and Enforcement Directorate of the Insolvency Service to investigate Whyte's takeover.[279]

Alastair Johnston, the former Rangers chairman, has requested that the government's Intelligence and Enforcement Directorate investigate Craig Whyte's acquisition of the Ibrox club. Johnston, who was the chairman at Rangers when Whyte bought out Sir David Murray last May, has been open about his scepticism towards the club's owner. It was confirmed last week that Whyte mortgaged Rangers' future season-ticket income to the tune of £24m, although he denies part of that funding was used to settle a £18m debt to the Lloyds Banking Group. Speaking to the Guardian on Thursday evening, Johnston said:

> I have had numerous approaches following the recent revelations in the press about the acquisition of Rangers Football Club and the use of future season-ticket money. I am not in a position to answer all the questions put to me but I do recognise the issue is causing much concern. I believe this is a prevalent view amongst Rangers stakeholders who are now demanding full transparency about the funding of the acquisition of the club, its current financial status and, most importantly, the way forward. In order to allow all of the options potentially available to stabilise the club to be explored, there must be total disclosure of all the underlying obstacles. Therefore, in my capacity as the chairman of the club during the period when it has been alleged that certain

financial arrangements of concern were executed by the buyer, I have formally requested that the Intelligence and Enforcement Directorate investigate and clarify this matter once and for all which is surely in the interests of all concerned.

At this stage, it seems that The Rangers Football Club plc was 'paralysed' by events. Whyte took further advice regarding entering administration. The legal advice was that the company had to serve a Notice of Intention (NoI) to put the said company into administration and then they had two weeks to plan if they were actually going to go into administration. This action would stall any creditor payments for those two weeks.

Duff & Phelps state that — in view of anticipated failure to meet future funding requirements of the company — Whyte filed a NoI to Appoint Administrators with Court of Session on 13 February 2012.[280, 281] Shortly afterwards, HMRC lodged a Creditors' Petition to appoint an Administrator in respect of unpaid taxes, which had accrued since August 2011 of £9M. After discussions between parties, HMRC decided to withdraw its petition, consenting to the appointment of Paul Clarke and David Whitehouse of Duff & Phelps as JAs.[282]

On Tuesday 14 February 2012, The Rangers Football Club plc was placed in administration. The SPL then confirmed that Rangers FC would be docked 10 points.[283] Extensive analysis, in this regard, is offered by The Daily Telegraph of 14 – 18 (Tuesday – Saturday) February 2012. It is instructive to reproduce it below.

Tuesday 14 February 2012:[284]

The Rangers owner, Craig Whyte, is on the brink of tipping the club into administration in an attempt to avoid the ruinous impact of a £50million tax investigation that could also affect up to eight Premier League clubs. The Old Firm club yesterday filed notice of their intention to enter administration, citing the threat of a tax bill of between £5million and £50million - and possibly as high as £100 million - as the reason for a move that

140

would see an automatic 10-point penalty. Rangers' huge potential tax liability is the result of an ongoing tax inquiry by Her Majesty's Revenue & Customs into the club's use of a complex tax avoidance device, Employee Benefit Trusts. HMRC is seeking as much as £49million in unpaid tax, interest and fines for Rangers' use of EBTs in the 10 years before Whyte bought the club last year. The Daily Telegraph understands that up to eight current or former Premier League clubs are facing a similar investigation into their use of EBTs, which were considered an efficient - and legal - means of reducing tax until relatively recently. Administration, which will come within 10 days of yesterday's notice, would leave Rangers 14 points behind Celtic in the Scottish Premier League and effectively see them concede the title. It will, however, provide significant protection for the club and Whyte, who remains the majority shareholder and largest secured creditor against HMRC's demands, and can be seen as a proactive, defensive measure. If we hadn't done that then liquidation could have been a possibility, Whyte said. This secures the long-term future of the club.

A tax tribunal is currently considering its verdict in the Rangers case, which if it went against them would be ruinous to the club and have a significant impact on Whyte.

Under EBTs companies pay money into a trust that then loans the money to the employee for benefits, typically pensions or for the purchase of shares, on the understanding that the loan is never repaid. HMRC alleges that Rangers' previous owners simply used EBTs to avoid paying millions of pounds in tax and National Insurance on the player payroll. Sources said last night that HMRC is investigating whether Premier League clubs operated in a similar way. Whyte has openly considered the prospect of administration since he took over at Ibrox, notably in an interview with The Daily Telegraph last September, and statements released last night suggested the latest move is part of a negotiation with HMRC. The chairman is Rangers' secured creditor after a company he controls cleared bank debts of £17million with a loan from one of his companies upon his takeover last year. In normal circumstances HMRC would be first in the queue for repayment of outstanding debtors, but in administration the taxman has no protection, and will have to join the line behind Whyte and the players to get its money back. If administration is successfully negotiated Whyte could emerge in control of the club, albeit through a new holding company, with any potentially crippling tax liability drastically reduced.

In a statement the club said they had already approached HMRC with proposals for a Creditors Voluntary Agreement - a deal to pay off outstanding debts - and were seeking a moratorium from further action. If approved the Rangers CVA would allow the club to emerge from administration within a month, crucially allowing them to hit UEFA deadlines for gaining a licence to play in European competition, a crucial revenue stream for the club. Rangers also said that Whyte, the majority shareholder, would continue to fund the club if the tax authorities agreed to "ring-fence" that funding from any tax issues.

Last night HMRC indicated it would not agree to any such deal, with sources claiming that the EBT issue was "entirely unconnected" with yesterday's move by Whyte, and a "red herring". Whyte said the opposite was the case.

> The fact is that Rangers' ongoing financial position and the HMRC first tier tribunal are inextricably linked. Rangers costs approximately £45million per year to operate and commands around £35million in revenue. From the outset I have made it clear that I do not think it is in the best interests of Rangers to throw good money after bad. Against a backdrop of falling revenues, costs have to be cut significantly. Painful as though that may be, it is the future of clubs such as ours. There is no realistic or practical alternative to our approach because HMRC has made it plain to the club that should we be successful in the forthcoming tax tribunal decision they will appeal the decision. This would leave the club facing years of uncertainty and also having to pay immediately a range of liabilities to HMRC which will be due whatever the overall result of the tax tribunal.

Tuesday 14 February 2012:[285]

> SCOTTISH football was rocked yesterday by the news that Rangers Football Club is preparing to go into administration. The move by the Glasgow club, which is in dispute with the tax authorities and deeply in debt, represents the biggest crisis in its

140-year history. Legal papers were lodged at the Court of Session in Edinburgh, notifying its intention to appoint an administrator. The club said it now had 10 days to confirm whether administrators had been appointed. The legal process was put in motion by the club's owner, Craig Whyte, before a tax tribunal decision that could land it with a bill of more than £50 million.

Mr Whyte, who was heckled by fans, said last night the club was facing massive financial challenges and the best way to secure its long-term future was to go through a "formal restructuring process". The appointment of an administrator will result in a moratorium on the club's debt. But there could be redundancies and players could be asked to take a wage cut. Ally McCoist, the Rangers manager, admitted recently that there was a "crisis" off the park. A judge previously ruled there was a real risk of insolvency at the Ibrox club if the tax bill went against them.

Wednesday 15 February 2012:[286]

Owner Craig Whyte placed the club into administration after Her Majesty's Revenue and Customs went to court in Edinburgh to force the move on its terms, which would have allowed the government to appoint the executives overseeing the bankruptcy. Whyte had filed papers on Monday giving him 10 days to decide whether to put the club into administration over a claim by HMRC for as much as £75 million, including penalties involving unpaid tax relating to the use of employee benefit trusts. Rangers yesterday appointed Duff & Phelps as administrators. Rangers set up the trusts under the previous owner, Sir David Murray, who sold his 85 per cent stake in the club to Whyte in May for £1 in return for Whyte repaying £18 million of loans to Lloyds Banking Group Plc. However, it is the inability of Whyte to fund the club's business on a weekly basis which has brought them to this stage. In a statement on Rangers' official website, Whyte said:

> Due to its cost structure, the club has been loss making for many months. This situation has resulted in increasing liabilities and the club has been in discussion with HMRC regarding these liabilities. These liabilities combined with the threat of the outcome of the first-tier

tax tribunal left the club no option but to formally restructure its financial affairs.

Whyte stressed the administrators would work in the club's interests. He added:

It remains our firm belief that the club's future can be secured and we hope this period of administration will be as short as possible.

Wednesday 15 February 2012:[287]

The Daily Telegraph was told two weeks ago that administration papers had been drawn up then but the suggestion could not be confirmed at that stage. Yesterday's moves did, though, suggest that Whyte had made his move at what he saw as an opportune moment to thwart the revenue's attempt to prevent him naming his own administrator.

Wednesday 15 February 2012:[288]

The club signalled its intention to go into administration on Monday, when it said it had 10 days to make a decision. The taxman went to court over unpaid VAT and PAYE bills of £9 million that have accrued since Craig Whyte's controversial takeover of the club last May. The action was not linked to the dispute over a potential tax bill of £50 million, which was the subject of a recent tribunal over the club's use of an Employment Benefit Trust scheme to pay players between 2001 and 2010. A decision on that case, which could force Rangers into liquidation, has still to be reached. A spokesman for HMRC said:

We can't discuss specific cases for legal reasons, but tax that has been deducted at source from the wages of players and support staff, such as ground keepers and physios, must be paid over. Any business that fails to meet that basic legal requirement puts the survival of the business at risk.

144

The tax authorities told the court they were concerned about the possible perception among creditors that an administrator chosen by the directors would be too close to the club.

But after legal debate, they accepted the appointment of Paul Clark and David Whitehouse, of Duff and Phelps, as the club's preferred administrators. They are now responsible for the day-to-day running of Rangers and Mr Clark said they would "fully recognise the great history of the club" and what it meant to fans "throughout the world".

He added:

> Whilst today is a sad day for Rangers, it also addresses the terrible uncertainty that has been hanging over the club. The administration period, while difficult for all involved, will give stability to the club in order to move forward. I can assure all Rangers supporters that all aspects of the administration will be carried out with the interests of the club firmly in mind.

He added that as a first step the administration team would make sure Saturday's match against Kilmarnock at Ibrox could go ahead as planned.

Friday 17 February 2012:[289]

> Craig Whyte's methods of running Rangers have already set alarm bells ringing with the administrators brought in by the Ibrox owner to run the club, it emerged yesterday. Their anxieties were aroused by the fact that £24million of cash advanced against four years of Ibrox season-ticket sales was not paid to Rangers and also because £9 million of PAYE and VAT monies deducted at source were used to fund the club's cash flow.

> At a media conference at Ibrox, David Whitehouse, one of the two administrators from Duff and Phelps, was asked if it was common for companies to use money due to the Government, and replied: "That's not common practice."

When Whitehouse was asked if he and his colleague, Paul Clark, were concerned about what they had found, he said:

> Yes. All financing of the business will be subject to proper investigation. Our understanding is that the funds from Ticketus didn't come through the company's account. They went through a parent company account, so we haven't got visibility on that and that's what we're trying to get through Companies House. We believe the debt to Ticketus is £24 million.

On the subject of the sum owed to HMRC in respect of PAYE and VAT, Clark said:

> Payments just weren't made. Exactly why - and whose decision that was - isn't something we are yet able to confirm.

The immediate news for Rangers fans appears to be better than expected - several inquiries about a possible purchase of the club were said to have been received and it was also stated by Clark that liquidation of the business is less likely because of the attitude of HMRC, who could yet be owed up to £50 million, depending on the outcome of a tax tribunal - but there will be redundancies, including those of players.

At this stage, it is also worth reviewing the Murray International Holdings Limited Annual Report to 30 June 2011 (published on 4 April 2012):[290]

> As events unfolded, it is with profound regret that we sold the club to Craig Whyte and Wavetower.

> Despite extensive marketing of its interests in Rangers, MIH had previously been unable to secure an offer considered to be in the interests of the Club, its shareholders and its fans. Notwithstanding that it had received no consideration for the sales of its controlling shareholding, and acting entirely in good faith, MIH considered that the transaction with Craig Whyte satisfied these criteria as it provided an immediate and substantial improvement in the club's financial position as well as a significant investment in the playing squad. The acquirer

also stated its intention to invest a further £20m over a four year period. As part of the transaction, Craig Whyte's company also secured the indebtedness of the secured creditor and was under an obligation to convert this into shareholder funds in the future.

Given its high profile and nature, together with the vested, and often conflicting interests of various parties the sale was never likely to be straightforward. The acquirer and his advisors were, following requests, provided with financial, management and operational information given by the Independent Committee of the Board of the Club subject, as one would expect, to appropriate confidentiality undertakings. The information was then utilised to perform due diligence before finalisation and completion of the transaction. Having ultimately secured ownership and control, it was for Craig Whyte and the new owners to determine the strategic and operational direction of the Club while continuing to honour and fulfil their various contractual obligations and responsibilities. They patently failed to do so.

I have also been gravely disappointed and staggered at the revelations that have materialised since the beginning of 2012. Neither Murray Group nor myself had any knowledge in the role of Ticketus in the acquisition of the Club. Indeed, this conflicts with the independent assurances given to us prior to and at the time of sale and is hardly consistent with the shareholders circular issued. We are also astonished that the £9.5million deposited in the client account of Craig Whyte's lawyers and held to the order of the club appears to be unaccounted for. These funds were earmarked for squad investment (£5.0m), settlement of a tax liability (£2.8m), and expenditure on the infrastructure of the stadium (£1.7m). The inability to account for these monies is particularly disturbing given the independent conformations obtained from Craig Whyte's lawyer at completion and as recently as 3rd January 2012.

Following the appointment of the Administrators, we brought their attention to this matter and provided a not unsubstantial amount of documentation and evidence relating thereto. We are eager to learn of the findings of their investigation.

3.3 Academic Frameworks

3.3.1 Organisational: Six Stages of Organisational Decline and Renewal

For the purpose of this chapter, I will consider the third and fourth stages, namely diagnostics and retrenchment.

McKiernan suggests a careful diagnostic routine that explores the complex relationship between symptoms, secondary causes and primary causes of decline. In this respect, in his book (*INTO THE BEAR PIT*), Whyte offers that this was his main task in the period May 2011 – August 2011. In detail, he examined and attempted to diagnose:

- Symptoms: physical, managerial, behavioural and financial.
- Causes: primary and secondary (including a revised leadership).

I do give him the benefit of the doubt here. I consider that Whyte thought that he could 'make it work' i.e. The Rangers Football Club plc and Rangers FC. He would try and break even without Europe. He would have to sort out all costs (i.e. Murray contracts) and increase revenue. If he lost the FTTT, he would consider administration (certainly, the previous Board of Directors of The Rangers Football Club plc had considered this) and leave creditors behind. He had, of note, experience in 'failing businesses.' In this respect, and in terms of his motivation, he was a businessman who specialised in turning around companies. Although a Rangers fan, he was — I suggest — somewhat naïve about the resultant public scrutiny.

The big problems, however, were:

- Delays to the FTTT and uncertainty over associated appeals: May 2011, November 2011 and January 2012.

- Elimination from European football i.e. no additional revenue and disappointment/frustration.

And:

- He had very difficult PR (for example, the BBC documentary *Craig Whyte Uncovered: Rangers Thousandaire & His Dodgy Past*)
- Considerable 'sniping' from others.
- No credit line i.e. nobody would give them/him money. Whyte himself states that it was difficult to get a bank account. Banks did not want association with football clubs and the said BBC documentary led to further uncertainty.[291]

Like Sir David Murray, it appears that he did, however, try and resolve this (i.e. EBT liability) with HMRC.

In general and returning to Leavy & McKiernan 's views on retrenchment, organisations have a natural tendency to retreat to what they know best when crisis hits. Autocratic management, tighter control, cost reduction/cutting, rationalisation and other retrenchment policies seem to be the automatic first choice options for organisations to travail. Whyte wanted The Rangers Football Club plc to, at least, break even without additional revenue from, for example, European football. On purchase, he offers that the revenue was £35M but the cost was £45M. Clearly, he needed the additional revenue from European football — especially the Champions' League income. When Rangers FC was eliminated from Europe and further much-needed revenue was lost, Whyte looked for survival and the achievement of a positive cash flow. Once 'safety was reached', I suggest that Whyte would strive for a 'slimmed down' form of some version of the previous strategy [a response in terms of efficiency] and the pursuance of growth and development with a new strategy [an entrepreneurial response].

Smith evidences such retrenchment:[292]

The association (SFA) painted a picture of a club where the board was not presented with accounts and where financial controller Ken Olverman had his authorisation limit for signing checks slashed from £10 000 under the previous regime to £100 under Whyte. Olverman was told to ditch the previous practice of settling bills within 30 days and extend that to 60 days. He was ordered to withhold payments to HMRC and had no knowledge of the multimillion invoice issued to Ticketus for the deal Whyte had brokered. According to the SFA, the invoice to the firm did not follow standard Rangers format and looked as though it had been generated using computer clip art.

3.3.2 Stakeholder: The Change Curve

For the purpose of this chapter, I will consider the first two elements of The Change Curve, namely denial and shock. I suggest that the denial continued as Whyte was portrayed as a billionaire — any issues with The Big Tax Case liability would also be 'sorted' by him. The final 'shock', however, happened on 14 February 2012 i.e. this is real!

The emotion of shock is evident below:

1. NO HEADLINE
Sunday Herald
February 19, 2012

> AMID the anger and despair of seeing Rangers plunge into administration, the club's more prominent fans have vowed to rally behind the crisis-hit Scottish champions. Wet Wet star Graeme Clark, a life-long Rangers supporter, said: The events of the last few days have caused great sadness and despair for all Rangers fans. I was always in denial about Rangers going into administration I just never thought it would happen. Professional snooker player, and Rangers fan, Graeme Dott, was confident the club would fight back. He said: The whole thing is a bit of a mess and, more than anything, it's been embarrassing. All the fans knew it was coming, but you never expect a club the size of Rangers to go into administration.

2. Rangers fans 'shocked' and 'devastated' by move towards administration; Rangers fans were left in a state of shock after the club lodged legal papers signalling their intention to enter administration, according to Rangers Supporters Assembly president Andy Kerr.
telegraph.co.uk
February 13, 2012

> Kerr said the news was perhaps expected but no less "devastating."
> "I am shell-shocked," he said. "Every message I have had on my mobile has mentioned how sad it is. Some of us fans had expected that we might face this day but that it has happened so quickly has been shocking. It is devastating and it leaves us with more questions than answers. I wonder what the trigger was? People want to know what it means. How quickly can we get out of the situation? Where do we start with the debts and playing squad? There are around 200 employees at Ibrox, what will happen to them?"

3. Rangers administration creates 'shock waves' in football world; Scottish Premier League champions Rangers effectively surrendered the league title to Glasgow rivals Celtic as they fight for their future after being put into administration.
telegraph.co.uk
February 14, 2012

> The crisis facing such a big club, champions a world record 54 times, has sent shock waves through British soccer where many smaller teams face a precarious existence.
> "Really what it proves is that nobody is immune from this and I think it sends shock waves into football.

4. CARNAGE; RANGERS' DARK DAY BUTCHER IN SHOCK AT CLUB'S PLIGHT
The Mirror
February 15, 2012

RANGERS legend Terry Butcher fears the club face "pure carnage" after they went into administration yesterday. "I just can't believe it. I came here 26 years ago and never thought I'd witness Rangers go into this kind of area."

Blame and anger then commenced...

3.4   Chapter Summary

3.4.1   Rangers FC: 2010 to 14 February 2012

In 2008, Craig Whyte bought several stockbroker and asset management companies under the umbrella of the Merchant House Group.

In 2010, there was a suggested desperation — by Sir David Murray — to sell The Rangers Football Club plc. Indeed, it was reported that anyone with money could meet with Sir David. The asking price, at this time, was £33M.

Whyte used Ticketus to finance the purchase of The Rangers Football Club plc. Initially, there was an equity element of £5M to buy the shares.

31 March 2011 was also the deadline for a license — by the SFA — to play European football for Season 2011/2012. To obtain such licenses, it was important for 'applying clubs' that they must not owe tax. On 1 April 2011, The Rangers Football Club plc produced the delayed mid-term accounts and admitted openly for first time that two separate tax cases were hanging over the company i.e. The Small Tax Case and The Big Tax Case. Moreover, Alistair Johnston admitted the other ongoing tax probe (Big Tax Case) could leave the company with a bill they could not afford to pay.

On 19 April 2021, Johnston casted doubt on Whyte's ability to immediately transform the club's fortunes and revealed an Ibrox Director had proposed an alternative £25M investment.

3.4.2   The 'finance deal'.

In April 2011, Whyte states that he was told about The Small Tax Case /DoS liability of £2.8M and that £1.75M would be required to be spent on the stadium (public address system and catering) to ensure that it was ready to open in Season 2011/2012.   As such, the previous £5M that was demanded for equity (shares) was reduced to £1. The 'deal' was effectively, then, about debt financing.

On Friday 6 May 2011, it was announced that Craig Whyte had acquired the 85.3% shareholding in The Rangers Football Club plc from Murray MHL Limited for £1 after the Takeover Panel had ratified the deal. Wavetower was an 'acquisition vehicle' for the takeover of the Rangers Football Club plc. Wavetower and Liberty Capital gave a guarantee to Ticketus. Craig Whyte and Phil Betts were Executive Directors and had full authority. In addition, the securities that Lloyds held over The Rangers Football Club plc's principal tangible assets were assigned to Whyte's companies.

The Share Purchase Agreement (for £1) was as follows:

- The debt owed to Lloyds (£18M) — by The Rangers Football Club plc — was now owed to Rangers FC Group Limited.
- Wavetower Limited would been renamed The Rangers FC Group Limited on 12 May 2011.
- £5M would be invested in the playing squad and a further £20M would be invested in the team by 2016.
- Provision of a further £5M in working capital would be provided to the club to provide capital expenditure to bring the catering facilities and the public address system at Ibrox up to date.
- A confirmed agreement was made to cover the £2.8M liability owed from The Small Tax Case (plus charges/penalties) was made.

3.4.1 Rangers FC: 2010 to 14 February 2012

On 24 May 2011, changes in the Boardroom of The Rangers Football Club plc commenced. On 27 May 2011, Phil Betts was confirmed as a Director. Gary Withey replaced Donald McIntyre as Company Secretary and Andrew Ellis was a Director of The Rangers FC Group Limited

154

During late July and August of 2011, results in Europe were most significant in the history of Rangers FC. Whyte was 'banking' on the revenue from such European football. The business plan was most limited. In addition, The Rangers Football Club plc did not have a credit line.

On 18 October 2011, John Greig and former chairman John McClelland resigned from the Board.

Whyte attempted to 'sort out' the problem with HMRC. He offered that there was a high probability that administration was highly likely. Indeed, he discussed a solvent restructure with the SFA/Harper McLeod in October 2011 in case the FTTT was lost.

On 7 November 2011, the FTTT reconvened. However, on 16 November 2011, it was postponed to January (16 -18) 2012. This did cause further uncertainty. Whyte reflects that he should have 'gone for administration' in October 2011. Moreover, and later in this month, The Rangers Football Club plc confirmed to the PLUS Stock Exchange that Whyte had previously been disqualified as a Director.

Throughout December 2011 and January 2012, Duff & Phelps was requested by The Rangers Football Club plc to recommence discussions with HMRC in respect of the Small Tax Case liability and arrears in PAYE/National Insurance and VAT that had accrued since August 2011.

On 9 January 2012, The Rangers Football Club plc shares were suspended from trading on the PLUS Stock Exchange for its failure to submit audited accounts.

On 13 January 2012, Phil Betts resigned from The Rangers FC Group Limited. On 20 January 2012, he resigned as a Director of the Board of Rangers Football Club plc. He was replaced by Andrew Ellis on the Rangers Football Club plc Board on 20 January 2012.

In late January 2012, it became apparent that — in absence of significant working capital or an agreement with HMRC — the company would be unable to meet its liabilities as they fell due and the company could not avoid formal insolvency proceedings. Whyte filed a NoI to Appoint Administrators with Court of Session on 13 February 2012. Shortly afterwards, HMRC lodged a Creditors' Petition to appoint an Administrator in respect of unpaid taxes, which had accrued since August 2011 of £9M. After discussions between parties, HMRC decided to withdraw its petition, consenting to the appointment of Paul Clarke and David Whitehouse of Duff & Phelps as JAs. On Tuesday 14 February 2012, The Rangers Football Club plc was placed into administration. The SPL then confirmed that Rangers FC would be docked 10 points.

3.4.3 Academic Frameworks

Organisational: although Whyte tried to diagnose the situation (both symptoms and causes), there were significant problems:

- Delays to the FTTT and uncertainty over appeals.
- Elimination from European football i.e. no additional revenue and disappointment/frustration.

And:

- He had very difficult PR.
- There was considerable sniping from others.
- Credit was limited. It was difficult to get a bank account.

Like Sir David Murray, it appears that he did, however, try and resolve the potential EBT liability.

Whyte looked for survival and the achievement of a positive cash flow.

Stakeholder: denial continued, as Whyte was portrayed as a billionaire — any issues with the Big Tax Case liability would also be 'sorted' by him. The final 'shock', however, happened on 14 February 2012 i.e. this is real. Blame/anger then commenced.

3.5   Reflection

My reflection of A Descent into Chaos is in four parts:

- Murray International Holdings Limited/Sir David Murray
- The Rangers Football Club plc
- Craig Whyte
- HMRC

Murray International Holdings Limited/Sir David Murray

Rangers FC was operated by The Rangers Football Club plc. This company was part of the wider Murray International Holdings Limited group of companies. It is not clear if all Rangers FC stakeholders were clear of the 'other' companies that linked the plc to Murray International Holdings Limited i.e. Ranges FC Investments Limited, Murray Sports Limited and Murray MHL Limited. Indeed, during the period 1998-2011, very few voices expressed concern with the relationship between Rangers FC, The Rangers Football Club plc and Murray International Holdings Limited.

Moreover, were all aware that Murray International Holdings Limited owed Lloyds almost £1B?
Did supporters, therefore, realise how 'exposed' Rangers FC was to Murray International Holdings Limited and Lloyds? Were many stakeholders too lazy to enquire or simply in denial?

The Global Financial Crisis had a most significant effect on Murray International Holdings Limited. In the resultant credit crunch, Lloyds wanted their money back as they, too, feared for their own position.

Simply:

- It is understood that Lloyds told Sir David Murray that if he wanted to get Murray Metals into Murray Capital (his 100 percent-owned company), he could buy it back for £1 provided he sold The Rangers Football Club plc by 30 April 2011. In this respect, Ian Shanks confirmed that a deal had been in place since April 2010 for Sir David Murray to buy back his metals business. This was an agreement in Project Charlotte.

- Lloyds 'wanted out' of football/The Rangers Football Club plc. They threatened to withdraw bank facilities if the IBC did not sanction the transaction with Craig Whyte. Moreover, it seems that Sir David put pressure on IBC to sell saying that Whyte was threatening to withdraw.

The Rangers Football Club plc

Although Craig Whyte was blamed for the administration of The Rangers Football Club plc, Donald McIntyre did reveal that the plc was in financial pearl. The Alastair Johnstone-led Board was considering administration — they had no money.

When Sir Murray felt induced to sell The Rangers Football Club plc, there was one main problem — few, if any, wanted to buy the company. The potential EBT liability did not help: potential buyers were certainly put off by the possibility of an unpaid tax bill running to tens of millions. Many companies across Britain had used EBTs for tax-avoidance purposes but, in the case of The Rangers Football Club plc, it proved most difficult with HMRC remorselessly pursuing the company.

Craig Whyte bought the company and football club for £1. In many respects, perhaps Craig Whyte was a solution i.e. he was an insolvency expert and had, of note, experience in falling businesses.

Craig Whyte

I consider that Craig Whyte thought that he could make the Rangers project work. He could try and 'break even' without Europe. He would have to sort out all unnecessary costs and increase revenue.[293] This is echoed in a report from The Daily Telegraph:[294]

> Whyte recognised the contribution of Murray but promised changes in the running of the club, which had two representatives of Lloyds Banking Group on the board before Whyte took over. Whyte said:
>
>> I firmly believe the changes I have implemented will be in the longer-term interest of the club, which must always come first. Perhaps the biggest change that has been effected since the takeover in May has been the repayment of all bank borrowings. The club is no longer reliant on bank funding, nor does any bank control our operations on a daily basis. I hope fans would share my view that, looking ahead, the club should do everything to live within its means and operate on a commercially viable basis. I firmly believe that is the only sustainable, long-term strategy for Rangers.

He did, however, expect bad news from the FTTT in October 2011. If the FTTT had found against The Rangers Football Club plc in late 2011, Whyte could have filed for administration and would have been relatively blameless. But more time was needed to conclude the FTTT and instead of concluding in October 2011, it had to resume in January 2012.

He, however, had further and ongoing difficulties: a loss of European revenue; sniping from previous Members of Board; and an unhelpful media. In this respect, was someone 'back briefing'? Did this previous Board want it to fail so that they could buy it back?

Whyte — I consider — also had a problem with working capital. The plc was bought by someone (i.e. Whyte) who did not have the money to bankroll it.

Finally, he was politically naïve — did he know what he was getting into? It was not just another company to be restructured. It was Rangers FC. Did he understand this fully?

HMRC

Were HMRC at fault too? It is understood that both Sir David
Murray and Craig Whyte offered a 'settlement'. Like Sir David
Murray before him, Whyte states that he did try and resolve the
EBT/FTTT issue with HMRC but to no avail.[295]

It is understood that HMRC refused to negotiate on The Big Tax
Case, The Small Tax Case and outstanding PAYE arears. Did
the resultant chaos need to happen?

A resultant chaos: 14 February 2012 – to 29 July 2012

Chapter Four

Administration to Liquidation: 14 February 2012 – to 29 July 2012

Resultant chaos

Retrenchment

Anger and
Depression

14 Feb 2012: Administration   29 July 2012: Rangers FC v Brechin City FC

Chapter Contents:

4.1 Introduction

> For the reasons set out in the Proposals, the CVA Proposal and this report, this appointment is considered to be the highest profile sports club Administration in Scotland (and probably the whole of the UK) and has involved a large number of complex elements. The Administration was reported and commentated upon in many national newspapers in Scotland for much of the duration of the appointment.
>
> Duff & Phelps Interim Report to Creditors dated 10 July 2012.

In the period 14 February 2012 – 29 July 2012, three inter-related and complex themes were at play:

- The Administration process of The Rangers Football Club plc through Duff & Phelps.
- The sale of Rangers FC to Sevco Scotland Limited.
- The eventual entry into the SFL Third Division of Rangers FC.

In addition, there was also:

- The SFA Independent Committee (chaired by Lord Nimmo Smith) that led to disciplinary charges that would play out all spring/summer and would be resolved via the 5-Way Agreement.
- The SPL Commission/Harper McLeod.
- The proposed Financial Fair Play amendments issued by the SPL.

This is shown at Figure 14.0 — A General Storyboard.

	February	March	April	May	June	July
Admin Process:	13: Notice of Intention to Appoint Administrators 14: Administration	16: Indicative Offers 29: Sevco 5088 Limited incorported	4: Best and Final Offers 5: Duff & Phelps suggest amount owed to creditors = £134M	4: Sevco 5088 Limited provided Indicative Offer 12: Duff & Phelps granted Sevco 5088 Limited exclusivity 29: Sevco Scotland Limited incorporated	6: Charles Green appointed to day-to-day management 14: CVA fails	31: Sevco Scotland Limited changes name to The Rangers Football Club Limited. The Rangers Football Club plc changed its name to RFC 2012 plc
SFA:	17: Independent Committee/Nimmo Smith		17-23: SFA Disciplinary Tribunal			4: Vote on SPL share transfer help. Rejected by 10-1 13: 25 SFL member clubs voted to place Rangers FC in Third Division
SPL:		2: Hugh Adam allegations/SPL Commission	6-9: Financial Fair Play amendments	30: Financial Fair Play amendments. SPL clubs themselves could decide how to deal with New co Rangers		

Figure: 14.0: A General Storyboard

In this chapter, I draw principally on the material published at Companies House for The Rangers Football Club plc.[296] In detail, I make specific reference to the five Duff & Phelps Reports. I do accept that a significant literature was produced during this period; however, Duff & Phelps were appointed by the Court of Session and it is, therefore, sensible that communication from them is given credence. Moreover, the Duff & Phelps JAs (Paul Clark and David Whitehouse) were licensed to act as insolvency practitioners by their regulatory body, the Insolvency Practitioners' Association.[297] I, therefore, place credibility to the authenticity and accuracy of this material.[298]

The said five Duff & Phelps Reports are as follows:

- *Report to Creditors* dated 5 April 2012.
- *Proposal for a Company Voluntary Arrangement by the Joint Administrators of The Rangers Football Club plc to its Creditors and Shareholders* dated 29 May 2012.
- *Interim Report to Creditors* dated 10 July 2012.[299]
- *Progress Report to Creditors* dated 24 August 2012.
- *Final Progress Report to Creditors* dated 27 September 2012.

In addition, and where required, I refer to material from the broadcast and print media.

4.2 Administration to Brechin City Football Club.[300]

After The Rangers Football Club plc was placed in administration, and of worry to many stakeholders, Craig Whyte 'disappeared.' As such, and as Calvin Spence points out, Rangers FC was somewhat rudderless, leaderless and wholly dependent on Paul Clark and David Whitehouse.[301]

In their (first) *Report to Creditors* dated 5 April 2012, David Whitehouse states that the Purpose of Administration was to achieve one of the following hierarchical objectives:[302]

166

- Rescuing the Company as a going concern; or
- Achieving a better result for the Company's creditors as a whole than would be likely if the Company were wound up (without first being in administration); or
- Realising property in order to make a distribution to one or more secured or preferential creditors.

Certain sections of this (first) Report are worthy of comment. For example:

6.2 The first objective is to rescue the Company as a going concern. Given the levels of liability in the Company, both contingent and actual, this would most likely take the form of a CVA or a Scheme of Arrangement. A CVA or Scheme of Arrangement would enable the Company (legal entity) itself to continue to trade in the future. A CVA or Scheme of Arrangement would also require monies to be introduced to the Company which would be used in satisfaction of creditor claims. It is likely that funds would be made available by selling the assets of the Company to a purchaser or by shareholder investment.

6.3 In order for a CVA or Scheme of Arrangement to be successful it is likely that any purchaser would wish to take ownership of all or substantially all of the Company's share capital. A CVA or Scheme of Arrangement would also need to be approved by creditors.

6.4 Should a CVA or Scheme of Arrangement not be possible, the Joint Administrators would look to pursue the second objective which would involve a going concern sale of the business and assets of the Company. This would enable the business to continue, subject to approval by the relevant football authorities, under a different company registration number.

At this stage (i.e. February 2012), it was important for the JAs to 'trade' the business whilst seeking a purchaser. The JAs offer that valuation advice confirmed that a sale of the business and assets — as a going concern — would realise a far higher value than if the company were first to be wound up. In detail, there were a number of 'classes of asset' including the player contracts, Ibrox Stadium and Murray Park whose value would have been significantly impaired should the company have ceased to trade in the first instance.[303] Thus, for the JAs, maintaining trading operations would maximise value in the business and assets of the company and/or facilitate a rescue of the company as a going concern through a CVA/Scheme of Arrangement.

The JAs state that this was important for six reasons:[304]

- The ability of the Club to complete its outstanding fixtures for the remainder of the 2011/2012 season and trade as a going concern.
- Preservation of value in player contracts.
- Preservation of employment and corresponding reduction in unsecured, preferential and non-preferential claims against the Company.
- Preservation of Club's status as member of SPL and SFA.
- Safeguarding of SPL prize money due to the Club in May 2012.
- The enhanced 'going concern' value of the Club.

This was, indeed, to be a complex and complicated process.

Throughout the early stages of administration, ongoing discussions took place with HMRC. In addition, the JAs were involved in regular meetings with UEFA, SFA and the SPL regarding the relevant football regulations and the implications of the company's insolvency on the current season, the sale process and the ability of the club to play in European competitions.

At this juncture, it is, however, instructive to introduce two separate inquiries that commenced in the spring of 2012: a) the SFA Independent Committee; and b) the SPL Commission.

a) SFA Independent Committee

Shortly after entering administration on 17 February 2012, the SFA appointed an Independent Committee (IC) to review the insolvency of the club (I suggest company) in the context of the governance of Scottish football clubs. The IC was led by Lord Nimmo Smith and the SFA CEO Stewart Regan. Also on this IC were Bob Downes and Professor Niall Lothian.[305] The SFA claimed that their previous efforts in obtaining information relevant to the Fit and Proper Person requirement had been restricted by the club's solicitors' continued failure to share information in a timely or detailed manner.[306]

The outcome of this IC was a Notice of Complaint (NofC) against Craig Whyte and the club. In this respect, Graham notes:[307]

> Within two weeks, it had completed its investigation into breaches of Articles of Association and submitted a report to SFA. On 8 March 2012, only one month after Rangers had entered administration and when Duff & Phelps were attempting to find a buyer, the SFA Board considered Whyte not to be a fit and proper person to run Rangers and that the Club would face a Disciplinary Tribunal to determine any punishment for these alleged breaches.

The said NofC against the Club included five breaches of disciplinary rules:

- Failure to disclose that Craig Whyte had been disqualified as a company Director.
- Failure to ensure that Craig Whyte had acted in accordance with the disciplinary rules in respect of the above.
- Suffering an insolvency event.
- Bringing the game into disrepute.
- Failure to pay ticket monies to Dundee United FC for a Scottish Cup tie at Ibrox Stadium on 5 February 2012.

169

These breaches were due to be heard at a Disciplinary Tribunal on 29 March 2012. The Judicial Panel Members were Gary Allan QC, Eric Drysdale (Director of Raith Rovers FC) and former freelance football journalist Alistair Murning. However, it was decided to conjoin the Tribunal of the above charges (the five 'breaches') with the Tribunal of two separate charges against Craig Whyte (bringing the game into disrepute and not acting in the best interests of Association Football). The re-scheduled Disciplinary Tribunal was set for 17, 18, 20 and 23 April 2012. [308,309]

The determination of the Disciplinary Tribunal was thus:

- The Football Club:

  - £160,000 fine.
  - 12-month transfer embargo, which meant that the club could not adequately replace the 20 or so first team squad players that it was about to lose.

- Craig Whyte:

  - £200,000 fine
  - Banned for life from Scottish Football.

These charges, particularly against Rangers FC, would 'play out' all summer and reach a conclusion in the 5-Way Agreement in July 2012.

In their *Interim Report to Creditors* dated 10 July 2012, the JAs offer further analysis.

Disciplinary Matters

4.18 As has been widely reported, several charges were brought against the Club for breaches of the SFA Articles and these charges were heard by the Disciplinary Tribunal in a hearing held on 17, 18, 20 and 23 April 2012.

4.19 Of the seven charges brought against the Club, one was found not proven. However, the remaining six were found proven resulting in three censures, fines totalling £160,000 (payable within 12 months) and a Transfer Embargo.

4.20 Following a review of the Disciplinary Tribunal's Note of Reasons and having taken legal advice, the Club appealed the Disciplinary Tribunal's determination in respect of the Transfer Embargo. This appeal was on several grounds, most notably that the Disciplinary Tribunal had acted out with its powers in determining such a sanction.

4.21 The Club's appeal was heard by an Appellate Tribunal (i.e. a new group of individuals drawn from the SFA Judicial Panel pool) on 16 May 2012.[310] However, the Appellate Tribunal's decision was to unanimously affirm the decision of the original Disciplinary Tribunal.

4.22 The impact that the Transfer Embargo would have on the Club's football operations, and in particular on the ongoing sale process, was significant. Given that the Club's firm legal advice maintained that the Transfer Embargo was out with the scope of the Disciplinary Tribunal's powers, the Club sought legal advice on further steps that could be taken to challenge the Transfer Embargo.

4.23 Consequently, the Club sought a Judicial Review of the Appellate Tribunal's decision at the Court of Session and this Review was heard by Lord Glennie on 29 May 2012. In accordance with the Club's legal advice, Lord Glennie's opinion was that the Transfer Embargo was a sanction that was out with the powers of the SFA Judicial Panel Protocol and he, therefore, concluded that the sanction could not be held against the Club and the matter should be returned to the Appellate Tribunal for reconsideration.

4.24 The Appellate Tribunal has yet to be reconvened to consider this matter further and, given the recent sale of the Company's business and assets noted above, a timescale for resolution of this matter by the Appellate Tribunal is unclear.[311]

b) SPL Commission

On 2 March 2012, allegations were made in the Daily Mail newspaper by Hugh Adam.[312] The allegation was that to make the EBT work, The Rangers Football Club plc operated a two-contract system for players but only lodged one contract with the SFA and SPL. Just after the publication of this article, the SPL Board instructed an investigation into the alleged non-disclosure to the SPL of payments made by — or on behalf of — The Rangers Football Club plc to players since 1 July 1998.[313] On 18 June 2012, the SPL announced that The Rangers Football Club plc had a *prima facie* case to answer in respect of league rules over payments to players. This announcement followed an investigation by the Scottish law firm Harper Macleod.

Returning to the administration process, and to reduce the cost base, negotiations with playing staff, PFA Scotland and players' agents took place about temporary salary reductions. It was important for the JAs to avoid significant redundancies amongst playing staff as such redundancies would have resulted in players — with a potential transfer value — leaving the club without a fee being received. In their *Report to Creditors* dated 5th April 2012, the JAs state that as playing staff were the highest earners, logic would have been to remove most of them and only keep the players that had the highest transfer values. Of note, this would have resulted in a detrimental effect on team performance and, thus, reduced SPL prize money and the value of the Club. After lengthy discussions, salary reductions for first team of 25% — 75% were put in place, which led to monthly cost savings of £1M.[314, 315] For non-playing staff, the Director of Football (Gordon Smith) and the Chief Operating Officer (COO) (Ali Russell) left on 29 February 2012. In addition, on 9 March 2012, a further two redundancies were made: the PA to the COO; and the Global Partnership Director who was based in London.

On 29 March 2012, a key event took place that did not appear in the mainstream media. Sevco 5088 Limited (Company number 08011390) was incorporated. The founding Director was Samuel George Alan Lloyd. It is, of note, still trading to this date.

On 30 March 2012 (prior to the 31 March 2012 deadline), the club submitted its annual license request to SFA. This submission was required to comply with SFA requirements and to be assessed for a license to compete in UEFA competitions for football season 2012/2013. In their *Report to Creditors* dated 5 April 2012, the JAs state that the UEFA Club Licensing and Fair Play Regulations 2010 required certain confirmations from licence applications in relation to financial management matters.[316] Amongst the key requirements are that the club needs to:

- Have audited accounts signed off on a going concern basis — given the uncertainty of club's financial position, the accounts to 30 June 2011 had not been signed off on a going concern basis.
- Pay in full, or agree a payment plan, for all "social taxes" (to include all PAYE/National Insurance as a minimum). The Club was unable to pay, by 31 March 2012, the outstanding PAYE/National Insurance as of 31 December 2011 and it had not been possible to agree a payment plan (i.e. a CVA) in sufficient time to meet the 31 March 2012 licensing deadline.

This was a key requirement for UEFA and the absence of these signed accounts meant that participation in European competition would not be possible in the 2012/2013 season. The JAs discussed the matter with UEFA directly on 27 March 2012 at which point it was confirmed by UEFA that there would be no exception available to the club. A further question arose as to whether European participation would be possible for any of the purchasers wishing to acquire the business, history and assets of the company (The Rangers Football Club plc). The usual UEFA requirement is for 3 years of trading history to be presented to them. Any newly incorporated company acquiring the business, history and assets of the company would not be able to meet this requirement. No commitment was received from UEFA in this regard.

Of interest, the following detail remains on the Companies House website for The Rangers Football Club plc (SC 004276):

> **Accounts overdue**
> Next accounts made up to **30 June 2011** due by **31 December 2011**
> Last accounts made up to **30 June 2010**
> **Annual return overdue**
> Last annual return made up to **27 January 2012**

In their *Interim Report to Creditors* dated 10 July 2012, the JAs offer further insight:

> 4.16. As noted in the Proposals, the Club submitted a licence application to the SFA for both national and UEFA licences prior to the 31 March 2012 deadline. However, both licence applications were refused by the licensing committee of the SFA due principally to the fact that because of the Company's insolvency it could not complete its annual, audited accounts for the year to 30 June 2011. In addition, in breach of UEFA licensing regulations, the Company had overdue sums due to other football clubs and overdue PAYE/NIC amounts, which had arisen as a consequence of the Company's insolvent position.

> 4.17. Due to the Administration, it was not possible for the Company to satisfy these outstanding matters in order to obtain the licences, however the failure to receive a national licence had no practical effect on the Club's playing activities for the remainder of the season. The failure to obtain a UEFA licence for the following season did however impact upon the level of interest from prospective purchasers.

In their *Report to Creditors* dated 5 April 2012, we also start to see the 'initial thinking' that took place with respect to selling the company i.e. The Rangers Football Club plc.

For example, in Section 9:

9.1: Due to the high level of media coverage, the proposed sale has become known throughout the wider football and business community.

9.2. Contact was also made with parties who were known to have previously expressed an interest in acquiring businesses in similar and associated sectors.

9.3: An Information Memorandum was prepared and released to those interested parties upon receipt of a signed Non-Disclosure Agreement.

9.4: A virtual data room has been created for those prospective purchasers who were able to demonstrate that they had the funding to enable them to perform initial due diligence on the business and assets of the Club.

9.5: The Joint Administrators requested Indicative Offers from interested parties by 16th March 2012. A deadline for Best and Final Offers was set for 4th April 2012.

9.6: It is likely that sale will be either via exit from Administration via CVA or Scheme of Arrangement or there will be a going concern sale of the business and assets. Sale structure will be dependent on, amongst other things, the preference of the prospective purchaser and the ability to obtain control of RFC Group's majority shareholding.

The majority shareholding in the RFC Group was held, at this time, by Craig Whyte. The key dates — for the timeline — were thus:

- Indicative Offers from interested parties by 16 March 2012.[317]
- Deadline for Best and Final Offers was set for 4 April 2012.

It is also interesting to note that that although the JAs were trying to meet their hierarchical objectives, several other issues were 'at play'. For example, notwithstanding the SFA issues:

Arrestment Orders (Sections 9.23 – 9.25)

The JAs reached a settlement with Martin Bain which saw a release of funds from the Bank of Scotland Company account. In addition, an out of court settlement was also reached with Donald McIntyre, which resulted in the release of certain arrested funds.

Arsenal Holdings Shares (Sections 9.33 – 9.36).

In January 2012, The Rangers Football Club plc instructed Pritchard Stockbrokers Limited (Craig Whyte was Company Secretary) to sell the 16 ordinary shares that it held in Arsenal Holdings for £223,214. Monies were not transferred to The Rangers Football Club plc. Of note, Pritchard Stockbrokers Limited was placed in Special Administration Regime in March 2012. At this time (5 April 2012), the JAs had contacted Joint Special Administrators to recover this money.

Collyer Bristow (Sections 10.7 – 10.11)

Immediately following appointment of the JAs, investigations regarding acquisition of the company by The Rangers FC Group Limited were commenced. This led to various proceedings against Collyer Bristow (CB).[318] On 1 March 2012, the JAs applied to have all monies held by CB — which belonged to or were held to the order of the Company — to be paid to the JAs or alternatively to the Court. The Court ordered that £3, 667, 846.59 be paid to JAs' English solicitors Taylor Wessing (TW). In addition, and on 5 March 2012, all CB files — in relation to the purchase of the Company by The Rangers FC Group Limited — were passed to TW.

Ticketus (Sections 10.12 – 10.16)

Ticketus thought that they had some form of proprietary rights to the relevant seats and the proceeds of their sale such that those rights would 'hold good' against the Club in the event of the latter suffering an insolvency event and against any successor to the Club.

On 15 March 2012, the JAs applied to the Court of Session for directions as to the nature of these rights. On 23 March 2012, Lord Hodge (at the Court of Session) directed that Ticketus had no property rights in the seats nor in the proceeds of their sale. Their rights were of a personal, contractual nature only. This was important — it meant that if Ticketus made a claim for damages against the Club for breach of contract, the claim would rank as an ordinary unsecured claim in administration.[319]

In Section 14 (Dividend Prospects/Prescribed Part) to the *Report to Creditors* dated 5 April 2012, the JAs detail, in some depth, the Charges Registered against the Company and the Unsecured Creditors (both Preferential and Non-Preferential). The 'Charges' included: Floating Charge Creditor (The Rangers FC Group Limited); and Fixed Charge Holders (Kelvinside Academy War Memorial Trust and the Trustees of Kelvinside Academical Club Charitable Trust, The Scottish Sports Council, Kelvinside Academy War Memorial Trust and Another, The Governor and Company of the Bank of Scotland, Premier Property Group Limited and Close Leasing Limited). The Non-Preferential Unsecured Creditors included: Trade and Expense Creditors, Ticketus, HMRC (excluding Big and Small Tax cases), Supporter Debenture Holders and Football-related Creditors.

Of note, the JAs suggest that the amount owed to the non-preferential creditors was £55 415 632. HMRC was owed £14 372 042, which represented 25.93% of the non-preferential creditors. In addition, they (the JAs) estimate:

Small Tax Case

14.28 The Small Tax Case was bought against the Company by HMRC in respect of outstanding amounts owed from the use of a discounted options tax scheme for payments made to Tore

Andre Flo and Ronald De Boer between the tax years 2000/01 and 2002/03.

14.29 The total amount determined as due by HMRC in respect of this case is in the region of £4,000,000 after interest and penalty charges.

14.30 The Small Tax Case has not progressed as far as Tribunal and has been settled based upon advice received.

Big Tax Case

14.31 The Big Tax Case was brought against the Company by HMRC in respect of outstanding amounts owed from the use of the EBT scheme to make payments to employees of the Company between the tax years 2000/01 and 2009/10.

14.32 The total amount determined as due by HMRC in respect of this case is in the region of £75,000,000 including interest and penalties.

14.33 The Big Tax Case is disputed by the Company and is subject to first tier tax Tribunal Proceedings instigated by HMRC. An outcome has yet to be determined by the Tribunal.

Therefore, and at this date (5 April 2012), with the Big and Small Tax cases included, the amount owed to Creditors came to £134M.

In their *Report to Creditors* dated 5 April 2012, the JAs also offer options for an 'End of the Administration'. The options include:

- Company Voluntary Arrangement (CVA).
- Scheme of Arrangement.
- Creditors' Voluntary Liquidation (CVL).
- Compulsory Liquidation.
- Dissolution of the Company.

At this stage (i.e. 5 April 2012), the JAs had yet to form a view as to the exit route as this would depend upon the levels of interest from prospective purchasers, the offers received, and the structure of these offers.

Sub-Sections 16.3 – 16.13 offer a detailed analysis of each of these options. A summary of a CVA and CVL is detailed below. It is instructive to include this to develop the ongoing CVA/CVL narrative.

16.3 A CVA is an agreement between a company and its creditors. It must be supported by more than 75% in value of those voting. A CVA will require funds to be introduced to the Company, usually by way of shareholder investment and/or selling assets. These funds will be used to pay creditors of the Company a percentage of their total claim in full and final satisfaction of what is owed to them.

16.4 A Scheme of Arrangement is a court sanctioned process whereby a company proposes an arrangement, which can bind both creditors and shareholders. The court orders the calling of affected parties to consider a meeting of the proposal. The proposed arrangement must be supported by more than 75% of value and more than 50% of creditors in each class. There is then a subsequent court hearing for the court to sanction the arrangement. As set out above in respect of a CVA, funds will be used to pay creditors of the Company a percentage of their total claim in full and final settlement of what is owed to them through a Scheme of Arrangement.

16.5 Should a CVA or Scheme of Arrangement be proposed and agreed the Company will effectively return to a solvent position and continue to trade on out of any formal insolvency process, although it may still be subject to sanctions from the football authorities.

16.6 It is likely that any purchaser wishing to invest monies into the Club to fund a CVA or Scheme of Arrangement will require the shareholding or substantially all of the shareholding of the Club. The Joint Administrators are investigating whether there are mechanisms by which they can compel existing shareholders to transfer shares to a purchaser, but no representation has been made that this can happen to purchasers. A formal request has been made of the current majority shareholder RFC Group which holds circa 85.3% of the shares to make these available to a purchaser.

16.7 An alternative arrangement would see a CVA approved without a purchaser acquiring the shareholding. Once the CVA is approved the Joint Administrators could then seek to transfer the assets and/or liabilities of the Club into a wholly owned subsidiary and offer the purchaser the option to acquire the shares in that subsidiary. This does mean that the business would trade with a new company registration number and this also may have implications with the various football authorities.

16.8 Purchasers have been made aware that although the Joint Administrators have sought clarification on these issues from the SFA, the SPL and UEFA, it is not possible to confirm the position. The ultimate purchasers will be required to undertake their own discussions once they obtain preferred bidder status.

16.9 If a CVA is not pursued, a going concern sale of the Club's business and assets is likely to result. Should a going concern sale be achieved, the business and assets will transfer to a newly incorporated company. This will most likely result in the Company (the legal entity in which the business and assets currently sit) to enter into Creditors' Voluntary Liquidation and a liquidator to be appointed. A liquidator will fully investigate the financial affairs of the Company and undertake a detailed review of transactions over the years prior to the Company's Administration. Certain stakeholders of the Company have expressed their support for these investigations. It should be noted that a liquidator also has extensive powers to call all previous officers and management of the Company to account and to recover monies which were obtained from the Company by means inconsistent with their statutory obligations.

16.10 Should this be the case, any liabilities of the Company itself remain with the Company and therefore the newly formed company can continue to trade as a football club albeit with a new company registration number.

16.11 Depending upon the offers received, the Joint Administrators may proceed with any of the above options. There is also the possibility of CVA or Scheme of Arrangement followed by a Creditors' Voluntary Liquidation, or in the alternative a business sale conducted alongside a CVA/Scheme of Arrangement.

16.12 The Joint Administrators are duty bound to achieve the best financial return to creditors that they can and their choice of how to proceed is subject to the requisite majority of creditor approval.

In their *Interim Report to Creditors* dated 10 July 2012, the JAs note that a large number of unsubstantiated offers were received. Each party that sought to submit an offer was asked to provide proof of available funding and an outline of the terms of the offer. Of the offers received, three credible Indicative Offers were received on the 16 March 2012 deadline and one further credible offer was received on 23 March 2012. The key terms of each of these offers are summarised below:

- Offer 1 – Party 1. A sale of the company's business and assets for £25m. No CVA proposal required.
- Offer 2 – Party 2. Consideration of £5m to be introduced to the company subject to a successful CVA proposal.
- Offer 3 – Party 3. Consideration of £10m to be introduced to the company subject to a successful CVA proposal. Party 3 would obtain company's shares directly. Ticketus would not claim as an unsecured creditor in the process.
- Offer 4 – Party 4. Consideration of £10m to be introduced to the company subject to a successful CVA proposal. Party 4 would obtain company's shares directly.

At this stage i.e. 23 March 2012, the JAs considered that Offer 1 produced the highest return to creditors by a substantial margin. These offers could not, however, be finalised by the prospective purchasers until clarity was reached on several issues, the critical ones being:[320]

i)   Whether the Ticketus agreement could be terminated.
ii)   How the company's (i.e. The Rangers Football Club plc) shares would be acquired if the offer required a CVA.

iii)   How the company's major creditors would vote in a CVA.

iv)   The extent of any additional sanctions to be levied against the club by the SPL and SFA — if any.

v)   If a CVA was not possible, whether the SPL would permit the transfer of the club's Member Share from the company to a newly incorporated entity.

vi)   Whether the club would be eligible for participation in European Football during the 2012/2013 season and beyond.

This was, indeed, a complicated process. In the *Interim Report to Creditors* dated 10 July 2012, the JAs offer further explanation of each of these points. It is important, I consider, to reproduce these points below:[321]

i) The Ticketus Agreement. The JAs had already submitted a 'directions application' to the Court of Session in order to seek clarity on the Ticketus agreement. On 23 March 2012, Lord Hodge provided his guidance which confirmed that the JAs were able to terminate the agreement, if it was in the best interests of creditors to do so. Whilst this guidance did confirm the position as the JAs had previously asserted, the uncertainty as regards the status of Ticketus in the intervening period caused concern to purchasers.

ii) The Company's Shares. Party 3 and Party 4 both stated that their offer would assume that they would come to a separate arrangement with the company's major shareholder in order to acquire the shares to facilitate a CVA. This would not require the JAs to take steps to obtain the company's shares. Offer 1 was not conditional upon a successful CVA being proposed and, therefore, acquiring the shareholding was not relevant for this party. Party 2's offer required the JAs to facilitate a share transfer as part of the offer received. Legal advice was sought and it was confirmed that there are no provisions within the Act which could enable the JAs to compel delivery of the company's shares from the company's major shareholder(s). It was also confirmed that whilst there were other courses of action available, including a Scheme of Arrangement, these would take several months to implement and there was no guarantee of success. With the end of the season a target date for completion, the JAs could not, and did not, undertake to deliver the company's shares to any purchaser and, therefore, the interested parties were asked to make their own arrangements with the majority shareholder(s) directly. The other sanction available to the JAs would have been to enforce against the majority shareholder, The Rangers FC Group Limited, in relation to monies due to the club.

iii) CVA Proposal. Ongoing dialogue was maintained with the company's major creditor (HMRC) as it was apparent that HMRC's vote would most likely prevent any CVA proposal being approved due to the size of HMRC's unsecured claim *(emphasis added by author (W B Howieson))*. HMRC's stated position was that it would consider any CVA proposal put to it but would not commit to any decision until a CVA proposal had been formally put to all creditors.

iv) Extent of Further SFA & SPL Sanctions. The club was subject to a number of ongoing disciplinary proceedings. Prospective purchasers wished to understand the implications of any sanctions being imposed on the club before being in a position to commit to an acquisition of the club and/or its assets. As a number of these proceedings had yet to conclude, it was unclear what these sanctions would be and when they would be instigated.

v) Transfer of the Member Share and SFA Requirements. In the event that a CVA was not possible, prospective purchasers wished to understand how the club's member share transferred from the company to a new corporate entity. This transfer would be required to enable any newly incorporated company to participate in the SPL league. Prospective purchasers also wished to understand whether there were any implications with the SFA and its registration requirements. The JAs wrote to the SPL and SFA on a confidential basis in order to understand the processes, any limitations and the criteria which would be applied. Following responses received from both of these parties, all prospective purchasers were advised to contact the SPL and SFA for guidance. A number of the parties spent some time with the Scottish football authorities. Other bidders made no contact whatsoever.

vi) Participation in European Competition. The company's auditors were unable to finalise and sign off on the company's financial statements for the 12 months to 30 June 2011 as a consequence of the company's financial position.

Of note, it was apparent that although Offer 1 offered the highest return to creditors, given these uncertainties (i – vi), there were no unconditional offers, nor were there any offers which were deliverable at this stage in the process. Despite the inherent uncertainty, and to progress matters, all parties were well-informed of the risks and Best and Final Offers were invited on 4 April 2012 with a view to announcing the preferred bidder shortly thereafter.

The JAs state that the following Best and Final Offers were received by the deadline of Wednesday 4 April 2012:[322]

> Offer 1 – Bill Miller. Following further negotiation, Mr Miller declared himself to be the only individual remaining from Party 1 and subsequently lodged an offer of £10m for a purchase of the company's business, history and assets. There was no requirement for a CVA.
> Offer 2 – Party 2. No further offer was received; however, the original offer was not withdrawn.
> Offer 3 – Party 3. The original offer was reconfirmed.
> Offer 4 – Party 4. A revised offer of £12m plus additional deferred consideration contingent upon future European participation/success.
> Offer 5 – Party 5 (a new bidder). Consideration of £30m subject to a successful CVA proposal. No proof of funding was provided.

An announcement as to the preferred bidder was scheduled to be made during the week commencing Monday 9 April 2012. However, during the Easter Bank Holiday weekend of 6 - 9 April 2012, the JAs were formally advised of the proposed Financial Fair Play amendments to be issued by the SPL. A SPL vote was scheduled to be cast on 30 April 2012. The SPL made it clear that new rules (Financial Fair Play) would be brought into sanction clubs that went into administration and emerged with a

New Co structure — the preferred method for several Rangers bidders. The proposed rule changes were to give higher points deduction penalties for administration than the 10 points already suffered by Rangers FC and to impose penalties in exiting administration via New Co. The proposal was that, on formation of New Co, clubs should incur 10-point penalties for two years following the transfer of their SPL license and a reduction of 75% of the SPL income due to that club for those two years. This, understandably, created further uncertainty with bidders. Imposition of these penalties would make future title challenges difficult and significantly reduce income during that period. Several bidders attempted to seek clarification from the SPL on whether sanctions were likely to be applied but the SPL procrastinated.[323, 324]

During this time, Bill Miller confirmed that he would pay a refundable £500k deposit for exclusivity; however, his offer was entirely contingent upon an outright rejection of the SPL resolutions on 30 April 2012.[325] Party 2 did not make a further offer or increase the quantum of its offer at this time. Party 3 comprised of a consortium of individuals whose offer was to be underwritten by a third-party investor ('the Investor'). During a telephone call on 12 April 2012, the JAs were told that terms had not yet been agreed either between the individuals in the consortium or between the consortium and 'the Investor.' This cast considerable doubt over the ability of Party 3 to complete upon any agreement within the terms it had stipulated. However, the said Investor confirmed that it would provide the JAs with a £500k non-refundable deposit in order that Party 3 be given a period of exclusivity to complete the transaction. On 13 April 2012, Party 3 withdrew its offer of a non-refundable deposit just prior to a likely decision to grant them preferred bidder status. Party 4 withdrew its offer on 20 April 2012 citing the uncertainties facing the club and the difficulties surrounding the acquisition of the company's shareholding, which would be required for a CVA. However, its advisors verbally confirmed that it would contemplate making an offer for the business and assets of the club later via a Sale and Purchase Agreement

(SPA)[326] should a CVA not prove possible. Party 5 failed to provide proof of funding or disclose details of its professional advisors. This party was the least advanced of the bidders.

At this stage, Duff & Phelps state that Bill Miller's offer and Offer 3 were the offers which delivered the best return to creditors.[327] On 23 April 2012, however, and to add further complexity to an already complex situation, the SFA published its disciplinary hearing outcome that imposed the Transfer Embargo. This sanction caused a further delay to the process whilst the prospective purchasers considered the implications.

Bill Miller asked for further time to consider his position. Party 2 also requested further time from the JAs with which to formulate a revised bid and undertake due diligence despite using the media to call for the JAs to announce the name of a successful purchaser. On 28 April 2012, Party 2 and Party 3 together submitted a joint second offer, subject to a CVA, of £5.5M. The Investor had, by this point, stepped away from the consortium of individuals. This offer assumed that pre-existing football debtors be included in the sale. Football debtors held a value of approximately £3.8M which left this offer at a level of £1.7M, when compared to competing bids. In addition, a proposal was requested from Party 2 as to how the club would be funded whilst a CVA proposal was put to creditors. No such funding offer was received. This new offer was made on the basis that this purchaser could, and would, facilitate the transfer of the company's shares.

The SPL delayed voting on these sanctions on two dates: 30 April 2012 and 7 May 2012. Of note, the SPL proposals — as they were drafted — would have had far reaching consequences for any of the purchasers of the company and/or its business whether it was to be via a CVA or otherwise. As such, no preferred bidder announcement could be made as originally hoped whilst prospective purchasers looked to fully understand the implications and reformulate their offers accordingly. The SPL clubs reconvened on 30 May 2012 and offered that a club should be dealt with on a case-by-case basis. [328]   So, the remaining 11 SPL clubs could decide — by themselves — how to deal with a New Co Rangers. There were, theoretically, any number of penalties available to them, including the one that they ultimately took which was to reject the application to transfer the SPL share to the new company running the club.

Following further discussions and analysis of the remaining offers, the JAs concluded that Bill Miller's offer provided the best return to the company's creditors and was most likely to proceed to completion. As such, and on 3 May 2012, he was announced as the preferred bidder but with no exclusivity arrangement.

One day later, and on 4 May 2012, a late entrant into the sale process — Sevco 5088 Limited — provided an Indicative Offer setting out the terms on which it would acquire the company, which following several discussions was agreed upon as follows:

> Offer 6 – Sevco 5088 Limited. Consideration of £8.25m on successful implementation of a CVA contingent upon Champions League participation during the next three seasons. Should the CVA fail, a binding agreement to purchase the business, history and assets of the Club for £5.5m using a newly incorporated company. Trading the Club whilst a CVA was proposed was to be funded utilising future revenue and football debtor monies, as appropriate.

On the early May Bank Holiday weekend, following dialogue with the SFA and the SPL, it became apparent that Bill Miller was considering the withdrawal of his offer. As such, a draft SPA was sent to Party 4 and Sevco 5088 Limited. An SPA was not sent to Party 2/3 as it had not indicated that it would consider submitting any offer other than in conjunction with a CVA.

Final Sale Process[329]

On 8 May 2012, Bill Miller withdrew his offer.[330] On 10 May 2012, Party 4's advisors made a verbal offer of £5M for the

187

business and assets of the club at which point Party 2/3 submitted a funding proposal for trading the club whilst a CVA was proposed; however, the quantum of this party's offer remained below the Sevco 5088 Limited offer.

The final remaining offers were therefore:

> Offer 2/3. The final offer was for £5.5m; however, the purchaser wished to retain the football debtor balance of £3.8m leaving a net benefit to the estate of £1.7m. A funding proposal was put to the JAs whilst a CVA was proposed to creditors; however, this offer remained uncompetitive.
> Offer 4. A verbal offer for the business and assets of the company was received for £5m. No CVA proposal was required.
> Offer 6. £8.25m to fund a CVA. If the CVA failed, then it would revert to an SPA with a sale price of £5.5m. An exclusivity payment of £200k and provision of funding whilst a CVA was proposed.[331]

Having considered the offer from Sevco 5088 Limited and compared it to other offers received for the company/business and assets, the JAs determined that the Sevco 5088 Limited offer was preferable because it secured the best available return to creditors of the company and proposed a CVA in respect of the company. Consequently, on 12 May 2012, the JAs agreed and signed an Offer Letter with Sevco 5088 Limited and granted Sevco 5088 Limited exclusivity to complete a takeover of the company or a purchase of the company's business and assets by Monday 30 July 2012. Sevco 5088 Limited made a payment of £200,000 to the company for such exclusivity.

In the *Proposal for a Company Voluntary Arrangement by the Joint Administrators of The Rangers Football Club plc to its Creditors and Shareholders* dated 29 May 2012, it states that the Offer Letter was confidential between Sevco 5088 Limited and the company but the principal terms were as follows:[332]

- In addition to the £200,000, Sevco 5088 Limited agreed to advance to the company the sum of £8,300,000.

£8,300,000 would be available for draw down by the company no later than 31 July 2012 but only once certain conditions were satisfied.

- The company would repay the loan together with interest on it on or before 31 December 2020.
- The loan would, subject to the laws of Scotland, be secured by standard securities and a floating charge over the assets and undertaking of the Company.

From 6 June 2012, Charles Green was appointed to assist in the day-to-day management of the business of the company (at no cost to the company or the JAs) to manage the ongoing trading costs of the company and to allow for a smooth transition in ownership. The relevant Conditions of the Offer Letter included:[333]

- Sevco 5088 Limited acquiring the shares of The Rangers FC Group (Sevco 5088 Limited holds an irrevocable written undertaking from The Rangers FC Group to sell their shares to Sevco 5088 Limited for £1, conditional upon approval by the creditors and members of the Company (i.e. The Rangers Football Club plc) of a CVA).
- The Takeover Panel confirming that Sevco 5088 Limited shall not be required to make any offer for any share capital other than the Group Shares, under Rule 9 of the City Code on Takeovers and Mergers notwithstanding the acquisition of the Group Shares.
- All consents or other requirements of the SPL and SFA having been obtained or complied with so that Rangers Football Club can continue to participate in such domestic leagues and competitions as it currently participates in.
- In the event that either this CVA is not approved, or the other Conditions of the loan are not satisfied or waived by 23 July 2012, Sevco 5088 Limited is contractually obliged to purchase the business and assets of the Company for £5,500,000 by 30 July 2012.

At this stage, it is important to understand the 'arrangement' between Craig Whyte and Charles Green. In his book, *INTO THE BEAR PIT,* Whyte offers the following explanation.[334]

He met with Charles Green in London in March 2012. Whyte offers that he could not get involved; therefore, he needed someone to raise money and 'front up' a deal. With his colleague Aidan Early, Whyte bought a shelf company called Sevco 5088 Limited (Company number = 08011390).

Whyte appointed Green as a Director of Sevco 5088 Limited on 3 May 2012. The plan was that Green would front up an offer to Duff & Phelps. In addition, Green signed a Resignation Form and two blank appointment Forms (and blank Share Transfer Forms). Whyte also loaned Green £250,000 for legal fees. Whyte then paid the first tranche of that into Imran Ahmad's mother's account to pay the deposit to Duff & Phelps. According to Whyte, he then introduced Paul Clark to Charles Green.

Green's offer price for the club was £7.5M if there was a CVA and £5.5M for the assets alone if the CVA did not go through.[335] In addition, the idea was that Whyte (as he told Paul Clark) would give Green his (Whyte's) shares in The Rangers Football Club plc. Duff & Phelps announced Green's interest publicly on 12 May 2012 and said that he had a period of exclusivity to purchase the club. Green said that he was fronting a consortium of unnamed backers and had done a deal to purchase Whyte's shares for £2.[336, 337]

As the CVA Proposal failed on Thursday 14 June 2012, Green — as planned — paid £5.5M for the company's assets (Stadium, Murray Park and Albion Car Park) which were to be transferred into a new company, which Whyte believed to be Sevco 5088 Limited. Unbeknown to Whyte, Green had set up another company called Sevco Scotland Limited (Company number SC425159) on 29 May 2012 and transferred the rights from Sevco 5088 Limited to it.

Whyte states: "Green then unilaterally decided to move the deal."

This is shown diagrammatically at Figure 15.

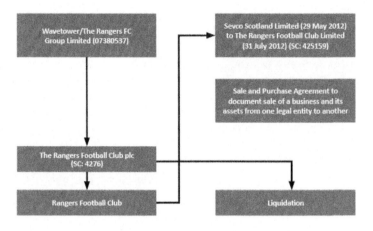

Figure 15.0: Green's Acquisition of Rangers Football Club

Once he had the business and assets, Sevco Scotland Limited changed its name to The Rangers Football Club Limited on 31 July 2012 — this is the company that operates Rangers FC today. It is not fully understood exactly what happened and, in particular, why the purchase was made by Sevco Scotland Limited and not Sevco 5088 Limited. The Sun newspaper later published the article *Green: I shafted Whyte to Get Gers.*[338] Whyte believes that he (and other investors in Sevco 5088 Limited) was defrauded by Green.[339, 340] Perhaps, however, the answer is contained in the Rangers International Football Club plc Annual Report of 30 June 2013.[341] In Notes to the Financial Statements, 28. RELATED PART TRANSACTIONS, it states:

> On 14 June 2012, Sevco 5088 Limited entered into agreements for no consideration to legally reassign its beneficial interest in

funding placing letters held and to novate the trade and assets purchase agreement with RFC 2012 plc (in administration), to Sevco Scotland Limited (now The Rangers Football Club Ltd)

This is, again, a key area of debate. As such, I invite my colleague, Dr Mathew Bonnett, to offer further insight.

Sevco 5088 was incorporated on 29 March 2012. It was incorporated by 7Side Secretarial Limited (7Side) in Cardiff with total share capital of one share with a nominal value of £1. 7Side are a company offering company formation and secretarial services of use to the legal profession. Businesses like 7Side set up many companies and then sell them onto people who want a ready-made company without the 'hassle' of setting one up. These companies are also called (off-the-) shelf companies or vintage companies. The only Director appointed at the time of incorporation was a Managing Director of 7Side Sam Lloyd who took the role as a formality to start the company's existence by enabling the incorporation to be recorded at Companies House, home the Register of all UK companies. If you look at the Companies House website you will find that Sam Lloyd started many companies and often used the name Sevco followed by a 4-digit number. So, the term Sevco, which is now synonymous with Rangers FC, was in fact a term used by a secretarial company in south Wales for its newly incorporated companies. Charles Green was appointed as Director of Sevco 5088 Limited on the 3 May 2012 at the same time as Sam Lloyd resigned and the registered office of the company was changed from that of 7Side to an address in London. There are no filings showing any share transfers so officially the shareholding continued to be owned by 7side Limited as it had since incorporation. According to filings at Companies House, there was - at this point - only one Director of the company and that was Charles Green. Subsequent filings show that Craig Whyte and Aiden Earley were appointed as Directors of Sevco 5088 from 9 May 2012. However, these filings were not made until the following April (i.e. documents were filed in 2013 but were backdated to 9 May 2012). There is clearly a disagreement at this point which Companies House is silent on. As discussed in the main text, there appears to have been forms signed by Green which were blank at the time and disputes over which ones submitted to Companies House were real. The narrative is that Whyte appointed

Green to raise money and 'front up' the Sevco 5088 Limited bid on Whyte's behalf. However, the position is unclear. Green was the only Director of Sevco 5088 Limited according to Companies House and Whyte was not listed as a shareholder in the company. If you were Duff & Phelps, who would you accept as a representative of Sevco 5088 Limited? Green incorporated Sevco Scotland Limited two months after Sevco 5088 Limited was incorporated on 29 May 2012. But unlike Sevco 5088 Limited, it was not set up as an off-the-shelf company by an agent but was incorporated with Green as the sole Director. The filings on Companies House show Green in the incorporation documents taking the first ever Directorship of this company. Green is on record as saying it was important to have a Scottish Company as the legal form of Rangers FC. It is true that there are some differences and, indeed, Scottish companies must have their registered address in Scotland. Equally Sevco 5088 Limited was clearly not a Scottish company and was variously based in Cardiff and then London. But why call it Sevco Scotland Limited? We can see from the above that 'Sevco' was a name used by a secretarial firm in Wales, so it would seem a deliberate use of the same name by Green. Sevco Scotland Limited may be the first 'Sevco' to ever be incorporated in Scotland.

Novation means that all parties agree that one of the parties in an existing contract will be replaced by one of the other parties to the Novation agreement. In this case Sevco 5088 Limited, Duff & Phelps and Sevco Scotland Limited all agreed that Sevco Scotland Limited would replace Sevco 5088 Limited in the agreement that in exchange for £5.5M Duff & Phelps would assign the rights to the assets of The Rangers Football Club plc to Sevco Scotland Limited instead of Sevco 5088 Limited. The signatories to the Novation agreement, or deed, would have been Charles Green, the only official Director of Sevco 5088, a member of Duff & Phelps, probably one of the Joint Administrators, and Charles Green the only Director of Sevco Scotland Limited. Whyte was not involved as officially he held no position in any of the parties to the Novation. In company law, Directors have a duty to act in the best interest of the members of the company and to avoid conflicts of interest. In the case of Sevco 5088 Limited, whatever the informal understandings between Whyte and Green, the official shareholder was still 7Side and the only listed Director at that time at Companies House was

Charles Green. It is, therefore, difficult to argue Green was breach of this duty to members of Sevco 5088 Limited when he novated the contract with Duff & Phelps and bought the business and assets of the company (i.e. Rangers FC) using Sevco Scotland Limited instead of Sevco 5088 Limited. There may well be other contracts and agreements behind the scenes but Companies House - at the time of the purchase - was silent on the matter. If Duff & Phelps were relying on official records to keep a track of who was representing who then they were entitled to believe that Green could legitimately novate the agreement on behalf of Sevco 5088 Limited and Sevco Scotland Limited.

Simply, as Director of Sevco 5088 limited, this was in Green's gift i.e. to novate the trade and assets from Sevco 5088 Limited to Sevco Scotland Limited. At this stage, I am left wondering if Whyte was 'too far removed' from proceedings to be aware of this 'novation' by Green. Green incorporated Sevco Scotland Limited as a Scottish company on 29 May 2012 – perhaps he had realised that by this date that the CVA would fail. A Scottish-incorporated company also helped with the ongoing Rangers Scottish 'identity.' It is also interesting to note that in the CVA proposal, the JAs use Sevco 5088 Limited. In their *Interim Report to Creditors* dated 10 July 2012 (and thereafter), the JAs use Sevco Scotland Limited.

Returning to the Duff & Phelps administration, this arrangement with Sevco 5088 Limited led to the Proposal for a CVA dated 29 May 2012. Such a CVA was likely to provide for a greater distribution to be made to creditors than would have been possible if: [342]

> (1) the business and assets of the Company were sold absent a CVA; and/or
> (2) the Company was put into liquidation.

In addition, the JAs believed that this CVA would ensure the continuation of Rangers FC in its current corporate entity. This would provide the maximum opportunity to avoid additional football regulatory sanctions and would allow the enhanced prospect of a successful application for a UEFA licence, which was required to compete in UEFA competitions (subject to satisfying the necessary UEFA regulations) thereby enhancing the business' value and satisfying the strong preference of the supporters that the football club continued to trade within its current corporate entity.

The JAs, therefore, believed that it was in the best interests of the creditors to approve the CVA Proposal.

In their *Interim Report to Creditors* dated 10 July 2012, the JAs reported that the club continued to trade under the control of the JAs up to the date of the sale of the business and assets of the company to Sevco Scotland Limited on 14 June 2012. During this period, Rangers FC was able to complete all its remaining SPL fixtures and achieved second place in the final SPL standings for the 2011/2012 season. Moreover, the continuation of trading operations enabled the JAs to put the said CVA Proposal to the creditors of the company. After the CVA Proposal was rejected by creditors, the JAs were able to secure a going concern sale of the business, history and assets of the Company to Sevco Scotland Limited.

Following the sale of business and assets of The Rangers Football Club plc, the responsibility for maintaining all trading operations passed to Sevco Scotland Limited, which continued to operate the club. The JAs then completed a handover of operational matters to Sevco Scotland Limited and undertook an exercise to finalise all outstanding issues relating to the Administration trading period. The corporate entity which remained under the control of the JAs i.e. The Rangers Football Club plc was placed into CVL once all outstanding issues had been attended to. Some five months later, Duff & Phelps announced, in October 2012, that creditors had approved an end to their administration and that they had applied to the Court of Session for BDO to be appointed as liquidator. This appointment was legally approved on 31 October.[343] Of note, following the CVA creditors' meeting on 14 June 2012, the JAs were approached by a party verbally offering £6M for the business and assets of the company. No offer had been received by this party in the previous 17 weeks. The person making the offer was believed to be part of the Party 3 consortium. Notwithstanding the verbal offer, the JAs confirmed that a binding contractual agreement had been reached and the business, history and assets were subsequently transferred from the company (The Rangers Football Club plc) to Sevco Scotland Limited.[344]

The purchaser (Sevco Scotland Limited), however, required membership of the SFA and either the SPL or SFL to continue to operate Rangers FC and participate in a senior football competition in Scotland. Therefore, it sought agreement with the football authorities. The company (The Rangers Football Club plc) was required to be a party to such agreements to assist Sevco Scotland Limited, as required by the SPA.

A most significant and intense period of negotiations followed in terms of proposed SPL and SFL entry. It is instructive, then, to offer three pieces on analysis to understand fully this period: Wikipedia, Chris Graham and Duff & Phelps.

Wikipedia
(https://en.wikipedia.org/wiki/Administration_and_liquidation
_of_The_Rangers_Football_Club plc):

The financial collapse of Rangers resulted in a great deal of discussion within Scottish football. Initially it was proposed by the Scottish Premier League (SPL) that Rangers should be allowed to play in the SPL, despite the failure of the CVA. This failure meant that Rangers' membership share in the SPL had to be transferred to the new company, along with its other assets and that transaction required the approval of a two-thirds majority of the 12 SPL clubs. Kilmarnock chairman Michael Johnson had stated that it was likely that he would vote in favour of re-entry, but after consultation with their fans he decided to abstain. The chairmen of Aberdeen, Hearts, Dundee United , Hibernian, Inverness CT and St Mirren all publicly stated that they were likely to vote against. St Johnstone chairman Steve Brown declared that he would in principle oppose an automatic re-entry depending on the extent of the sanctions and conditions, while Motherwell chose to vote on the basis of fan and shareholder opinion. Newly promoted Ross County were relatively quiet on the issue, claiming that they would take into consideration the views of other clubs before making their decision.

When the vote on the share transfer was held on 4 July, it was rejected by a 10-1 majority. Only the old Rangers company voted in favour, and Kilmarnock abstained. Celtic were the only SPL club not to announce their voting intentions prior to the ballot taking place, but later released a statement confirming their "no" vote and stating that "the integrity of the game was of paramount importance" and that the "decision to refuse access into the SPL was an overwhelming one and demonstrates the depth of feeling amongst everyone involved in Scottish football".

Following the vote by rival clubs to reject the application for direct entry of Rangers to the SPL, SFL and SFA executives proposed a direct entry to the Scottish Football League First Division.

Scottish Football League clubs felt that they were being forced to deal with a situation which was not of their making. Notable opponents to direct entry included Raith Rovers chairman Turnbull Hutton, who said that lower league clubs were being "bullied, rail-roaded and lied to" and described the conduct of the governing bodies as being corrupt". Clyde and Falkirk also voiced strong disapproval of Rangers entering the First Division, with the Falkirk chairman Martin Ritchie claiming that parachute entry would be "totally unacceptable".

On 13 July, 29 out of 30 SFL member clubs voted to give Rangers associate membership but 25 of them also voted to place Rangers FC into the Third Division of the Irn-Bru Scottish Football League from the start of the season. Agreement was subsequently reached on the transfer of SFA membership.
Sevco Scotland Ltd agreed to accept all conditions relating to charges against Rangers FC of bringing the game into disrepute, including a 12-month transfer embargo, the payment of all outstanding fines and football debts, and agreement on broadcasting rights. The Scottish Premier League retained its

right to the potential application of sanctions, including an investigation into the club's use of EBTs and any penalties that may be applied as a result of it.

The decision allowed the relaunched Rangers to complete their first fixture just two days later, a Ramsdens Cup tie against Brechin City at Glebe Park.

Chris Graham (Taking on the Establishment: Rangers and the Scottish Football Authorities)[345]

The CVA was rejected by HMRC on 12 June 2012 and Green announced that the New Co route would be taken to allow the club to rebuild. Thus, this left Rangers at the mercy of 11 other SPL clubs. They (football authorities) issued dire warnings about what was, effectively, their own actions. The SPL Board heaped pressure on the SFL to 'parachute' Rangers into the First Division – a move which would lessen the financial impact on the SPL of Ranger's absence, as it would effectively only last for one year, but would allow them to pander to the vocal sections of their fan bases who demanded Rangers removal from the topflight of Scottish football.

Both Stewart Regan and Neil Doncaster issued veiled threats of financial implications if the SFL did not comply. Fans took to the internet message boards to warn the 11 SPL club chairmen that they would vote with their feet if Rangers were allowed to continue in the SPL. This 'No to New Co' movement lobbied Chairmen to vote Rangers out of the league but not without a little help from Stewart Regan. The first few days of July 2012 saw feverish talks behind closed doors. It was clear that SFL clubs were being put under huge pressure to accept Rangers into the First Division and lessen the impact of removing them from the SPL.

On 3 July 2012, an SFL briefing note from Stewart Regan and Neil Doncaster provoked outrage amongst SFL Chairman. Regan had indicated that the SFA would veto any attempt to accept Rangers into the SPL by refusing to transfer their SFA membership. The same day, the Rangers Fans Fighting Fund published a poll which confirmed what the Rangers fans had been telling the football authorities this for weeks. Seventy-five per cent of Rangers fans voted that the club should resume playing in the Third Division. On 4 July, the SPL clubs finally took decision to remove Rangers from SPL. More clubs issues statements heavily criticising the SPL and SFA handling of the matter.

Finally, on 13 July, Rangers fate was known. The SFL clubs voted to admit Rangers into the Third Division. The rest should have been straightforward but the SPL and SFA stepped in to complicate matters. The authorities demanded that Rangers accept a 'Five-way Agreement' between SPL, SFA, SFL and Rangers' old and new companies.

Two weeks of negotiations took place until the Club were finally forced into accepting a range of sanctions for the SFA to transfer their membership to the new company. Rangers had to accept the registration embargo, starting on 1st September 2012, despite it having been ruled legally unenforceable in the Court of Session. Rangers had to pay all outstanding fines and costs to the SFA, including the costs for the Court of Session challenge to the registration embargo, which the club won, and all outstanding debt to clubs both within and out with Scotland. They also had to accept being part of a hastily cobbled deal to keep the Sky and ESPN television contracts alive. This granted the broadcaster rights to show 15 Rangers games as part of the SPL contract, with the SFL receiving a token sum to be distributed to all their member cubs.

Furthermore, the SPL retained all prize money due to the club for their second place finish the previous season and reserved the right to pursue potential stripping of titles for the years in which Rangers had used EBT loans to players.

Administrator's Progress Report of RFC 2012 plc dated 24 August 2012[346]

As has been widely publicised, the Purchaser was unsuccessful in its application for the transfer of the Rangers Football Club plc's SPL share and following further negotiations with the Football Authorities, ultimately agreed such terms as were necessary to obtain the transfer of the Rangers Football Club plc's SFA membership and gain membership of the SFL.

The terms of these agreements were inter alia:

- That the Company's SPL share was transferred to Dundee Football Club.
- That the Company's SFA membership was transferred to the Purchaser.
- That the SFA Appellate Tribunal, which was due to be reconvened following the Interlocutor of Lord Glennie on the Club's Judicial Review, was empowered to impose the Transfer Embargo.
- That the Purchaser was required to assume liability for all football-related creditors, being all creditors of the Company that are football clubs, the Football Authorities or clubs of the other national football associations. This includes outstanding transfer fees and SFA disciplinary fines arising from the SFA Disciplinary Tribunal commented on in previous reports.

In terms of 'TUPE transfer of the Playing Staff', certain players objected to the transfer of their employment contracts to Sevco Scotland Limited.[347] The position of The Rangers Football Club plc was that these employees were transferred to Sevco Scotland Limited under the provisions of TUPE. It was considered that the objection by these players about their employment transfer was a matter for Sevco Scotland Limited to deal with under the provisions of TUPE. TUPE did not cover the position of the SFA player registration and, therefore, this was a separate matter for Sevco Scotland Limited to discuss with the football authorities. While the manager, Ally McCoist, and several players were willing to transfer, other first team players such as team captain Steve Davis, Steven Naismith and Steven Whittaker refused to have their contracts transferred under TUPE regulations and became free agents. The Rangers Football Club Limited subsequently agreed a fee for Davis with Southampton FC, while Charles Green pursued claims in relation to Naismith and Whittaker.

On 31 July 2012, The Rangers Football Club plc changed its name to RFC 2012 plc. This was in accordance with the SPA. The company changed its name as per Companies House records on 31 July 2012 so that the purchaser (i.e., Sevco Scotland Limited) could take the name The Rangers Football Club Limited. With the 5-way Agreement signed, transfer of membership was approved although as Rangers FC was still officially an SPL club at the time, an unprecedented 'conditional membership' for which there was no proviso in the SFA's Articles of Association had to be granted in order that the Ramsdens Cup Tie at Brechin City FC on could go ahead on 29 July 2012.

Full membership of the SFA was confirmed the following week in advance of the Third Division match at Peterhead FC on 11 August 2012.

4.3 Academic Frameworks

4.3.1: Organisational: Six Stages of Organisational Decline and Renewal

For the purpose of this chapter, I will remain with the fourth stage, namely retrenchment. I suggest that retrenchment continued beteem 14 February 2012 and 29 July 2012. In terms of cost reduction, there was clearly: a reduction in expenditure; stronger financial controls; and an intensive effort to reduce all production costs. In addition, and in line with the administration process, assets (where possible) were sold, debt was reduced (again where possible) and, sadly, staff left the organisation. Most of this retrenchment was overseen by Duff & Phelps and latterly by Charles Green. At the organisational level, then, we witnessed: directive (perhaps autocratic) management, tighter controls, cost cutting and other retrenchment policies. Simply, these actions and behaviours were central to the turnaround process as the plc was in significant decline.

4.3.2: The Change Curve

For the purpose of this chapter, I will consider the second two elements of The Change Curve, namely anger and depression.

After the feelings of shock and denial, anger is often the next stage. A scapegoat, in the shape of an organisation, group or individual, is commonly found. Focussing the blame on someone or something allows a continuation of the denial by providing another focus for the fears and anxieties the potential impact is causing. Common feelings include suspicion, scepticism and frustration.[348] I suggest that scapegoats included: Sir David Murray, Craig Whyte and the SFA/SPL.

The lowest point of the curve comes when the anger begins to wear off and the realisation that the change is genuine hits. It is common for morale to be low and for self-doubt and anxiety levels to peak. Feelings during this stage can be hard to express and depression is possible as the impact of what has been lost is acknowledged. This period can be associated with apathy, isolation and remoteness. At this point, performance is at its lowest.[349]

The emotions of anger and depression are evident below:

1. Rangers' humiliation will be savoured by Celtic supporters but they must be careful what they wish for; No surprise but unquestionably a major shock. That was the impact of the news that Rangers - one of the oldest clubs in the world, with a history that stretches back to 1872 - had petitioned the Court of Session for the appointment of an administrator.
The Telegraph
February 13, 2012

> There are already signs of seething anger amongst lifelong adherents of Rangers who want to know how their club could conceivably have been brought to this pass.

2. MURRAY: THERE IS NO WAY FOR ME TO COME BACK AS OWNER
Daily Record
February 15, 2012

EX-BOSS RULES OUT RETURN AS FANS VENT THEIR FURY

Sir David tells of his sadness at plight of Rangers SIR David Murray ruled out buying back into Rangers yesterday - and told of his "huge disappointment" at the club going into administration.

In a statement, the former Rangers owner confirmed there was no "legal mechanism" for him to reacquire the Ibrox club from Craig Whyte. He added: "Words cannot express how hugely disappointed I am with news of today's appointment of administrators to The Rangers Football Club PLC."

But furious fans were in no mood to let Murray off the hook as they descended on Ibrox to voice their despair and anger. Allan Thomson, 55, of Balornock, Glasgow, said: "Murray stayed at Rangers for too long, but he has made the worst decision ever in selling the club to Whyte and he needs to stand up and be counted." And he was scathing about Whyte, too, adding: "None of the millions Whyte got from Ticketus, or from any sales of players, has been reinvested in the club - so where is it? "He may have paid just pounds 1 for the club but it looks like he is going to walk away with millions of pounds after leaving us destitute. "The club will never die, the fans will make sure of that, but Whyte must go right now."

Robin Lowey, 56, of Penilee, Glasgow, said: "Whyte is not even a football man, never mind a Rangers man. He is nothing but a chancer - simple as that. He wasn't banned from being a company director for seven years for nothing. If he hasn't been paying the tax since he got here, then that isn't on and he has brought this great club to its knees. Whyte didn't even have the decency to spare five minutes for the fans - the people who have supported the club through thick and thin. All he had to do was be honest with the fans. But we are left wondering what happened to the Ticketus money and from the money from the sale of Jelavic. He shouldn't be playing games with the club. It's more than just a business, it's a way of life for a lot of people."

Gavin Kerr, 29, of Cessnock, Glasgow, said: "It is a sad, sad day for Rangers - 140 years of history, including 54 league titles, is going down the pan. We want to keep our club and its history, we don't want to end up being Rangers United. Whyte knew what he was taking on when he came to the club. But to find out he has cheated the club as well is sickening and he must go now. It is absolutely ridiculous he could have thought that Rangers fans would settle for starting out all over again following another team." Lee Smith, 19, of Thornliebank, said: "Craig Whyte has brought shame on Rangers. The club should never have been allowed to get anywhere near this situation. Maybe he has walked all over whoever he has done business with in the past, but it looks like that isn't going to be the case here."

3. Sport - Tartan Talk - Rangers hardcore respond with anger
The Irish News
April 28, 2012

Amid the fear and uncertainty surrounding the future of Rangers Football Club, the final Glasgow derby of the season will again take place against a backdrop of threats and intimidation. Rather than reflect on the punishment meted out for decades of financial mismanagement, the gut response of a hardcore of the Rangers support has been one of outrage and aggression. Rather than face the situation in a positive manner, some fans have chosen to lash out with misguided anger, others issuing threats or planning for boycotts against the unseen multitude of enemies that have threatened their very existence. Jardine had spoken of a unified group of fans rising up against injustice.

4. Rangers liquidation: Shareholders anger after club's last rites
The Scotsman
June 15, 2012

SHAREHOLDERS in Rangers have long since been forced to accept they hold little influence on how the club is run. Their share certificates, some of them passed down from generation to generation, were more about emotional investment than anything else. Yesterday, around 250 of those small shareholders attended the final meeting of The Rangers Football Club plc. It lasted little more than 20 minutes, a sense of futility and despair engulfing those present.

5. Anger and frustration as Rangers close to liquidation
Irish Independent
June 15, 2012

Rangers administrators Duff and Phelps faced heckling and jeers at a meeting of shareholders at Ibrox yesterday after a Company Voluntary Arrangement (CVA) was formally rejected at a creditors meeting earlier in the day. Around 150 shareholders gathered in the middle tier of the Bill Struth Main Stand at 1.0 for what should have been the formality of a vote, albeit effectively redundant by that stage, on the CVA proposal. However, frustrated and angry members of the audience took the opportunity to demand answers from administrators on a day when Rangers edged closer to liquidation and shareholders lost their stake in the club.

4.4   Chapter Summary

On Tuesday 14 February 2012, HMRC consented to the appointment of Paul Clark and David Whitehouse of Duff & Phelps as JAs. It was important for the JAs to 'trade' the business whilst seeking a purchaser. This was a complex and complicated process.

At this time, two separate inquiries commenced: the SFA Independent Committee; and the SPL Commission.

In their *Interim Report to Creditors* dated 10 July 2012, the JAs note that many unsubstantiated offers were received in the Spring of 2012. Each party that sought to submit an offer was asked to provide proof of available funding and an outline of the terms of the offer. Of the offers received, three credible Indicative Offers were received on the 16 March 2012 deadline and one further credible offer was received on 23 March 2012. An announcement as to the preferred bidder was scheduled to be made during the week commencing Monday 9 April 2012. However, during the Easter Bank Holiday weekend of 6 - 9 April 2012, the JAs were formally advised of the proposed Financial Fair Play amendments to be issued by the SPL. A SPL vote was scheduled to be cast on 30 April 2012.

One day later, and on 4 May 2012, a late entrant into the sale process — Sevco 5088 Limited — provided an Indicative Offer setting out the terms on which it would acquire the company. Having considered the offer from Sevco 5088 Limited and compared it to other offers received for the company/business and assets, the JAs determined that the Sevco 5088 Limited offer was preferable because it secured the best available return to creditors of the company and proposed a CVA in respect of the company. Consequently, on 12 May 2012, the JAs agreed and signed an Offer Letter with Sevco 5088 Limited and granted Sevco 5088 Limited exclusivity to complete a takeover of the company or a purchase of the company's business and assets by

Monday 30 July 2012. Sevco 5088 Limited made a payment of £200,000 to the company for such exclusivity.

On 14 June 2012, following the sale of business and assets of The Rangers Football Club plc, the responsibility for maintaining all trading operations passed to Sevco Scotland Limited. The JAs then completed a handover of operational matters to Sevco Scotland Limited and undertook an exercise to finalise all outstanding issues relating to the Administration trading period.

The corporate entity which remained under the control of the JAs i.e. The Rangers Football Club plc was placed into CVL once all outstanding issues had been attended to. Some five months later, Duff & Phelps announced, in October 2012, that creditors had approved an end to their administration and that they had applied to the Court of Session for BDO to be appointed as liquidator. This appointment was legally approved on 31 October.

The purchaser (Sevco Scotland Limited), however, required membership of the SFA and either the SPL or SFL to continue to operate Rangers FC and participate in a senior football competition in Scotland. Therefore, it sought agreement with the football authorities. The company (The Rangers Football Club plc) was required to be a party to such agreements to assist Sevco Scotland Limited, as required by the SPA.

A most significant and intense period of negotiations followed in terms of proposed SPL and SFL entry. On 31 July 2012, The Rangers Football Club plc changed its name to RFC 2012 plc. The company changed its name as per Companies House records on 31 July 2012 so that the purchaser (i.e. Sevco Scotland Limited) could take the name The Rangers Football Club Limited. With the 5-Way Agreement signed, transfer of membership approved although as Rangers FC were still officially an SPL club at the time, an unprecedented 'conditional membership' for which there was no proviso in the SFA's Articles of Association had to be granted in order that the

Ramsdens Cup Tie at Brechin City FC on could go ahead on 29 July 2012.

Full membership of the SFA was confirmed the following week in advance of the Third Division match at Peterhead FC on 11 August 2012.

4.3 Academic Frameworks

4.3.1: Organisational: Six Stages of Organisational Decline and Renewal. Retrenchment continued beteem 14 February 2012 and 27 July 2012. Most of this retrenchment was overseen by Duff & Phelps and latterly by Charles Green.

4.3.2: The Change Curve. We witnessed — in the Spring/Summer of 2012 — significant anger and depression. Scapegoats included Sir David Murray, Craig Whyte and the SFA/SPL.

4.5   Reflection

This was a complex and complicated period of time in the history of Rangers FC. Indeed, of all the chapters in this book, I spent the most time researching this chapter in reading, thinking, and trying to understand what actually happened. I now think that I understand most of it.

During the period, 14 February 2012 – 27 July 2012, three inter-related and complex themes were at play:

- The Administration process of The Rangers Football Club plc by Duff & Phelps
- The sale of Rangers FC to Sevco Scotland Limited.
- The eventual entry into the SFL Third Division of Rangers FC.

In addition, there was also:

- The SFA Independent Committee that led to disciplinary charges that would 'play out' all spring/summer and would be resolved via the 5-Way Agreement.
- The SPL Commission/Harper McLeod
- The proposed Financial Fair Play amendments issued by the SPL.

In everyone's defence, although it appeared that 'things were made up as they went along', we had — in the context of Scottish football — not seen anything like this before. The administration process created shock for all, not just Rangers FC stakeholders: "This was Rangers — this does not happen to them." In this respect, I do recall how prominent this story was in such non-traditional Scottish sports programmes as *Today* (BBC Radio 4) and the Channel 4 News. Certainly, the administration process was conducted under the glare of (the world's) media. As such, I do consider that the JAs had a very difficult and demanding job.

In terms of academic frameworks, we witnessed retrenchment throughout. There was also significant anger and depression by many (if not all) Rangers FC stakeholders.

For me, questions remain surrounding Sevco 5088 Limited and Sevco Scotland Limited. It is interesting that the CVA on 29 May 2012 referred to Sevco 5088 Limited but all Duff & Phelps reports, thereafter, refer to Sevco Scotland Limited. I am not sure if I understand fully what happened here. The answer is probably in the novation and Green wanting a company registered in Scotland.

But there were positives — a lot was achieved, by many, to resolve fully this very difficult situation by 29 July 2012. Perhaps, however, the most significant actors were (and continue to be) the supporters and the leadership of the various social movements — the lifeblood of the game. As Jock Stein once said: "Football without fans is nothing." This remains as true today as it was when originally stated.

An emergence from chaos: 29 July 2012 – 6 March 2015

Chapter Five

Brechin City Football Club and onwards: 29 July 2012 – 6 March 2015

Emergence from chaos

Recovery

Acceptance

29 July 2012: Rangers FC v Brechin City FC

6 March 2015: Dave King and regime change

Chapter Contents:

5.1   Introduction

In this chapter, I will examine the recovery of 'corporate Rangers' and Rangers FC to the period 6 March 2015. On this date (6 March 2015) — with regime change — I suggest that 'corporate renewal' commenced.

As such, I will examine over a three-year period:

- 5.2: 29 July 2012 – 30 June 2013
- 5.3: 1 July 2013 – 30 June 2014
- 5.4: 1 July 2014 – 6 March 2015

In this first period (i.e. 29 July 2012 – 30 June 2013), two companies emerged: The Rangers Football Club Limited and Rangers International Football Club plc. Simply, The Rangers Football Club Limited was incorporated on 29 May 2012 (previously called Sevco Scotland Limited). In the period to 30 June 2013, a total of 33 415 000 shares were issued in The Rangers Football Club Limited for a total consideration of £13 294 000. The entire share capital of The Rangers Football Club Limited was purchased — in a share-for-share exchange — on 19 December 2012, the date of the parent company's (i.e. Rangers International Football Club plc) IPO.

We can, therefore, analyse Rangers at three levels: strategic, operational, and tactical. Two companies and a football club offer a 'levels approach' to analyse and understand this recovery. This is shown at Figure 16.

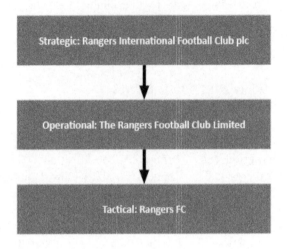

Figure 16.0: Rangers at Three Levels: Strategic, Operational, and Tactical

Rangers International Football Club plc is the holding company of The Rangers Football Club Limited. In turn, The Rangers Football Club Limited operates Rangers FC – the football club. In addition to this significant corporate restructuring, during this period (2012 – 2015), Rangers FC ascended from SFL Division Three to the SPFL Championship. But there was also a significant 'fight' for the ownership of the plc (Rangers International Football Club plc). Indeed, and as cited in Wikipedia:

> Rangers boardroom politics were a fractious force, causing a constant flux with change after change of various directorial positions, rival factions attempting to take control of the company and the emergence of Mike Ashley as the major stakeholder and power broker in late 2014.[350]

In this chapter, each section (5.2 – 5.4) will report on/offer analysis of:

- The football club (i.e. Rangers FC) including key descriptives.
- Rangers International Football Club plc.
- The Rangers Football Club Limited where required.

5.2   29 July 2012 – 30 June 2013

5.2.1 The Football Club

Rangers FC played in SFL Division Three in Season 2012/2013. Their first home league match in this Division was a 5–1 victory over East Stirlingshire FC on 18 August 2012 in front of a crowd of 49,118 — a world record for a football match in a fourth-tier league. According to Wikipedia, Rangers FC were defeated in the third round of the Scottish Challenge Cup by Queen of the South FC at Ibrox on 18 September 2012, in the quarter-finals of the Scottish League Cup at home to Inverness Caledonian Thistle on 31 October 2012 and in the fifth round of the Scottish Cup by Dundee United FC on 2 February 2013.[351] Rangers won the Third Division title on 30 March 2013 after a goalless draw at Montrose FC.

From The Rangers Football Club Limited Annual Report (page 4) to 30 June 2013, the Key Performance Indicators are shown at Table 11.0:[352]

	13-month period to 30 June 2013
Turnover (£000s)	17 696
Operating Loss (£'000s)	(17, 608)
Wages/Turnover Ratio	99%
Number of games played (total)	49
Number of games played (SFL Home)	18
Number of games played (SFL away)	18
Number of games played (Cup home)	7
Number of games played (Cup away)	4
Number of games played (Friendlies)	2
Number of season tickets sold 2012/13	38 228
Average season ticket price (£)	210
Average attendance (all home matches)	39 335

Table 11.0: The Key Performance Indicators for The Rangers Football Club to 30 June 2013

5.2.2   The Rangers Football Club Limited

In the autumn of 2012, the holding company (Rangers International Football Club plc) did not exist. Therefore, the story commences with The Rangers Football Club Limited. The Rangers Football Club Limited was incorporated on 29 May 2012 under the previous name Sevco Scotland Limited. On 14 June 2012, Sevco Scotland Limited purchased the trade and assets of RFC 2012 plc (i.e. Rangers FC), which was in administration. Under the sale and purchase agreement, the total acquisition and cost was recorded at £5.5M. Sevco Scotland Limited became The Rangers Football Club Limited on 31 July 2012. The principal activities of The Rangers Football Club Limited were the operation of a professional football club in Scotland together with related commercial activities. During the period 31 July 2012 – 30 June 2013, the football club was 'run' by the Rangers Football Club Limited.[353]

A timeline for The Rangers Football Club Limited from Companies House information is shown at Table 12.0

29 May 2012	14 June 2012	31 July 2012	17 August 2012	31 October 2012	18 December 2012	22 April 2013	29 May 2013	31 May 2013
Incorporation. Share structure: 2 shares at £1/share. New share structure: 200 shares at £0.01/share.	Sevco Scotland Limited purchased the trade and assets of RFC 2012 plc, which was in administration. Brian Stockbridge appointed as Secretary and Director. Imran Ahmed and Malcolm Murray appointed as Directors.	Name Change: Sevco Scotland Limited to The Rangers Football Club Limited.	Allotment of shares: 29 340 200.	Allotment of shares: 33 415 200.	Termination of Appointment of Malcolm Murray as Director.	Craig Mather appointed as Director.	Termination of Appointment of Imran Ahmed as Director.	Termination of Appointment of Charles Green as Director.

Table 12.0: Timeline for The Rangers Football Club Limited

In the Annual Return of The Rangers Football Club Limited (dated 29 May 2013), the Statement of Capital states that the total number of shares was 33 415 200. These 33 415 200 ordinary shares were held by Rangers International Football Club plc. At this stage, then, it is important to recognise the history of Rangers International Football Club plc. Simply, there was an Initial Public Offering (IPO) on 19 December 2012, which offered the following:

Placing shares:	24 242 857
(Institutional)	
Offer shares (i.e. new ordinary share):	14 285 714
Acquisition shares:	33 415 200
(The Rangers Football Club Limited)	

38 528 571 shares (i.e. 24 242 857 + 14 285 714) were 'on offer' via the IPO. Shares in The Rangers Football Club (i.e. 33 415 200) would be purchased by The Rangers International Football Club plc.[354]

This IPO was reported in various media outlets. For example:

The Daily Telegraph. 20 September 2012: *Rangers fans offered shares.*

> Rangers fans could be asked to register their interest in a share issue as early as next month. The Rangers board have in recent weeks appointed Cenoks Securities as brokers for their initial public offering (IPO) while Capita has been contracted to deal with supporters enquiries and for registration purposes. Rangers newco chief executive Charles Green said:
>
> > What we plan to do now in the next few weeks is put an information pack together and in early October there will be further information put out to fans and they can register their interest.

The Daily Telegraph. 12 October 2012: *Rangers plotting £20m stock market flotation.*

RANGERS Football Club has kicked off its plan for a £20m stock market flotation as it tries to recover from the embarrassment of administration and demotion to the fourth tier of Scottish football. The club said that the funds raised will be used to strengthen its squad, improve facilities and provide additional working capital. Rangers will aim to list about 50pc to 60pc of its shares on London's junior AIM market, targeting institutional investors as well as fans. Cenkos is acting as the club's adviser. An initial public offering (IPO) prospectus is expected to be published by the end of the month. Charles Green, chief executive, who led a £5.5m buy-out of Rangers in June, said:

> Rangers is debt-free and a huge club with enormous support and a 140-year track record of success in the domestic and international arenas. Our aim is to return the Club to its glory days while ensuring it is run efficiently and profitably.

BBC: 5 December 2012: Rangers share issue aims to raise £27m.

Rangers Football Club hopes to raise up to £27m in its forthcoming share issue, it has emerged. Ahead of the launch on the Alternative Investment Market (AIM), the club said it had already received pledges of £17m from business investors. It hopes to attract another £10m of investment from supporters, bringing the total value of the club to £50m. The Third Division club will be floated on the AIM as Rangers International Football Club plc. The information is contained in a document lodged with the London Stock Exchange. Companies make these announcements 10 business days ahead of their first anticipated day of listing. The document also states:

> Upon admission, Rangers International Football Club plc will acquire Rangers Football Club Limited on the basis of a one for one share exchange and after admission Rangers International Football Club plc will be the holding company for the group.

Full details of the Rangers International Football Club plc IPO are at: *IPO (untitled (wordpress.com))*. Key details are thus:

Major Shareholders.

As at the date of this Prospectus, the following shareholders had notifiable interests of more than 3 per cent in RFCL:

No of Shareholder Ordinary Shares	Percentage
Charles Green	
5,000,200	14.96%
Blue Pitch Holdings	
4,000,000	11.97%
Mike Ashley	
3,000,000	8.98%
Margarita Funds Holding Trust	
2,600,000	7.78%
Richard Hughes	
2,200,000	6.58%
Imran Ahmad	
2,200,000	6.58%
Craig Mather	
1,800,000	5.39%
Norne Anstalt	
1,200,000	3.59%

So far as the Company is aware, immediately following Admission, the following persons will hold directly or indirectly three per cent or more of the Company's voting rights, assuming no Offer Shares are issued:

No of Shareholder Ordinary Shares	Percentage
Charles Green	
5,000,200	8.67%
Hargreave Hale Limited	
4,949,000	8.58%
Artemis Investment Management LLP	
4,286,000	7.43%
Blue Pitch Holdings	
4,000,000	6.94%

Mike Ashley
3,000,000   5.20%
Margarita Funds Holding Trust
2,600,000   4.51%
Cazenove Capital Management Limited
2,450,000   4.25%
Richard Hughes
2,200,000   3.82%
Imran Ahmad
2,200,000   3.82%
Legal & General Investment Management
2,000,000   3.47%
Limited
Insight Investment Management (Global)
1,900,000   3.30%
Limited
Craig Mather
1,800,000   3.12%

After the IPO, the story continues. For example:

BBC. 18 December 2012: *Rangers share issue raises £22m.*

> Rangers Football Club has raised half its target investment from
> fans, following the deadline for its share offer. It had aimed to
> raise £10m of investments in the club from small-scale retail
> buyers of shares. There was already a commitment to the major
> part of the share offer, with rich individuals and institutional
> investors signing up to at least £17m. The club announced on
> Tuesday evening that it had raised a total of £22.2m. On
> Wednesday morning, the shares in Rangers International
> Football Club plc will start trading on London's Alternative
> Investments Market (AIM). It is part of the London Stock
> Exchange, on which shares in Celtic Football Club are also
> traded. The deadline for fans to buy new shares in the club
> passed on Tuesday afternoon. A statement from Rangers said:
>
>> A total of £22.2 million has been raised from
>> professional and institutional investors and supporters
>> which will be used to take the club forward, strengthen
>> the squad when appropriate and improve facilities.

The Daily Telegraph. 20 December 2012: Rangers IPO is 'springboard for rebirth' of club.

> Rangers chief executive Charles Green has promised manager Ally McCoist money for new players after claiming the club's share issue can act as "the springboard for the rebirth" of the Glasgow giants. The Ibrox outfit on Tuesday night announced over £22 million - including more than £5million from fans - had been raised from their listing on the Stock Exchange, and dealings on the Alternative Investment Market began yesterday morning. A successful flotation is set to be good news for McCoist, who said after Tuesday night's 3-0 win over Annan that he was hoping for some cash to spend on his squad. A signings embargo means Rangers are unable to register free agents until Sept 1 and will have to wait until the following January to buy new players, but Green has promised a healthy transfer kitty when the restrictions are lifted. Green said:

> > In the presentation we did when we were selling the shares, and also in the prospectus, we said that, of the £22million, £10million is put to one side for Ally. Of course, we can't buy players at the moment, we can't do that until January 2014. But, between now and then, we'll also have another season's worth of season ticket sales so the cash position will increase. We're not saying it's £10million and only £10million. If Rangers fans, as we expect, come out and buy their season tickets next year, there is perhaps another £20 million there and that is a fantastic position for the manager, the club and its fans to be in. When we are allowed to go into the market, this club will take the right players and take the right action.

> He added:

> > This is definitely the springboard for the rebirth of Rangers.

In Summary, and from this IPO of Rangers International Football Club plc:

- 38 528 571 shares were allotted at £0.7/share. This formed the basis of the Proposed Placing Offer and Application for Admission to AIM.

- With 33 415 200 from The Rangers Football Club Limited, Rangers International Football Club plc was valued at £50M (i.e. 71 943 771 shares at 0.7/share).

- Of the 38 528 571 shares, 24 242 857 shares were offered to Institutional Investors (£17M). With their 33 415 200 shares from Rangers Football Club Limited, they had 57 658 075 shares.

- Off the 38 528 571 shares, 14 285 714 shares were offered to individuals – again at 0.7/share. 7 437 981 were not sold which meant that on 18 December 2012, Rangers International Football Club had 65 096 056 shares. This was also apparent in Annual Return of 16 November 2013.[355]

Ultimately, Rangers International Football Club plc was formed and listed on the Alternative Investment Market of the London Stock Exchange and became the holding company for The Rangers Football Club Limited, which, in turn, owns and operated the football club i.e. Rangers FC.

The Board of Directors of Rangers International Football Club plc for the period December 2012 – June 2013 was as follows:

- Brian Stockbridge (from 4 December 2012).
- Philip Cartmell (from 7 December 2012).
- Charles Green (4 December 2012 – 31 May 2013).
- Ian Hart (from 7 December 2012).
- Craig Mather (from 24 April 2013).
- Malcolm Murray (from 7 December 2012).
- Bryan Smart (from 7 December 2012).
- Walter Smith (from 7 December 2012).

A simple timeline for Rangers International Football Club plc is detailed at Table 13.0 below.

16 November 2012	26 November 2012	4 December 2012	4 December 2012	14 December 2012	18 December 2012	18 December 2012	19 December 2012	24 April 2013	4 June 2013
Incorporation as Rangers Football Club plc. Public Company Limited by Shares. Articles of Association. Share structure: 1 share at £1/share. FFW Securities Limited appointed as Secretary and Director. Edward Laurence Lumb appointed as Director.	Name Change: Rangers Football Club plc to Rangers International Football Club plc	Termination of Appointment of FFW Securities Limited as Secretary and Director. Termination of Appointment of Edward Laurence Lumb as Director. Charles Green appointed as Director. Brian Stockbridge appointed as Secretary and Director. Sub-division of £1 ordinary share into 100 ordinary shares at £0.01 each.	Ordinary Resolution to allot Placing, Offer and Acquisition Shares. Articles of Association adopted by Special Resolution	Appointment of Ian Hart, Bryan Smart, Malcolm Murray, Walter Smith, and Philip Cartmell as Directors.	Allotted Placing Shares: 241 100 001. Total number of shares: 24 242 957	Allotted shares: 33 415 100 Total number of shares: 57 658 057	Allotted shares: 7 437 999. Total number of shares: 650 096 056	Craig Mather appointed as Director.	Termination of Appointment of Charles Green as Director.

Table 13.0: A Timeline for Rangers International Football Club plc

The Interim Results of Rangers International Football Club plc were reported on 4 March 2013. The key points are as follows:[356]

Operational Highlights

- Sustainable long-term structure now in place:

    o   Assets and intangibles purchased from Administrators of former Rangers Football Club plc for £5.5m on 14 June 2012
    o   Successful IPO on AIM market of London Stock Exchange raised £22.2m in December 2012 to fund growth strategy, and bringing the total raised share capital since incorporation to £35.2m

Chairman's Statement

This has been a period of extraordinary progress for the Club and I am pleased to announce the financial results for Rangers International Football Club plc. These interim results cover the seven-month period to 31 December 2012 and reflect the fact that the Club is successfully rebuilding one of the UK's most renowned football institutions. The acquisition of the trade and assets of the then Rangers Football Club plc by a consortium of investors was completed on 14 June 2012 and heralded the end of a traumatic period for the Club, during which the then Rangers Football Club plc had been placed into administration by the previous owner. Following the rejection of a Company Voluntary Arrangement by creditors, the Rangers Football Club plc was put into liquidation and subsequently Rangers International Football Club plc was created, incorporating The Rangers Football Club Ltd into the Group.

Malcolm Murray
Chairman
4 March 2013

Charles Green, CEO of Rangers, commented:

This has been a significant period in the Club's history, in which vital steps were taken to ensure the survival and rebuilding of

225

one of the UK's most venerable football institutions. The priority for the Company to date has been to stabilise the business and put in place solid financial foundations for the future. To this end, revenue streams have been enhanced, and costs cut. In addition, important strategic steps have been taken, such as the agreements now in place with Sports Direct, Puma and Blackthorn Cider. These achievements have been made whilst retaining the important fabric and structure of the Club. We will continue to execute our growth plan, and investors and supporters can have confidence in the development of operations as the Club progresses. Undoubtedly, challenges lie ahead but the Club is now well equipped to meet them successfully. Above all, the Club and its supporters are resolute in the belief that, both on and off the pitch, Rangers can look to the future with confidence and pride.

Financial Review

It was clear from Rangers' league status this season there would be a resultant impact on turnover at the Club. It was essential, therefore, that costs were substantially reduced and this was achieved. Operational costs have been reduced to £15.7m for the reporting period, compared with approximate previous costs of similar periods of £22m in the then Rangers Football Club plc (now in liquidation). Reductions in costs have been largely achieved through the review of commercial contracts and a reduction in player payroll costs. Overall operational costs are expected to continue to decline as further cost saving initiatives and efficiencies take effect. Work continues on further enhancements to the quality and sustainability of revenue streams. Overall, we have achieved these operational changes whilst retaining the fabric and structure of the Club which is necessary given the scale of our operations. I am glad to report that, as of the date of this announcement, only £251,000 remains to be paid in relation to the £2.8m of football debts we undertook to pay in the SFA licensing agreement, and these amounts are not due to be paid until October 2013. The Company has reported a profit of £9.5m which should be viewed in the context of recognising a negative goodwill credit of £20.5m. The Company is expected to report an operating loss at year end in accordance with the business plan and broader growth strategy.

226

A revaluation process was undertaken during the period; Ibrox stadium and Murray Park were revalued at £40m, and intangibles were valued at £19m on acquisition. We have embarked on a programme of infrastructure improvements at Ibrox. Initial investment has been made in groundskeeping equipment and expenditure on LEDs and stadium jumbotrons is underway. The Club has also acquired the Albion car park and Edmiston House which will be redeveloped to improve the match day experience for supporters and both these acquisitions are expected to produce near term returns on investment through future revenues.

The raising of £22.2m capital is an excellent outcome from the flotation of the Company on AIM and the funds, along with the £13m of other share capital provide the Club with a sound financial footing going forward. It is essential, however, that the Club does not over-extend itself in future as such an approach is unsustainable, regardless of the playing environment. The priority for the Company to date has been to stabilise the business and put in place solid financial foundations for the future. This work will continue and investors and supporters can have confidence in the development of operations as the Club progresses with its core business of playing football.

Brian Stockbridge
Finance Director
4 March 2013

From the Annual Report of the Rangers International Football Club plc – published on 30 June 2013 – some interesting information does emerge. For example:

Page 6:

In August 2012, Rangers announced a partnership with retail giants SportsDirect.com to enable the Club to control its retail operation and give supporters the chance to buy direct from the Club and in doing so, continue to invest in the future. Rangers Retail, a subsidiary company of Rangers International Football Club plc was formed with SportsDirect.com to enable the Club to utilise the huge buying power and resources of

SportsDirect.com while maintaining the majority stake holding in the partnership.

<u>Page 38</u>:

The company's subsidiary undertakings are The Rangers Football Club Limited, the main activity of which is the operation of a Professional Football Club and Ranges Media Limited which is a dormant company. The Rangers Football Club Limited holds investments in the following companies:

Garrison Security Services Limited (Security).   100%.
                      Preference Shares.
Rangers Retail Limited (Retail).   51%
                      Ordinary Shares.[357]

Returning to The Rangers Football Club Limited, and in terms of governance, the Board of Directors was as follows:

- Imran Ahmad (14 June 2012 - 29 May 2013).
- Charles Green (29 May 2012 - 31 May 2013).
- Brian Stockbridge (from 14 June 2012).
- Craig Mather (from 22 April 2013).
- Malcolm Murray (14 June 2012 - December 2012).

From the Annual Report of The Rangers Football Club Limited — published on 30 June 2013 — key insight does again emerge. For example:[358]

<u>Page 3</u>:

Exceptional operating costs (£3.695m) include: £2.7m of repayments in respect of football creditors taken on from RFC 2012 plc, which TRFCL was committed to paying; investigation expenses of £0.6m relating to fees incurred by the Company after the Board committed to an independent investigation following legal claims by Craig Whyte and Aiden Earley.

<u>Page 6</u>:

Purchase of Albion Car Park from Lloyds Banking Group for £1.6m and Edmiston House from Murray International Holdings Company for 0.8m.

Page 9:

On 15 April 2013, the Board of RIFC announced it was commissioning an independent examination and report relating to allegations made by Craig Whyte, the previous owner of RFC 2012 plc, concerning RIFC's former CEO and former Commercial Director. A letter before claim was received by RIFC plc from legal advisors to Craig Whyte and Aidan Earley. RIFC plc engaged the services of Allan & Overy LLP to defend against the possible claim. In addition, the NXDs of RIFC plc (the Investigating Committee (IC)) engaged the law firm Pinsent Masons LLP to investigate the connections between Craig Whyte and the former and current personnel of RIFC plc and its subsidiaries (the Investigation). The Investigation was overseen by Roy Martin QC.

On 30 May 2013, RIFC plc announced that the Investigation had been concluded on 17 May 2013 and Pinsent Mason and Roy Martin QC have reported to the IC. The IC is satisfied that a thorough investigation was conducted despite the inherent limitations of a private inquiry.

RIFC found no evidence that Craig Whyte had any involvement with Sevco Scotland Limited (now called The Rangers Football Club Limited) which ultimately acquired the business and assets of RFC 2012 plc from the administrator; nor which would suggest that Craig Whyte invested in The Rangers Football Club Limited or Rangers International Football Club plc either directly or indirectly through any third party companies or vehicles.

On 28 May 2013, a further letter before claim was sent to (inter alia) The Rangers Football Club Limited and Rangers International Football Club plc on behalf of Craig Whyte, Aidan Early and (purportedly) Sevco S5088 Limited. The Board is of the view that claims set out in the letter before claim are entirely unsubstantiated based on legal advice received to date by the Board and the outcome of the Investigation.

229

Page 10:

On 20 June 2013, Imran Ahmed intimated his intention to raise a claim in respect of alleged unpaid bonuses under a clause of his contract of employment. On advice from the Company's lawyers, the Directors consider that there is no substance to this claim and that no obligation to pay a bonus arises. Consequently, no provision for payment has been made in these financial statements.

Irrespective of the 'Investigation' detailed above i.e. the connection between Whyte and Green, more generally — and during his time with Rangers International Football Club plc, The Rangers Football Club Limited and Rangers FC — I consider that Green did provide, and evidence, leadership. For example, Kinnon states:[359,360]

> Green proved himself to be a real champion of the Rangers cause, standing up for the club's rights in a way that his predecessors had not.

And he (Green) did, of note, secure membership of SFL and took forward the IPO and listing on the AIM.[361] This was also reported in the print media. For example:
Talking Rangers Ibrox chief is winning support.[362]

> However, credit where it is due. He has provided far more funds for McCoist than many expected, and invested properly in the team. Yes, the wage bill will be hugely reduced from last term, but some of the top SPL players have been secured. Green has managed to provide McCoist with a team good enough to cruise to successive title successes. He's also given the supporters a quality of player which might just be enough to entice them to stick with their club this term after over 38,000 turned out for the League Cup encounter with East Fife on Tuesday night. There would have been less costly, and slightly more difficult, ways to achieve promotions, but Green hasn't tried to do this on the cheap. Already, he has committed to more in wages than the man he replaced, Whyte. It appears there is a united front at Ibrox and everyone working together is what the club needs to forge a successful future.

Ally happy with Green machine.[363]

ALLY McCOIST believes Rangers finally have a figurehead willing to stand up for the club. The manager has welcomed the return of leadership at Ibrox under Charles Green following the club's liquidation saga. He said:

> It's been sadly missing. For about four or five months there was nobody at all. It's long overdue that we have someone to represent the club and fight for the club and we've certainly got that at the moment.

Overall, a corporate strategy was emerging with a clear distinction between what was strategic and what was operational. Many problems, however, remained in the Boardroom of Rangers International Football Club plc. For example, from spring 2013, significant issues surfaced. A summary of these key issues is as follows:

- The leadership (or perceived lack of it) of by Rangers International Football Club plc Chairman Malcolm Murray – particularly in his dealings with Charles Green.[364]
- Charles Green himself:

  - 5 April 2013: *Rangers: Craig Whyte prepared to go to court over assets.*[365]
  - 8 April 2013: *Rangers chief Charles Green criticised for 'racist' remark.*[366]
  - 10 April 2013: *Rangers: SFA queries Charles Green's dealings with Craig Whyte.*[367]
  - 13 April 2013: *Rangers: Board orders investigation into Charles Green.*[368]
  - 19 April 2013: *Rangers: Charles Green steps down as chief executive.*[369]

- Rangers: Craig Mather appointed interim chief executive.[370]
- Boardroom divisions and lack of unity.[371]

231

- Walter Smith concerns.[372]
- The requirements of further investment.

In his Sunday Herald article of 28 April 2013, *Ibrox remains in flux, with parties inside and out jockeying for position,* Richard Wilson summarises the key difficulties:

> Rangers remain a club of deep uncertainty, with several interested parties moving into place with a view to buying a stake in the coming months. The members of the consortium that bought the club last summer can sell their shares in June. Charles Green and Imran Ahmad, who have both left, are unable to sell their stakes of 7.79% and 3.38% respectively until December, 12 months after the club was launched on the Alternative Investment Market. They appear, though, set on offloading them to James Easdale, the owner of McGill's buses with his brother Sandy. Up to 30% or more of the club could become available, effectively a controlling stake. The past week has been fraught for Rangers, but it might also allow for a period of respite. More revelations may emerge about the dealings between Whyte, Green and Ahmad. The board split was not entrenched, and there is the opportunity now for a greater sense of co-operation. Leadership is required in the boardroom, but there are people at the club trying to bring progress. The independent examination by Deloitte and Pinsent Masons began last Monday files and computers have been pored over all week and a verbal report will be delivered to the directors tomorrow. In the meantime, the willingness of the finance director, Brian Stockbridge, to support the likes of Walter Smith and Ian Hart on the board has been significant, as was Mather's appointment as permanent chief operating officer and interim chief executive.

In addition, 6 May 2013:

Reasons to be cheerful to the fore at Ibrox[373]

> Until the independent examination into Charles Green and Ahmad's running of the club, and the extent of their collusion with Craig Whyte, the former owner, has been completed, Rangers are in a state of uncertainty. There continue to be suggestions that less than £10m of the initial public offering

232

(IPO) money remains, despite statements to the contrary from Murray, Craig Mather, the interim chief executive, and Brian Stockbridge, the finance director. Those considering buying shares are certainly waiting until the forensic examination, by Pinsent Masons and Deloitte, is complete to be sure of the financial position and the assets owned. Yet Rangers have season tickets to sell and the next campaign to plan for.

8 May 2013:

Murray hangs on as Rangers hit self-destruct[374]

Rangers are virtually paralysed by boardroom infighting as Malcolm Murray stages a last-stand attempt to maintain his position as chairman, The Daily Telegraph understands. Murray's situation has been under threat for some time but he is determined to continue and there have now been several board meetings at which internal politics have absorbed the energies of the directors. Murray - who has the support of former manager Walter Smith and another director, Phil Cartmell - lost a vote of confidence at a board meeting on Monday but the meeting broke up without any statement to the Stock Exchange or a formal resolution on the chairman's position. Charles Green, the former chief executive, is still a director - at least nominally - until the end of May, but his position has been weakened significantly by his recent resignation, although he retains his eight per cent shareholding in the club. Smith was on the verge of quitting following Monday's events but an Ibrox investor told The Daily Telegraph:

> He was angry and frustrated but he has been persuaded that he can do more for Rangers by remaining on the board than standing down, so he has got the gloves on again.

16 May 2013:

Rangers shareholders try to overthrow chairman Malcolm Murray in bid to snatch control of boardroom[375]

A LEGAL letter was served on the club today which demanded Malcolm Murray's removal and for two businessmen to be

233

given seats on the board. THE war for control of Rangers took an explosive new twist today when shareholders launched a bid to overthrow chairman Malcolm Murray by forcing an extraordinary general meeting. We can reveal Blue Pitch Holdings - who helped bankroll Charles Green's original £5.5million buyout of the Ibrox club's assets - have teamed up with controversial bus tycoons James and Sandy Easdale to call for Murray's head. A legal letter was served on the club at around 3pm on Wednesday which demanded Murray's removal. It also called for businessman Chris Morgan of the mysterious Blue Pitch Holdings and James Easdale to be given seats on a new-look board. The club now have 21 days to agree to implement the changes or face yet more public turmoil, with the proposals going to a shareholders' vote at an EGM next month. Between them Blue Pitch and the Easdales - who have struck a deal to snap up shares belonging to both former chief executive Charles Green and shamed commercial director Imran Ahmad - control around 29 per cent of the club. They believe that by joining forces, they have enough power to push through the changes they want and grab control of the fractured Ibrox boardroom. In fact, they wrote informally to the club two weeks ago to request the removal of both Murray and non-executive director Phil Cartmell. It is not yet clear if Cartmell remains on their hit-list but what is certain is that they were enraged by the club's failure to respond or acknowledge their original request. A source close to the gathering crisis said tonight:

> Blue Pitch and the Easdales had already decided these changes were necessary but they have been outraged by what they see as a blatant disregard for basic protocol. As a result, they have formalised their demands and will force an EGM if that's what it takes. These people will not take no for an answer. The Easdales were promised a seat on the board by Charles Green when they invested in the flotation in December and they want what they paid for. The same applies to Blue Pitch, who backed Green from day one. They are unhappy with the direction the business is moving in and this is an aggressive move to protect their investments.

But the bombshell will further destabilise a board who have been split down the middle for many months now, following a

234

personality clash between Murray and Green. Ironically, all factions appear to agree that Murray's time as chairman is all but up. But former manager Walter Smith and Cartmell have been appalled at the manner in which others have tried to force the situation to a head - with Green still attempting to call the shots even after his resignation and a bumper pay-off from the role of chief executive. Now those rifts are set to deepen with the news that an EGM has been called as the battle for the heart and soul of Ibrox enters its closing stages.

17 May 2013

Murray clings on as directors close in at Ibrox[376]

Meanwhile, in a separate development, former club chairman Alastair Johnston said he believed a cancer is spreading throughout the club which will not go away until self-serving investors are rooted out. Mr Johnston, who was ousted in May 2011 by then owner Craig Whyte, has concerns about the jockeying for position at the club. He said:

> With so many investors in quotation marks trying to play an active role in the guidance of Rangers Football Club, I don t think that is a healthy situation. I don t know the people involved but I really wonder about their agenda. I really wonder in whose best interests are they working.

He added:

> A lot of people can say they have the best interests of the club in mind but it is easy to say that. There are people vying for control and influence and they have got to lay down their ambitions and be transparent about finances and investment. The board of Rangers whoever it is and however it is constituted has to come out and be transparent about the assets and the commitments and what that will mean to investors.

Mr Johnston said there was a power vacuum at the club, adding:

> Someone has to come out and show guidance. Until the supporters can see a line-up of people that they can get

behind then they have a dilemma. At some point somebody has to say to the fans we want you to spend money and here is what we're going to do.

He dismissed any suggestion that Rangers would close, saying:

The basic fabric of the club will ensure survival but it will need transparency for that to happen.
It is a difficult time at Ibrox, and the club needs leadership to move forward with purpose.

Leader needed to calm troubled waters before Rangers are engulfed[377]

THE search for clear, blue water goes on as storms continue to assail Rangers. It is likely, however, that Malcolm Murray will be thrown overboard as the club hopes to lurch from another crisis towards safer havens. The burden of chill reality continues to batter the club. Murray was last night clinging on to his post as chairman with Philip Cartmell, a non-executive director, also believed to be in peril. It is believed that an extraordinary general meeting may not be required to effect the removal of Murray, whose situation is hazardous despite support from city investors. His fate was described by one source as unavoidable. He has to go. Too many see him as a liability, he said. The upheaval at Ibrox was described last night by a city source, sympathetic towards Murray, as mud wrestling and everyone is going to be covered in it. The departure of Murray is seen as sad but inevitable even among those at the club who are kindly disposed towards him. Turmoil is thus assured whether he goes or survives with Rangers facing a highly critical period. Murray's position is defended by investors who believe he knows the workings of the City, has an interest in the long-term future of the club and was an integral part of the pitch to potential shareholders. Unfortunately for him, moves to remove him are not just driven by Charles Green, the former chief executive with whom he has had a volatile relationship, but by other elements on the board who have become frustrated at his failure to provide leadership and direction. This is particularly important when a board has so many differing factions and has the added problems of interference from outside. Broadly, Murray is largely isolated and faces such as Walter Smith,

236

increasingly disillusioned by what he has walked into, Green, who leaves his directorship soon but has a large shareholding, and former owner Craig Whyte, whose presence may be as insubstantial as his claims but who has still the capacity to cause severe mischief. If Murray goes, then the theory is that James Easdale, co-owner of McGill's buses, and Chris Morgan, who has links with Green, will be brought on board. The fit and proper person test may then kick in both officially and unofficially. For example, if Green is linked to Whyte, then Morgan may be unacceptable to both the Scottish Football Association and the fans. The board is also split on how to proceed. There has to be cost-cutting at Ibrox. This is easier for some to accept than implement. However, cash flow at Ibrox has been a trickle all season after the input of season ticket money. This is a club with a huge stadium to maintain and a top-class training facility to run. It also has a substantial wage bill. The figure of £10m or less is generally the one used to describe the remnants of the £22m gained through the share offer. This haemorrhaging of money cannot continue without funds being replenished by a wave of season-ticket money or by new investment. Both these avenues are obstructed by what is continuing to happen at Ibrox. The fans are keeping their hands in their pockets, wary of the fall-out from the fall outs. The Whyte connection is toxic to hopes of selling season tickets and although at least one prospective bidder and many inside Ibrox believe his claims have no merit, the one-time owner of Rangers still has the power to cast a cloud over the club. Some bidders for the club also want it to be clearly shown that Whyte has no claim on the assets before launching any bid for ownership. Thus the clear, blue water for Rangers needs Whyte to be painted out of the picture permanently. There is an argument the liquidation of Rangers ended his claims and that all further business involves him and Green on a personal, not Rangers, basis. Whatever way this deal is sliced, Whyte has to be clearly and obviously out of the Rangers equation. The next step is to end the board wrangling. This will be difficult, given the competing motivations of its members, with some keen on realising a return on investment quickly. The fight for control at Ibrox is in some ways a misnomer because there is a sense that no one is in control at the moment. Rangers desperately need a strong figure whose probity would not be questioned by financial or football institutions. This has to be a personality who can calm the City investors while not causing concern at the SFA. These figures are in short supply and will not be easily lured into the mayhem that reigns at Ibrox 2013. Without that strong, purposeful character, Rangers cannot address the problems that are most crucial to the existence of the club. One of the key issues dividing the board is the pace of cuts that have to be undertaken. The true blue corner will want to protect as many of the staff as possible and to help those they know at the club. However, the reality is that the outgoings are unsustainable and may be ruinous if season ticket money falters. The boardroom fight at Ibrox has been depicted as one for the heart and soul of the club but its very fabric is under threat unless both a peace is achieved and a viable way forward is charted.

On 29 May 2013, a Board meeting of Rangers International Football Club plc was held. At this meeting, Walter Smith was named as Chairman. An EGM was not called, and a Statement was released to the Stock Exchange.

Again, this was reported widely in the media. For example:

30 May 2013

Rangers: Club chairman Walter Smith urges board 'unity'[378]

> WALTER Smith has vowed to take a hands-on role as the new Rangers chairman after being charged with the daunting task of stabilising boardroom affairs at the troubled Ibrox club. The 65-year-old former manager took up the non-executive role, replacing Malcolm Murray, after a Wednesday night meeting of directors in London, which had been called in a bid to address recent acrimonious divisions on the board. Murray, who had survived previous attempts to remove him as chairman, stepped down at the meeting, which saw Smith unanimously elected as the new chairman. Smith said:
>
>> Although I have been on the board for some months this will be another departure for me but there are enough directors around to make sure we will make the kind of progress necessary and which our fans want. Unity among the directors is vital. We must all be on the same

page as often as possible. We won't always agree but Rangers, this club and our fans must always come first.

His new role was confirmed in a brief statement to the Stock Exchange shortly after 3pm yesterday afternoon.

The Rangers International Football Club plc today announced that Walter Smith has been appointed non-executive chairman of the board. Walter Smith is widely acknowledged as the club's most successful manager. Under his leadership, the club enjoyed two immensely productive spells.

Murray said after the announcement:

After a year as chairman throughout a period which has probably been the most turbulent in Rangers' history, I have decided to step down from my role so that our former manager, Walter Smith, can succeed me. Walter, who certainly doesn't need any recommendation from me, has my support and I believe he can bring stability and focus to the club.

Green resigned as chief executive last month and has agreed in principle to sell his shareholding to Greenock businessmen James and Sandy Easdale, owners of McGill's Buses. Blue Pitch Holdings, one of the original investors in Green's consortium last May, has called for an extraordinary general meeting to remove Murray and non-executive director Phil Cartmell and replace them with James Easdale and Green's associate Chris Morgan. So far, Rangers have yet to call an EGM as they "assess the validity" of the request.

Returning to the summer of 2012, the SPL had announced that an Independent Commission had been appointed to consider a case against the club on 17 August 2012. The Commission was chaired by Lord Nimmo Smith with Charles Flint QC and Nicholas Stewart QC. The Panel was due to sit in October 2012 but was delayed until 13 November 2012 due to the uncertainty over the date of the Big Tax Case result, which was to have a material bearing on the outcome. The Hearing was then further delayed due to an injury to Rod McKenzie of Harper Macleod.[379]

The Commission finally convened on 29 January 2013 and heard several days of evidence. Rangers refused to take part due to their misgivings over the attempt to strip them of five titles in an earlier draft of the '5-way Agreement'.[380] The Rangers Fans Fighting Fund (RFFF) had employed a lawyer and QC to contest the changes on behalf of the old company in what was ultimately a successful move.[381] In advance of the Commission, the FTTT had returned a verdict which found in the favour of The Rangers Football Club plc by 2:1 in November 2012. On 28 February 2013, the Commission gave their verdict: the use of EBTs conferred no sporting advantage — perhaps because they were at, this stage, legal and, therefore, open to all other clubs. The (The Rangers Football Club plc) was found to have not properly disclosed details of EBT loans to players. The club was only censured for this administrative omission and given a £250 000 fine levied on The Rangers Football Club plc. This result saw the SPL and SFA come under renewed pressure over the attempt to force the club into accepting title stripping in the summer of 2012.

5.3   31 July 2013 – 30 June 2014

> Any hope that the support had that the club might normalise after the departure of Whyte was already wafter thin. It would only deteriorate over the next 18 months as in-fighting, boardroom reshuffling and jostling for power became an almost weekly occurrence.
>
> Mark Cooper[382]

5.3.1 The Football Club

In Season 2013/2014, Rangers FC played in SPFL League One. They secured the League One title and promotion to Scottish football's second tier on 12 March 2014. Rangers also reached the final of the Scottish Challenge Cup, in which they lost to Raith Rovers and the semi-final of the Scottish Cup, in which they lost 3–1 at Ibrox to Dundee United.

From The Rangers Football Club Limited Annual Report to 30 June 2014 (page 4), the Key Performance Indicators are shown at Table 14.0:[383]

	13-month period to 30 June 2014
Turnover (£000s)	17 150
Operating Loss (£'000s)	8 147
Wages/Turnover Ratio	38%
Number of games played (total)	49
Number of games played (SFL Home)	18
Number of games played (SFL away)	18
Number of games played (Cup home)	4
Number of games played (Cup away)	8
Number of games played (Friendlies)	1
Number of season tickets sold 2012/13	36 039
Average season ticket price (£)	214
Average attendance (all home matches)	41 444

Table 14.0: The Key Performance Indicators for The Rangers Football Club to 30 June 2014

5.3.2 Rangers International Football Club plc

The general timeline for Rangers International Football Club plc (from Companies House) is shown at Table 15.0.

8 July 2013	9 July 2013	5 August 2013	10 October 2013	16 October 2013	7 November 2013	14 November 2013	20 November 2013	24 January 2014
Termination of Appointment of Malcolm Murray and Philip Cartmell as Directors.	Appointment of James Easdale as Director.	Termination of Appointment of Walter Smith as Director.	Termination of Appointment of Ian Harte as Director.	Termination of Appointment of Craig Mather and Bryan Smart as Directors.	Appointment of David Somers as Director.	Appointment of Norman Chrigton as a Director.	Appointment of Graham Wallace as Director.	Appointment of Philip Tudor Nash as Secretary. Termination of Appointment of Brian Stockbridge as Secretary and Director.

Table 15.0: A Timeline for Rangers International Football Club plc

On Friday 2 August 2013, it was revealed that Green, who had resigned as Chief Executive in April 2013 — while his business dealings with former owner Craig Whyte were under investigation (in addition to Green's use of a racial epithet to describe his colleague, Imran Ahmad) — would be returning to the club as a consultant.[384] On 5 August 2013, Walter Smith resigned as Chairman of Rangers International Football Club plc. Smith called the Board 'dysfunctional' and that the Board could 'rarely find consensus and agreement.'[385]

Green left Rangers on 20 August 2013 — some 18 days after his arrival. The official statement, issued by Rangers International Football Club plc to the Stock Exchange, read:[386]

> Following a board meeting this morning the club's directors decided to terminate the consultancy agreement with Charles Green. The decision was unanimous and takes effect immediately.

Of note, although no longer employed by Rangers International Football Club plc, Green still had a significant say in how the Ibrox boardroom would look after Christmas 2013. For example, he still held 5M shares which gave him a 7.7 % holding. At this time, it was understood that he had promised to sell his shares to another Rangers investor, Sandy Easdale.

On 21 August 2013, The Daly Telegraph reported that although Green left Rangers on 20 August 2013, in a move which pleased the club's supporters, it had not averted the likelihood of an Extraordinary General Meeting (EGM) being convened in September 2013. Simply, a group of disgruntled shareholders led by Clyde Blowers chairman Jim McColl called for the meeting in a bid to topple chief executive Craig Mather. They also wanted Brian Stockbridge and Bryan Smart removed from the Board and their directorships handed to accountancy expert Frank Blin and former Blue Knight Paul Murray. It was understood that:

There are those on both sides who favour a compromise, but the sticking point was Murray's presence in the opposition group. Murray, a former Director under his namesake, Sir David, is understood to have angered Mather, who is unhappy about the nature of leaks and speculation which have emanated from the other side. [387]

The Daily Telegraph noted that there was a possibility that the EGM and Rangers' Annual General Meeting could be held on the same night, probably in the third week of September 2013 and at a notable cost to the club. In respect of the call for an EGM, it was reported as:

> The directors can state categorically that they have always been open to adding to the current size of the board and are actively seeking a new chairman, one who will bring instant and significant benefits. In particular it will be necessary to connect strongly with corporate Britain if the board's ambitions for Rangers are to be fulfilled. This board has been working tirelessly to find an intelligent solution to the request for a general meeting and all of the directors are open to sensible and reasonable additions. For instance, the board are not against Frank Blin becoming a director but do have reservations about other proposals.

The last sentence was a reference to Paul Murray's bid to become a Director at Ibrox for the second time.

Continuing with the EGM, by 3 September 2013 a deal to spare the club the cost of an EGM had still not been reached but talks were continuing. Holding such an EGM would have cost the club around £80K and the plc Board had proposed that the motion lodged for discussion would instead be resolved at the Annual General Meeting (AGM), due to take place sometime in October. [388]

On 6 September 2013, reporting on the ongoing power struggle, The Daily Telegraph reported that Rangers confirmed on Wednesday (4 September 2013) they would consider a request to add former chairman John McClelland and three other men to their board.[389] A group of investors led by Jim McColl also proposed appointing Paul Murray, Sandy Easdale and Frank Blin as directors. McColl and his group had called for an extra meeting in a bid to have Chief Executive Officer Craig Mather, Finance Director Brian Stockbridge and Bryan Smart removed, but it appeared that they had signalled their intention to withdraw that in the event that the quartet led by McClelland was admitted to the Board. The group stated that shareholders deserved the right to vote on the re-election of any Director. In an agreement with the plc, the requisitioners EGM request was to be carried out at the AGM.[390] The condition was that the AGM had to take place by October 2013.

In this same period, Green agreed to sell 700K shares of his 5M to Laxey Partners Limited – the Isle of Man-based Hedge Fund. Sandy Easdale bought the remainder of his shares when the 'lock-in' ended in December 2013. He (Sandy Easdale) joined the Board of The Rangers Football Club Limited in September 2013. His personal shareholding had increased to 4.37% of Rangers International Football Club plc. As such, Easdale now had voting rights of 23.8% believed to be the proxies of Blue Pitch Holdings and Margarita Holdings.

In September 2013, Brian Stockbridge and Craig Mather flew to South Africa to meet with Dave King. King' preference was to invest in the club through a new share issue rather than buying existing shares. Brian Stockbridge and Craig Mather had offered him the possibility of becoming Charman.[391]

On 1 October 2013, The Scotsman newspaper reported on the Annual Accounts of Rangers International Football Club plc that were signed off by Crag Mather and Bryan Stockbridge on 28 September 2013.[392]

The key headlines were as follows:

- There was an operating loss of £14.4M.

- Revenue of £19.1M was generated over a 13-month period — the vast majority of this sum came from gate receipts. The plc spent £17.9M on staff costs.
- Many fans remained concerned about the spending. Of note, the accounts showed a total of £7.8M was spent on paying the players that won the Third Division title meaning the majority of wage costs were to non-playing staff. Green, who stepped down in April 2013, received wages of £333,000, a severance payment of almost £220,000 and a bonus of £360,000.
- Finance director Brian Stockbridge received more than £400,000, about half of which was a bonus, while former commercial director Imran Ahmad, who has launched legal action against the club over a bonus row, received £300,000.[393]
- Rangers International Football Club plc, which raised £22M from the IPO in December 2012, had £11.2M in the bank at the end of June — about £4.5M of which was from sales of 2013-14 season tickets.

Notice of the AGM on 24 October 2013 was also served.

On 14 October 2013, Paul Murray won — at the Court of Session in Edinburgh — an Interim Interdict blocking the said AGM meeting. Simply, the incumbent plc Board had attempted to block a motion for the election of potential new Directors (Paul Murray, Malcolm Murray, Scott Murdoch, and Alex Wilson).[394] Paul Murray also repeated his call for Craig Mather and Brian Stockbridge to go. Mather agreed — he resigned on 16 October 2013. Ian Hart and Bryan Smart also resigned as NXDs. Two new appointments were made: David Somers as Chairman and Graham Wallace as Chief Executive Officer.

Writing about Mather's departure, Tom English offered that Craig Mather was critical of Paul Murray for destabilising Rangers. Simply, (Paul) Murray, and the disaffected shareholders, wanted a democratically elected board at Rangers. They won a notable victory in their long-running pursuit of accountability in the Ibrox boardroom.[395] English also suggested that the Easdales were now the powerbrokers at the club (I suggest plc) and had been for some time. Although they had a relatively modest personal shareholding, they had proxies from other investors (upwards of 25 per cent of the shareholding). English states that — on certain Rangers' issues — they could call on as much as 50 per cent. He offers:

> The fact that nobody knows for sure is part of the problem. The mystery surrounding the Easdales and who they are in bed with is one of the on-going problems at this besieged club.

At this juncture, English offers key and relevant questions:

- How many shares do the Easdales own?
- How many shares are committed to them by proxy when things come to a vote in the AGM?
- Have they got the support of Margarita Holdings and Blue Pitch Holdings — two of the serious institutional investors?
- If they have, how did they get that support?
- Who are Margarita Holdings and Blue Pitch Holdings?
- What deals were done in order to secure the support?
- Who is involved with them? Is, by any chance, Charles Green, involved? Or Imran Ahmad? Or any other individuals who feature in the grim back story?

English also considers that the Easdales must have seen Dave King as a threat. King will not buy their shares and make them wealthier. He will issue new shares — if he gets the chance — and dilute their control of the plc. The Easdales could have done with his money, but it was the concession of power that was the problem. He (English) offers:

> Mather left yesterday the words in his statement hinting at the real story of his exit. The chief executive had "agreed to stand down". Agreed with the plc board, where only two men remain and only one of them matters. Stockbridge will serve a purpose for the Easdales in the short term. He will soak up the criticism

like a human sponge but the real target should be the ones behind him, the bus tycoons who claim all of the power and answer none of the questions.

Of worry to many, on 17 October 2013, former Rangers chairman Alastair Johnston also warned that ex-owner Craig Whyte may still be attempting to control the club: [396]

> Mather came into Ibrox during the Charles Green era and Green was linked to Whyte. My concern is Whyte's malevolent influence could be part of the eight-ninths of the iceberg hidden from view. I don't believe Mather... suddenly decided to resign. Somebody is pulling the strings and there are other people out there with their own agendas.

On 21 October 2013, three influential Rangers supporters' groups joined forces to demand answers as Rangers International Football Club plc remained in the grip of a power struggle.[397] Several questions were raised:

- When will the club's AGM be held? The delay resulting from the Court of Session on 14 October, followed by the resignations of Craig Mather and Bryan Smart, leaves the current Board of Directors extremely vulnerable.
- Given the level of concern among fans regarding the ownership and finances of the club over the recent past, and the various investigations that have been undertaken, it is important that the individuals that are behind Blue Pitch Holdings and Margarita Holdings were made known to remove any doubt that there are connections to either Craig Whyte, Imran Ahmad or Charles Green.
- What is the position of the Easdale brothers going forward?

The supporters groups stated (in relation to the Easdales):

> They are now in a prominent position, both in terms of their shareholding and influence on the Board, and it is important that fans understand their view of the future structure of the Board

248

and the running of the club. The club has adopted a very defensive position recently in efforts to rebuff allegations and clarify misinformation.

Laxey Partners Limited became largest shareholder in mid-November 2013 when it purchased an additional 3.3M shares. At their request, Norman Crighton became an NXD. Laxey had said that they would support the moves of Paul Murray and Jim McColl but, in end, backed the Board as the appointments of Somers, Wallace and Crighton and the departures of Green, Mather and Ahmad were — they considered — the necessary refresh that the club needed.

Continuing with the (significant) concerns with Green and Whyte, on 6 December 2013 — and in an open letter on the Rangers website — David Sommers offered:[398]

> Let me say categorically, that until I joined the Board a mere 4 weeks ago yesterday, I had never heard of Charles Green, Imran Ahmad, Craig Whyte, or any of the other characters in Rangers' history.

This statement followed the release of a draft 'constitution' for the club, proposed by Paul Murray, Malcolm Murray, Scott Murdoch, and Alex Wilson. The quartet (also known as the requisitioners) were seeking election to the Rangers board (Rangers International Football Club plc) at the AGM, which had been set for Thursday 19 December 2013.

Further discontent remained. For example, on 7 December — 12 days in advance of the AGM — the battle for control of Rangers intensified, with chairman David Somers dismissing the four rebel shareholders seeking election to the board at the upcoming AGM as "fanatics" who are "driven by their own personal self-interest."[399] The Paul Murray-led group — referred to by Somers as the "Gang of Four" but who call themselves "requisitioners" — had earlier launched a renewed attack on the current regime, warning that the end of Rangers is nigh under their stewardship and making numerous promises to the club

249

fanbase as to how they would manage the stricken club if they were to win the backing of voting shareholders on 19 December 2013. The Scotsman reported:

> The rebels, made up former oldco director Murray, Malcolm Murray, Scott Murdoch and Alex Wilson, told fans they would restore "trust and transparency" to the board if given the chance. As well as guaranteeing that Ibrox would never be sold on their watch, they pledged that there would be fan representation on the board, that directors and close associates should have no interest in any club contracts and that executive pay should be properly controlled and independently benchmarked.

In their letter to shareholders, the requisitioners, who each need 51 % backing from shareholders to secure their place, say:

> The very future of your club is now at risk.

In parallel, Rangers fans' group Sons of Struth wrote to the Ibrox club's top 50 investors in a bid to gain their support for boardroom change. Sons of Struth spokesman Craig Houston said:[400]

> We're saying to the major investors: Don't turn your backs on the fans. Working with all the organised fan groups and the response we had from the fans in the stands shows without doubt that the Board as currently composed does not enjoy popular support. To protect their investment and for the club to flourish the investors have to stand with the fans. It's time for change.

On Sunday 15 December 2013, and some 4 days before the AGM, the Scotsman offered detailed analysis as the Board contenders 'geared up for the AGM fight.' [401]

> In the board versus the requisitioners contest, as it stands, the board have to be considered strong favourites. There's the 26 per cent of shares represented by the Easdales, the 11.6 per cent from Laxey Partners Limited and the 4.6 per cent from Mike Ashley. The board reckon they have about 46 per cent of the shares in the bag. Not a guaranteed victory, but a pretty good

starting point in an increasingly hostile fight, a war of statement and counter-statement, insult and counter-insult. The board see the requisitioners as scaremongers and blowhards, a collection of characters, some of whom had their chance on the board in the past and blew it, and who now want back on the board despite a combined shareholding of less than two per cent.

The requisitioners talk of an impending financial calamity at the club, about the true nature of the peril being concealed, about a club heading for the rocks again under the stewardship of a board that does not want to engage with supporters and that revels in gratuitous mud-slinging, such as calling those seeking change a gang of "fanatics."

The fans, seemingly in large numbers, are on the side of the requisitioners. Does that make them fanatics, too? They want change. Above all, they want the removal of finance director Brian Stockbridge as their main, non-negotiable, item. And, if there is a second, it would be the dismissal of Jack Irvine, the club's communications man who has riled them more than once.

Both sides are now in an endgame. Sandy Easdale is doing interview after interview. On Friday he attempted to shoot down the view that Rangers are running out of money, but then spoke of a "fatal blow" to the club were supporters to boycott season ticket sales. A mixed message and a touch of moral blackmail. There was also a condescending tap on the head of the fans. They've been brainwashed, he said. "The supporters won't hurt the club they love. They'll see sense in the long run..." Patronising people 'isn't a great way of winning them over. The requisitioners have not been impressive either, it has to be said.

Moreover, a very useful summary of the key events of the year 2013 is offered in the said article (Rangers boardroom contenders gear up for AGM fight. Scotland On Sunday. 15 December 2013). It is instructive, at this stage, to detail these:

- In January, Green stated that "the quicker we can leave [Scottish football] the better". Green said he was contacting David Cameron.
- In February, Nimmo Smith's report was condemnatory of Murray's Rangers and their breaches of the SPL rulebook

on deliberate non-disclosure of payments. The old board, the verdict stated, "bear a heavy responsibility" for the offences.

- In the spring, Green got embroiled in a drama over a racist comment in a newspaper, then attempted to defend the comment about his "Paki friend", only to later apologise. The club was also cast into a nightmare of uncertainty over his possible links with Craig Whyte and the creeping horror that Green and Whyte were in some kind of cahoots after tape recordings emerged. Enter Pinsent Masons legal firm, exit Green.
- Enter Craig Mather, exit Ahmad, amid a surreal online controversy after it was reported that Ahmad had taken to social media, under an assumed name, in an attempt to dismantle Ally McCoist's managerial credibility.
- Whyte, meanwhile, had by then reported Green and Ahmad to the Serious Fraud Office in an attempt to get his hands on Rangers' assets.
- At some point, Stockbridge filmed a drunk Malcolm Murray in a restaurant.
- Alastair Johnston, former chairman, said that the power struggle was becoming a cancer spreading through the club.
- Enter Walter Smith as chairman. Exit Walter Smith as chairman, citing a dysfunctional board, a board that was spending money like there was no tomorrow, among the cash burned being the £825,000 salary to the manager. Later, there would be an announcement that McCoist's salary was going to be cut dramatically. Later still, another announcement that it still hadn't happened. Rangers had spent £7.8 million on their playing budget to win the Third Division. Smith shrugged his shoulders and said that's just the way things are at Rangers, as if the club was duty bound to flush money down the toilet.
- There is ducking and diving on both sides and, all the while, Sandy Jardine's words - "Don't embarrass our club" - have been drowned out.

In the run up to the AGM, Sandy Easdale had a further 3.1% of voting rights assigned to him by Beaufort Securities and he now held voting rights of 26.6%. Ally McCoist handed his voting rights (1M) to a local supporters' club — it was expected that they would vote against the Board. Ongoing concerns were also raised about the sale of Ibrox. This was reported in The Scotsman.[402]

'No sell-off'

Tuesday's reports also quoted Wallace vowing to ensure the ownership of Ibrox would be retained by the club - but Dinnie claims the strength of his assurance was not matched by football club chairman Sandy Easdale - who holds 26.62 per cent of the club's voting rights - when he spoke out last week. Now he wants the current PLC board to give a categorical promise that the stadium will not be sold off - a statement which has already been made by the four "requisitioners" - Paul Murray, Malcolm Murray, Scott Murdoch and Alex Wilson - who will also bid to win directorships on Thursday.

Dinnie said:

Wallace was insistent a sale and leaseback of Ibrox was not an option yet Sandy Easdale was quoted as saying 'at this present moment' it is not an option. The four nominees have promised to 'ring-fence Ibrox' and again we would ask the current board members to do similar on Thursday. Ally McCoist giving his proxy to supporters is excellent news as we, as the supporters trust, believe fans need an influential voice. It's imperative all fans who have a vote in Thursday's AGM use it, whether it's a proxy by the current manager or the fan in the street who owns a handful of shares.

The December 2013 AGM was angry. Graham Wallace stated that he was starting a 120-day Business Review to look at all costs. Moreover, the attempt by the Requisitioners failed. Polling was thus: Malcolm Murray (29.8%); Paul Murray (31.7%); Scott Murdoch (30%); and Alex Wilson (29.9%). Brian Stockbridge received 65.3% of votes — he left one month later. Wallace then recruited former Arsenal and Liverpool Finance Director Philip Tudor Nash as a Consultant. Wallace also assured the AGM that funds were in place to get to end of season; however, within weeks of the said AGM, McCoist was asked if players would take a 15% pay cut.[403] In addition, at the end of February 2014, it was announced that Rangers International Football Club plc had borrowed £500K from Sandy Easdale and £1M from Laxey Partners Limited. Both loans had to be repaid by 1 September 2014. In detail, it was understood that 'Laxey' wanted £150 000 interest on repayment. George Letham took over Laxey's loan but only wanted £75 000 instead of £150 000 and asked for the £75 000 to be converted into shares.[404]

The Interim Results of the Rangers International Football Club plc for the six-month trading period to 31 December 2013 were reported on 27 March 2014. The key points are as follows:

Operational Highlights

- Season ticket sales of approximately 36,000 for the 2013/14 season.
- Average home league attendance of over 40,000 during the period — seventh highest ranking UK football attendance.
- Revenue of £13.2M up by 38% (£9.5M for the 7 months ended 31 December 2012) — strong increase in sales from Sports Direct Retail partnership.
- Operating expenses of £16.8M (£16.6M for the 7 months ended 31 December 2012)
- Reduced loss before tax, excluding non-recurring items of £3.5M (£7.2M for the 7 months ended 31 December 2012).
- Cash of £3.5M as of 31 December 2013 (£21.2m at 31 December 2012).

Although there is, I suggest, evidence of ongoing recovery, concerns remained notably with: 'cash burn;' external influences on — for example — the purchase of season tickets; and the business requirement for all stakeholders to work together. These concerns are notable in the Statement by the, then, plc Chairman, David Somers reproduced in full below.

Chairman's Statement

The Interim Results cover the trading period for the six months ending 31 December 2013, one of the most tumultuous in the history of Rangers. Over that short time frame there were numerous changes to the Board, a postponed AGM and the appointment of new board members towards the end of the period to join James Easdale, who himself had only joined the Board in July 2013.

Against that background I was honoured to be appointed Chairman of Rangers in November 2013. Also joining the Board at that time were high calibre, professional directors, Graham Wallace as Chief Executive Officer and Norman Crighton as non-executive director. Together we were charged with stabilising the business and developing a long-term strategy for the Club, something that was urgently required following a period of boardroom instability.

The Board continues to deal with a number of legacy issues including a number of potentially costly legal cases, including the case referred to in note 15 of the Interim report.[405] The majority of the money raised from the IPO in December 2012 had been spent by June 2013 on IPO related fees and commissions, severance payments, the purchases of the Albion car park and Edmiston House and to fund ongoing operating losses. The Club incurred a further £7.7m of cash expenditure in the six months to 31 December 2013, funding additional fixed asset purchases and operating losses. In total the Club has spent over £4m on fixed assets since the IPO that are not yet generating incremental revenue. After the AGM, the Board conducted a detailed review of the business and established that the immediate financial plans needed to be re-assessed. In addition, operating costs had been running at a rate that could not be sustained by the revenue being generated by the Club. For example, in the period under review, nine players were signed at a time when the Club already had the second highest wage bill in Scottish football whilst playing in the third tier. When the Company was unable to generate short-term funding through planned asset refinancing and banking facilities, it was necessary to establish short term funding in February in order that the Club could continue to operate through the seasonal low point in its annual cash cycle. A solution was provided in the form of two credit facilities totalling £1.5m from shareholders.

Longer term it is the Board's aim to develop and implement an appropriate funding model that provides a platform for financial stability and supports the continued development of the Club's football team to ensure progression back to the top of Scottish football and to once again be competitive in Europe.

In implementing a professional basis for managing the Club, it remains a significant concern that external comment and ill-informed opinion continues to create uncertainty with regard to future income and cash flows. In particular, recent public comments suggesting season ticket holders divert payment away from the Club has caused a level of uncertainty over the timing and quantum of season ticket cash flowing into the Club, which as with many other football clubs, is Rangers' primary source of income. If this were to happen then there would be a negative impact on short-term cash balances and it is possible that the Club may need to seek alternative additional short term financing. This clearly would not be in the best interests of Rangers and would likely have a significant impact on our ability to progress the development of the Club in the planned manner. This possibility results in the existence of a material uncertainty which may cast doubt about Rangers' ability to continue as a going concern and therefore that the Company may be unable to realise its assets and discharge its liabilities in the normal course of business. Nevertheless, after making the appropriate enquiries and considering the uncertainties referred to above, the directors have concluded that there is a reasonable expectation that the Company has adequate resources to continue in operational existence for the foreseeable future. Accordingly, the directors continue to adopt the going concern basis in preparing the Interim results. Since the founding of the Club in 1872, supporters have, year after year, provided the working capital of the Club through ticket sales. Also providing capital were private individuals who subscribed for shares throughout the life of the Club. This model broke down when Rangers entered administration. The Club could only continue to survive and play football with the help of Rangers supporters and those who subscribed for shares at the IPO in December 2012. Many of those shareholders are fans and lifelong supporters. However, the bulk of the funds came from institutional investors. Both groups are stakeholders in the Company and must work together to help rebuild Rangers and ensure it has a successful, stable and sustainable future. The Club commenced a detailed business review during the period and this is nearing completion. The review will outline a clear strategic focus and vision for the future development of the Club, on and off the field, and the actions needed to deliver upon the vision. In addition, we have indicated previously that the Club will require additional investment to support our future plans. The outcome of the business review will allow the Board to assess the likely level of future investment and how best to structure this. The recent past has been a challenging time for everyone connected with Rangers.

David Somers
Chairman
27 March 2014

Post these Interim Results of the Rangers International Football Club plc (i.e. 27 March 2014), stability did not return. For example, Dave King suggested that fans pay their season ticket money for football season 14/15 into a Trust and the money would be released to the club on a 'pay-as-they-play' basis or season ticket money is placed in a Trust and released, in full, to the club against security of club property until all games are played. In this respect, King had the support of The Union of Fans.[406]

In general, season ticket numbers were down, supporters were becoming fatigued and disenchanted. Only Dave King appeared to have a vision — he stated that massive investment was required via fresh share issue. The answer was not to be asking players to take wage cuts in January 2014 and short-term loans. Of note, when the club needed to rebuild, the scouting and recruitment network was dismantled. The club did not have a single scout for the football team.[407]

The 13/14 season ended with the support and the plc Board in, it seemed, 'open warfare.' Significant wariness also ensued

257

amongst the support — by the end of May 2014, only 14 000 season tickets had been sold for the forthcoming season. Indeed, on 13 June 2014, the club announced that they had sold just 17 000 season tickets ahead of the new Championship season. Finishing this season/year, the Annual Report of the Rangers International Football Club plc — to 30 June 2014 and published on 26 November 2014 — does offer further insight. For example:[408]

> Business Review: Chairman's Report (pages 4-9)
>
> We all want to return to the top flight of our game, in the quickest possible time and with the on-going target of competing in European football. I am sure you will all agree that this will be more easily achieved if everybody who cares about the Club works together for the betterment of Rangers, which perhaps has not always been the case. Our path to restoring Rangers to where we all want the Club to be, can only be achieved with the continued support of all supporters, shareholders and business partners. Although much progress has been made in this financial year, I am also certain that there will be further testing times ahead, but I am confident that we will continue to successfully clear every hurdle put in front of us

5.3.3 The Rangers Football Club Limited

The Rangers Football Club Limited continued to operate Rangers FC. In addition, it remained 'subordinate' to Rangers International Football Club plc. Alexander Easdale was appointed to the Board of The Rangers Football Club Limited on 11 September 2013. From Companies House records, he did not have a seat on the Board of the Rangers International Football Club plc. In terms of the Statement of Capital, the total number of shares in The Rangers Football Club Limited was 33 415 200. These shares were held by Rangers International Football Club plc.

5.4   31 July 2014 – 6 June 2015

On the field, by the autumn of 2014, the journey through the leagues had become a slog. Two years of playing part-time opposition had taken its toll on the team. Even so, it seemed that the team was not up to speed in performance, preparation and professionalism as perhaps it should have been. It was looking unlikely that the team could actually win the Championship so would have to achieve promotion through the play-offs, if possible. There was no £20m share issue appearing over the horizon at the time. The club had signed 'onerous contracts,' said Graham Wallace, and the details of merchandising and retail contracts, naming rights going for a pound whilst the club lived seemingly off emergency loans every couple of months gave a depressing feel to the whole situation. It wasn't clear how the club was going to grow its way out of the situation as it felt like it was slowly being suffocated.

5.4.1 The Football Club

In season 2014/15, the league campaign began with a defeat to Hearts FC on 10 August 2014. Rangers reached the League Cup semi-final, being drawn against Celtic, and subsequently lost 2-1 on 1 February 2015. In the Challenge Cup, they lost 3-2 to Alloa Athletic FC on 3 December 2014 and Ally McCoist resigned soon after on 12 December 2014. He was, however, to serve less than a week of his notice period before being placed on gardening leave by the Board with his assistant manager Kenny McDowall being appointed Interim Manager until the end of the season. In the January 2015 transfer window, Rangers were also loaned five players from Newcastle United FC. After poor results in both league and Scottish Cup, Stuart McCall replaced Kenny McDowall as Interim Manager. The team failed to be automatically promoted to the Premiership — they successfully negotiated two play-off rounds before a 6-1 aggregate defeat to Premiership team Motherwell FC.

From The Rangers Football Club Limited Annual Report to 30 June 2015 (page 5), the Key Performance Indicators are shown at Table 16.0:[409]

	13-month period to 30 June 2015
Turnover (£000s)	15 408
Operating Loss (£'000s)	9 044
Wages/Turnover Ratio	40%
Number of games played (total)	54
Number of games played (SFL Home)	18
Number of games played (SFL away)	18
Number of games played (playoff home)	3
Number of games played (playoff away)	3
Number of games played (Cup home)	6
Number of games played (Cup away)	6
Number of season tickets sold 2012/13	26 515
Average season ticket price (£)	237
Average attendance (all home matches)	34 556

Table 16.0: The Key Performance Indicators for The Rangers Football Club to 30 June 2015

5.4.2 Rangers International Football Club plc

The general timeline for Rangers International Football Club plc is shown at Table 17.0.

Termination of Appointment of Malcolm Murray and Philip Cartmell as Directors.	Appointment of James Easdale as Director.	Termination of Appointment of Walter Smith as Director.	Termination of Appointment of Ian Harte as Director.	Termination of Appointment of Craig Mather and Bryan Smart as Directors.	Appointment of David Somers as Director.	Appointment of Norman Chrigton as a Director.	Appointment of Graham Wallace as Director.	Appointment of Philip Tudor Nash as Secretary. Termination of Appointment of Brian Stockbridge as Secretary and Director.

Table 17.0: A Timeline for Rangers International Football Club plc

The summer of 2014 summer saw continued discontent with various fans groups, alongside Dave King, attempting to influence the Board by withdrawing season ticket money.[410] Due to organised boycotts by the Union of Fans and Sons of Struth on the eve of new season, 21 000 season tickets had been sold — down 15 000 from previous season. Of note, the attendance at a Petrofac Training Cup match versus Clyde FC on 18 August 2014 was 11 190. The Scottish Cup exit to Raith Rovers FC on 8 February 2015 was watched by 11 422.[411]

Due to the reduced season ticket sales from the previous season (2013/14), the Rangers International Football Club plc required a 'financial injection.' The Board hoped that this would come from a share issue and announced this in June 2014. However, and of concern, the intention of raising up to £10M through an investment plan by the end of August 2014 failed when city investors did not purchase enough shares. The Board, therefore, relaunched a £4M share issue that was open to all existing shareholders — the initial plan was to try and raise £8M. 19M shares had been made available at £0.2/each. 5M were purchased by Laxey Partners Limited taking its stake to 16.3%

On 30 August 2014, Rangers fan discontent was demonstrated during a Championship game against Queen of the South FC at Ibrox with fans holding up red cards in the 18th and 72nd minutes. This situation was not improved when, on 3 September 2014, it was reported that Mike Ashley bought the naming rights to Ibrox Stadium for £1 in a deal with Charles Green in 2012. Concurrently, former Commercial Director Imran Ahmad finally succeeded in a bid to have £620 000 of assets frozen prior to pursuing litigation over an alleged unpaid £500 000 bonus. A few days later, the Board was granted leave to appeal this decision yet, on 12 September, it agreed to a settlement with Ahmad — much to the dismay of fans.[412] As some Rangers supporters' groups considered boycotting home matches in protest at the Board, it was reported that Ashley would not be participating in the share offer. Ashley's motives for not investing became clear in the following month.[413] At the end of the share issue, on 12 September 2014, it was announced that the plc had raised just over £3M which was still £1M short of its minimum target. The share issue was undertaken in order to allow Rangers International Football Club plc to continue to operate into the new year (i.e. 2015) but the failure to reach the target meant that further funding was required. Seeking an emergency loan, it is understood that Wallace spoke with Ashley. It is also understood that Ashley wanted ownership of the Rangers badge in return for a loan. Wallace refused. This is why — it is suggested — Ashley did not participate in the September 2014 share issue.[414] If he had, the money could have gone to the plc/club.[415] Instead, he purchased the 4.2M shares of Hargreave Hale for £840 000. He now had an 8.9% stake — second only to Laxey Partners Limited.[416] In addition, a few days later (on 16 September 2014), it was reported that Sandy Easdale had met with several investors that Rafat Rizvi, a (reported) convicted fraudster wanted by Interpol, had introduced him to.[417] This led to calls by the Union of Fans for Easdale to resign. This signalled the start of a crucial stage in the Boardroom power struggle at Rangers International Football Club plc with Dave King appearing to be outflanked by Ashley, who had secured the support of Sandy Easdale, David Sommers as well as the largest shareholder, Laxey Partners Limited.

Graham Wallace and Philip Nash met with Paul Murray, Dave King, and George Letham at the start of October 2014 to discuss the possibility of a cash injection. King's offer was £16M for 51% of Rangers International Football Club plc but he would also require a new share issue that would need to be approved by 75% of votes at an AGM. King's offer relied on 75% shareholder approval; however, with Ashley at 8.9%, Laxey Partners Limited, the Easdale and their proxies, they could easily get over 50% to oppose. Ashley reacted to the news by requesting an EGM vote on the removal of Graham Wallace and Philip Nash from the Board.[418] Nash resigned the day before the plc accepted a £2M loan from Ashley believing the loan not to be in the club's interest. Both Nash and Wallace had opposed this loan. Brian Kennedy returned and offered £3M in emergency funding with the condition of one seat on the Board.[419]

When offers of funding from Dave King and Brian Kennedy were rejected by Rangers' hierarchy, who instead opted for Mike Ashley's £2M loan offer, it was clear who was victorious. Particularly as Ashley's initial offer was insufficient and he had to be provide another £1M of funding less than a month later on 12 November 2014. In exchange for the initial funding, Ashley was granted critical power at Rangers International Football Club plc with the privilege to put forward the names of two nominees for appointment to the Board as well as security over Edmiston House and the Albion car park. As a consequence, Graham Wallace resigned.[420] Derek Llambias and Barry Leach were employed (initially) as consultants before being appointed Chief Executive and Finance Director respectively. Also, David Somers was named Executive Chairman but on a temporary basis in order to aid the transition. Financial respite was short lived as the Rangers International Football Club plc announced its preliminary results at the end of November 2014 indicating the club required another £8M of investment to see out the season.[421] In the Annual Accounts to 30 June 2014, the full extent of onerous contracts — stated by Wallace in his 120-day review — were becoming apparent. For example, Cooper suggests that fans had spent £7.6M on retail but the club had earned only £590 000 from Rangers Retail Limited, half of which was owned by Mike Ashley.[422] In addition, the main retail superstore at Ibrox and Rangers stores in Belfast and Glasgow Airport had been transferred to Sports Direct. Fifty-one staff would be transferred under TUPE to Sports Direct.[423]

The Rangers International Football Club plc AGM had been called for 22 December 2014. Eleven days beforehand, Norman Crighton — Laxey Partners Limited representative on the Board — left the Board. It would be a most significant move.

In advance of the December 2014 AGM, the Business Review (in the Annual Report of Rangers International Football Club plc to 30 June 2014) by David Somers (pages 4-9) summarises the historical and ongoing difficulties. It is instructive to reproduce it here:[424]

> We are asking at the 2014 Annual General Meeting for permission from our shareholders to enable us to issue shares for cash both on a non-pre-emptive and pre-emptive basis to ensure maximum flexibility for the Company to raise equity finance in the most cost efficient manner with a view to continuing to improve the long term financial stability of the Club. Permission to issue shares for cash on a non pre-emptive basis was not approved at the 2013 Annual General Meeting given the uncertainty over the strategic objectives for the Club at that time. This has limited the Company's ability to raise equity finance and has meant that since December 2013 Rangers has borrowed money to fund the Club. Very early in the 2014 calendar year, we borrowed money from George Letham and Sandy Easdale for a few months. This money has since been repaid, but I would like to publicly thank them for their support during the months in which we borrowed from them. More recently, since the end of the 2013/2014 financial year, we have again needed finance as operating revenue has been lower than anticipated. We were lucky that two individuals plus one consortium were willing to discuss offering Rangers financial support. There has been much recent speculation on these discussions and perhaps mainly with regard to the prospective support from a consortium which included Dave King and many questions as to why this proposal was not accepted by the Board. Given Rangers' history in doing deals with people, the Board agreed at the outset of any discussions with potential funders that it was very important that the Board undertook a high degree of due diligence in relation to any discussions. The Board also had a timeline set within which the best proposal would be completed.
>
> The first stage was a simple one of potential funders providing evidence that they had the uncommitted funds available and confirming the identity of the potential funders. Two of the potential funders were able to provide immediate proof of funds and identity details. The consortium which included Dave King was unwilling to provide proof of funds or identity details for consortium members until the condition to their funding had

been met. The Board were informed that the consortium comprised eight members in total and details of the identity of each consortium member was requested by the Board together with proof of funds. The consortium required the Board, as a condition of progressing these funding discussions, to obtain the prior consent of more than 75% of shareholders to support their proposal to provide equity funding. The Board were unable to obtain the comfort required by the consortium from shareholders without details of consortium members and the proof of funds, particularly as other proposals had provided this certainty and represented immediately available sources of finance. The consortium were principally interested in discussing a significant equity finance solution which would not have been capable of immediate completion given the need for either a pre-emptive offer to have been made first or for new authority to allot shares on a non pre-emptive basis to be granted at the 2014 Annual General Meeting. The Board were then in a position where the immediately executable proposals were assessed on their commercial merits and the Board consulted with significant shareholders as part of this process. Since the end of the financial year, two of our directors (Graham Wallace and Philip Nash) resigned. Philip was an interim Finance Director and originally was only asked to work for 3 months; so we always knew his was a temporary position. At the start of their tenure, Graham and Philip undertook a 120 day business review, the outcome of which required us to continue to operate at a significant loss until we returned to the Premiership. Although Graham had the full support of the Board and, the Board believed, of significant shareholders to implement this plan, in the event the Board found that shareholders appetite to support the level of losses envisaged in this strategic plan waned.

A. Operational Report.

It was made clear in the Business Review that if there was a substantial decrease in season ticket sales for the 2014/15 season, it would have a detrimental effect on our financial planning, and sadly this has occurred. We have seen a significant reduction in our season ticket numbers for the current season. Some fans decided not to renew their season tickets but stated that they will continue to support the team by attending on a match-by-match basis. We respect everybody's decision to make the choice they feel is right for them although it should be noted at the time of writing, that the number of fans attending our home league games so far this season is down year-on-year. This has had a large negative effect on our balance sheet and reduces our ability to move forward with the desired momentum and the Club has been compelled to seek additional funding to make up the shortfall.

In the post-reporting period the Board was pleased to announce the successful Open Offer for existing shareholders which resulted in 15,667,860 new Ordinary Shares being issued. This raised proceeds of £3.13m (before fees and expenses) and provided additional working capital which was required during the course of the current financial year. During the year we were able to secure short-term loans of £1.5m from the Club's shareholders Sandy Easdale and George Letham, and since the yearend we have secured a further credit facility of £3m from another shareholder MASH Holdings Ltd. As outlined in the strategic report, our forecasts indicate that a further capital raise will be required during the current financial year in order for the business to meet working capital requirements and for the Club to progress up the league pyramid

Page 9:

As at 30 June 2014, the Group held £4,607,000 of cash. Included within cash and bank balances is £3,069,000 (2013 – £946,000) relating to Rangers Retail Limited, which is not immediately available as working capital to the Group as a whole.

Paradoxically, as fans withheld their season ticket monies, this effectively left Rangers at the mercy of Ashley who could dictate the terms of, and source of, any future funding. Due to this power, the SFA issued Ashley with a Notice of Complaint for breaching a joint agreement that Ashley would not play a controlling role in Rangers and would maintain a stake of no more than 10%. Although Ashley did return the naming rights to Ibrox Stadium on Christmas Eve 2014, the SFA denied him permission to increase his stakehold further. Also in December 2014, the SPFL added to Rangers' financial woes by

267

withholding £250 000 of broadcast money the club was due in a bid to recoup a fine imposed by the Nimmo Smith Commission.

At the December AGM, Somers received just 61% of the ballot for re-election. It was enough but it reflected the widespread distrust of him a Chairman. Resolution 9 at the AGM had been to "enable the directors' authority for the disapplication of pre-emption rights." It had been proposed by the Easdales and would have allowed the company to have a share issue that would be open to the public. The Easdales then voted against it. Cooper suggests, of note, that the school of thought was that by rejecting it, the SFA would be forced into a position of allowing Ashley to increase his shareholding and effectively taking over the plc.[425] Llambias met with SFA to make the case for his (Ashley's) stake to increase from 8.9% to 29.9%. This was rejected by the SFA as they had, of note, become aware of another party which could provide credible funding — The Three Bears (Park, Letham, and Taylor). They (Three Bears) had offered to purchase all of the 40M shares in Resolution 8 & 9 for £6.5M.[426]

2014 ended with a significant shift in power:

- Laxey Partners Limited sold their 16.3% stake to Park/Letham/Taylor consortium for £2.6M. The Laxey Partners Limited boss Colin Kingsnorth said: "I sold because fans-based group were hopefully going to be best placed to take on Mike Ashley's power." Ashley had removed Norman Crighton. Asley, the Easdales and Somers were caught unaware.
- King purchased the share of Artemis and Miton giving him a 14.5% stake.
- Taylor, the Three Bears and King thus had 34.1% – a rival power base.

King called for an EGM on 16 January 2015. The original date set by the Board was 4 March 2015 in a hotel in London; however, this was then moved to Ibrox Stadium after two successive hotels refused to host the event and the date was confirmed for 6 March 2015. During the run up to the EGM, the incumbent Board agreed £10M funding deal with Sports Direct Limited (it is understood that £5M would be released immediately but £3M of that would go to repay Ashley for previous loans. If the second £5M was drawn down, it would be repayable within 5 years). The agreement saw Sports Direct Limited hold a floating charge over Auchenhowie, Edmiston House, the Albion Car Park and the club's registered trademarks. Sports Direct Limited was also transferred 26% of Rangers' share in Rangers Retail Limited (Rangers previously held 51% with Sports Direct holding 49%). The plc was bound to forego all shirt sponsorship revenue for the 2016/17 season and subsequent seasons until the loan was repaid.

In February 2015, there was a large volume of share purchases — Rangers supporters groups were heavily involved. On 25 February 2015, James Easdale resigned from the plc Board — just over a week before the EGM. On the same day, the Rangers Supporters' Trust (RST) purchased 450 000 shares from Beaufort Nominees, previously a proxy for Sandy Easdale. The RST now had shares and proxies of 4.4%. Rangers First, another supporters' group had 2.25%. Chairman David Somers departed with four days to go to the AGM. The SFA's investigation into Ashley concluded at the beginning of March 2015 with Ashley being deemed to have broken rules on dual ownership due to his influence on the affairs of Rangers. He was fined £7 500 and Rangers were subsequently fined £5 500 for their lack of governance. Just two days before the EGM, the club's Nominated Advisor, WH Ireland, resigned resulting in trading of the shares in the plc being suspended.

The outcome of the EGM was a decisive victory for King's consortium with Derek Llambias and Finance Director Barry Leach being voted off the plc Board and Dave King, Paul Murray and John Gilligan joining. Further board appointments were made with John Bennett and Chris Graham added to the plc board as Non-Executive Directors and James Blair was appointed as Company Secretary. On the same day as the appointments, Rangers suspended Llambias, Leach and Sandy Easdale from its football club Board pending an internal investigation.

5.5   Academic Frameworks

5.5.1. Organisational: Six Stages of Organisational Decline and Renewal

For the purpose of this chapter, I will consider the fifth stage of Organisational Decline and Renewal, namely Recovery. Leavy & McKiernan offer that Recovery follows retrenchment. An efficiency recovery/pathway is important when the main secondary causes of decline are internal and usually consist of, for example, liquidation or divestment. Many recovery pathways — governed by the old ways — are minor adaptations of what is already known. Any larger strategic response tends to be internal efficiency gains around the core business. Hence, the recovery strategies of many organisations are within their existing belief and rule systems rather than determined by a fundamental change in ideology.

Leadership is one of the critical elements of recovery. Not all turnarounds require a new CEO but fresh CEOs bring new vision, energy and 'way of doing things.' Symbolically, they signal the unfreezing of the old templates internally and a renewed stakeholder confidence externally. The CEOs style is significant — leadership traits differ at different stages of the business cycle and it is common to witness a more autocratic style during crisis and recovery as the conditions require direct control, short lines of command and clear vision.

With The Rangers Football Club Limited, we witnessed an efficiency recovery and leadership. For example, and in terms of efficiency, the successful IPO on the AIM market of The London Stock Exchange raised £22.2M in December 2012 to fund a growth strategy. In the Interim Results of March 2013, Charles Green states:

This has been a significant period in the Club's history, in which vital steps were taken to ensure the survival and rebuilding of one of the UK's most venerable football institutions. The priority for the Company to date has been to stabilise the business and put in place solid financial foundations for the future. To this end, revenue streams have been enhanced, and costs cut. These achievements have been made whilst retaining the important fabric and structure of the Club. We will continue to execute our growth plan, and investors and supporters can have confidence in the development of operations as the Club progresses.

Finally, recovery is evidenced by Brian Stockbridge:

It was clear from Rangers' league status this season there would be a resultant impact on turnover at the Club. It was essential, therefore, that costs were substantially reduced and this was achieved. Operational costs have been reduced to £15.7m for the reporting period, compared with approximate previous costs of similar periods of £22m in the then Rangers Football Club plc (now in liquidation). Overall operational costs are expected to continue to decline as further cost saving initiatives and efficiencies take effect. Work continues on further enhancements to the quality and sustainability of revenue streams. Overall, we have achieved these operational changes whilst retaining the fabric and structure of the Club which is necessary given the scale of our operations.

Although Green eventually left Rangers International Football Club plc, he did provide and evidence leadership. Not without fault, he, of note, secured membership of SFL and took forward the IPO and listing on the AIM. This (leadership) was also reported in the print media.

5.5.2 Stakeholder: The Change Curve.

For the purpose of this chapter, I will, again, consider the penultimate stage of The Change Curve, namely Acceptance. There was — in general — developing acceptance of the plight and situation of Rangers FC from 29 July 2012. This is evident below:

271

1. *I'm so glad Lee didn't quit like rest of Ibrox big guns.*
Daily Record and Sunday Mail
October 24, 2012

> It's amazing because it's the same fans I see at the away grounds.
> When you've been at a club for so long you see individual
> supporters who travel everywhere - from Forres to Berwick. I
> feel for them but I do see a better acceptance of what has
> happened to us as a club and where we are. There was an
> opinion, which was wrong, that we'd win every game in SFL3.
> I knew that wouldn't be the case.

2. *Ally McCoist: No shame in Third Division defeat.*
Scotsman
October 24, 2012

> It's no surprise that it has been proved to me. But I think people
> are now taking a wee step back and looking at the much bigger
> picture. I do not in any way want to make it sound like an
> excuse, but the facts of the matter are that we lost 28 players and
> had to bring in some young lads. These are facts and I do feel
> there is a better acceptance of now. That said, we still have to
> win the league and get promoted.

3. *Ally: Fans at last are accepting reality of third dimension life.*
Evening Times (Glasgow)
October 24, 2012

> ALLY McCOIST believes there is now a greater acceptance of
> the position Rangers are in from everyone involved at the club
> after their mixed start to life in the Irn-Bru Third Division. At
> this moment in time you do feel for them a little bit but, having
> said that, I do see a better, dare I say it, acceptance of what has
> happened and where we are, generally speaking.

4. *McCoist's underachieving stars owe him a big game.*
Sunday Life
September 23, 2012

> Certainly, the competition isn't the main item on the Ibrox menu
> this term, but the abject manner of the performance, lack of real

drive and meek acceptance of their fate sounded alarm bells - or at least, they should have.

5.6   Chapter Summary

In this chapter, the recovery of 'corporate Rangers' and Rangers FC in the period 29 July 2012 - 6 March 2015 is introduced. Three year periods were examined:

- 27 July 2012 – 30 June 2013
- 1 July 2013 – 30 June 2014
- 1 July 2014 – 6 March 2015

In this first period (i.e. 27 July 2012 – 30 June 2013), two companies emerged: The Rangers Football Club Limited and Rangers International Football Club plc. Ultimately, Rangers International Football Club plc was formed and listed on the AIM of the London Stock Exchange and became the holding company for The Rangers Football Club Limited which, in turn, owns and operated the football club. In general, a corporate strategy was emerging with a clear distinction between what was strategic and what was operational. Many problems, however, remained in the Boardroom of Rangers International Football Club plc.

Rangers FC won the SFL Third Division title on 30 March 2013.

In the second period (1 July 2013 – 30 June 2014), there were further 'movements' in the Boardroom of the Rangers International Football Club plc. For Rangers International Football Club plc, significant disunity ensued.

Rangers FC won the League One title and promotion to the Championship on 12 March 2014.

In the third period (31 July 2014 – 6 June 2015), notable change took place. The summer of 2014 saw continued discontent with various fans groups — alongside Dave King — attempting to influence the plc Board by withdrawing season ticket money. In addition, and throughout this period, Rangers International Football Club plc required additional money/working capital that

274

came from two principal sources: a share issue and a loan from Mike Ashley.

The AGM took place on 22 December 2014. Eleven days beforehand, Norman Crighton — Laxey Partners Limited representative on the Board — left the Board. It would be a most significant move.

2014 ended with a significant shift in power:

- Laxey Partners Limited sold their 16.3% stake to Park/Letham/Taylor consortium for £2.6M.
- King purchased the share of Artemis and Miton giving him a 14.5% stake.
- Taylor, the Three Bears and King thus had 34.1% – a rival power base.

An EGM was set for 6 March 2015.

In February 2015, there was a large volume of share purchases — Rangers supporters groups were heavily involved. Chairman David Somers departed with four days to go to the AGM.

The outcome of the EGM was a decisive victory for King's consortium. Further board appointments were made with John Bennett and Chris Graham added to the plc board as Non-Executive Directors and James Blair was appointed as Company Secretary. On the same day as the appointments, Rangers suspended Llambias, Leach and Sandy Easdale from its football club Board pending an internal investigation.

Rangers FC failed to be automatically promoted to the Premiership — they successfully negotiated two play-off rounds before a 6-1 aggregate defeat to Premiership team Motherwell FC.

5.7 Chapter Reflection

In the period 29 July 2012 - 6 March 2015, there was significant conflict at Board-level and, I suggest, three different Boards of Directors. There was, however, recovery from the horrors of 2011/2012. This is evidenced in The Interim Results of Rangers International Football Club plc that were reported on 4 March 2013.

In addition, we saw two companies emerge that were distinct from the football club: Rangers International Football Club plc (responsible for strategic direction/the development and sustainability of competitive advantage) and The Rangers Football Club limited (responsible for day-to-day operations especially of the football club i.e. Rangers FC).

I also suggest that — in line with The Change Curve — there was general 'acceptance' by all football club stakeholders/fans.

Perhaps, too, reaching the SPFL Premiership was too difficult for the management team of McCoist/McDowall. In their defence, however, it should be stated that the period 2011 – 2015 must have been very challenging indeed in terms of operational management especially when the Board of Directors continually changed.

I suggest also that it is important that football clubs are 'looked after' by business professionals who are also supporters. For example, prior to regime change in March 2015, were the various members of the Board of Directors 'Rangers men' at heart? One does wonder. Certainly, at the time of writing — and in the case of Roman Abramovich — many commentators are now asking about those who control clubs in UK.[427]

It is also, I suggest, very interesting (and concerning) how much control Mike Ashley was exerting on the plc. According to his Wikipedia entry, "He likes to park his tanks on people's lawns." Certainly, and in the case of Rangers International Football Club plc, he was 'tightening his grip' on the plc and, ultimately, the club. Although outside the scope of this book, there is clearly a further and separate study here.

As I attempted to chart recovery and acceptance in this period (2012 – 2015), I was drawn again to a quote by Paul Murray:[428]

> In my view, from May 6, 2011, it has all been wrong here. The minute the club was sold to Craig Whyte it was the wrong decision. I have made mistakes but hopefully people will recognise that I tried to do the right thing every time. I have certainly put Rangers' interests ahead of my own.

Cooper comments further in this respect:[429]

> If the King/Murray offer of April 2011 had been accepted, the club would have handled any impending storm much better than Whyte could ever manage. His business prowess couldn't even extend to running a football team for six months. If the First-Tier Tax Tribunal had delivered its verdict earlier. Yes, HMRC would have appealed (figures were still being disputed 10 years later) but the club could have had more time to prepare, to plan and to find alternative solutions. If the Murray Group and Lloyds had not accepted the first boat that went past. The entire episode had been an avoidable waste of time.

Chapter Six

Reflection

In this final chapter, I offer general and detailed reflections.

<u>General Reflection</u>

In Chapter One, I stated that the purpose of this book was to attempt to explain the complexity of the Rangers story in the period 1998 – 2015 in one location. This book does not seek to judge or to blame or to make recommendations. It is also not an investigative piece of journalism. This was a huge story in British football and Scottish society and, to date, there is not — to my knowledge — a book that encapsulates the context pre-Whyte (i.e. Sir David Murray/Global Financial Crisis) to regime change in March 2015. This is what I have endeavoured to do.

To help explain the complexity, I have offered A Framework for The Story of Rangers. This is again shown a Figure 17.0. This framework offers organisational (i.e. company decline) decline, diagnostics, retrenchment, and recovery. Decline, diagnostics, retrenchment, and recovery all affected the football club i.e. Rangers FC. Although Paul Murray talks about Recovery (see Chairman's Statement to Rangers International Football Club plc Interim Results dated 31 March 2015 below), I think that recovery actually started on 29 July 2012. For me, Renewal started on 6 March 2015. This framework also hopes to explain the emotional response of the many stakeholders: denial and shock; anger and depression; and acceptance. Integration, to me, commenced on 6 March 2015.

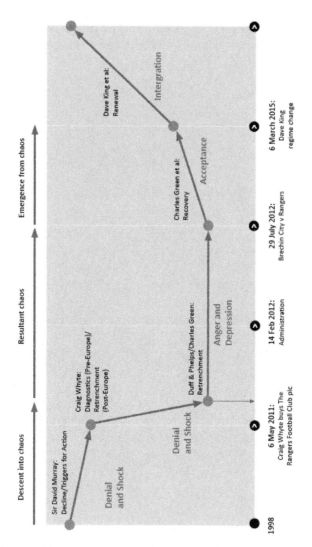

Figure 17.0: A Framework for The Story of Rangers

In addition, I have overlaid Figure 17.0 with the many companies involved — this is my 'Complete Story' and is shown at Figure 18.0

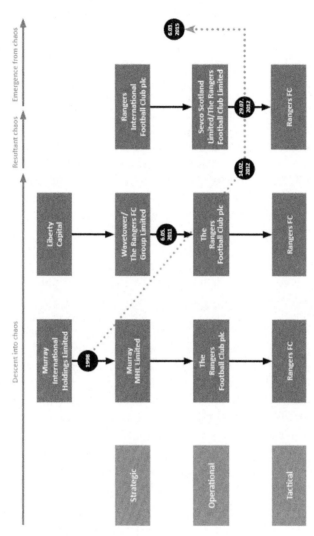

Figure 18.0: Complete Story

From Figure 18.0, once we understand the difference between a company and a club, the 'Rangers story' is about the companies that operated the club being sold and bought at the strategic and operational levels of analysis. Simply put, I suggest that it was distress/instability in the companies (i.e. corporate Rangers) that operated Rangers FC that caused a significant effect on the club and its many stakeholders at the tactical level of analysis. The Change Curve also helps us understand the emotional response of stakeholders. As an aside, I suggest, too, that we saw this (emotional response) in the Scottish Football Season 20/21 i.e. the stakeholders/supporters of Celtic Football Club transited through this Curve as they attempted — and were eventually unsuccessful in their efforts — to win 10 Premier League titles in a row.

This book does not offer the definitive answer; rather, it is an interpretation as to what happened. All cited material is from open source/what is in the public domain. I did, however, contact certain individuals who I considered were 'close' to certain parts of the story; however, for a variety of reasons it was difficult for these individuals to talk professionally. I do accept this. I do think, however, that I have detailed the key areas/themes: the decline in The Rangers Football Club plc in the first decade of this century; the EBTs and subsequent HMRC interest; a suggested dysfunctional plc Board to May 2011 (The Rangers Football Club plc); Craig Whyte (perhaps the right man in very difficult circumstances for The Ranges Football Club plc (i.e. he had some experience in corporate restructuring)); the resultant chaos that ensued in the Spring/Summer of 2012; and Charles Green/Recovery to March 2015. But – this story is 'ongoing.' At the time of writing i.e. March 2022 several themes continue to appear in the print and broadcast media. For example: Duff and Phelps;[430,431] BDO/HMRC;[432] Sports Direct;[433] and the role of the Crown Office.[434,435] One really does wonder when this story will finally cease.

As stated, the main area that is still difficult for me is May/June 2012 i.e. the relationship between Sevco 5088 Limited and Sevco

Scotland Limited. The Duff & Phelps CVA Proposal, dated 29 May 2012, clearly states that the Preferred Bidder was Sevco 5088 Limited. Once the CVA was rejected on 14 June 2012, Sevco Scotland Limited acquired the history and assets of The Rangers Football Club plc that included the football club. From here on in, Duff & Phelps refer to Sevco Scotland Limited. Perhaps, and politically, Sevco Scotland Limited made sense — it was a company registered in Scotland, thereby appealing to many stakeholders. I also understand that Sevco 5088 Limited would require both English and Scottish corporate lawyers for the transaction of Board minutes. In this respect, Sevco Scotland Limited also makes sense. But there is, I suggest, more to this relationship. Due to professional privilege, it is difficult for many to comment without the consent of the parties involved. I, again, do accept this.

To date, it is also interesting that RFC 2012 plc (formerly The Rangers Football Club plc) is not liquidated.[436]   If the parent company (i.e. RFC 2012 plc) is still not liquidated, and the football club was sold by Duff & Phelps to Sevco Scotland Limited (another company), one does wonder why so many folk consider that the club is 'dead.' This is, in my view, due to casual, lazy, and irresponsible journalism by many including the broadsheet newspapers.[437]

Detailed Reflection

Over the last three years, I have thought a lot about Rangers. From the outset, I was struck by how much money was spent by this football club — particularly in the Advocaat era. Most of it was not from Rangers FC/The Rangers Football Club plc; rather, the money was from Murray International Holdings Limited and, ultimately, the Bank of Scotland, which became part of the overall Murray International Holdings Limited debt to this bank. It should, however, be stated that the debt of The Rangers Football Club plc was reduced to £18M (i.e. an acceptable figure) at the time of purchase by Craig Whyte. In addition, in terms of governance, did many (all) of us realise how many companies operated/owned Rangers FC. I suggest five: The Rangers Football Club plc; RFC Investment Holdings Limited; Murray Sports Limited; Murray MHL Limited; and ultimately Murray International Holdings Limited.

In terms of governance, with Sir David Murray owning more than 85% of The Rangers Football Club plc, it was always going to be his 'train set.' Ultimately, it was his leadership that mattered. In this respect, was it right that one person/company owned so much of the plc that operated the football club? Was there, therefore, problems with the ensuing Board decisions/governance/leadership? Certainly, Paul Smith does echo this point about the history of governance at Rangers FC:[438]

> During more than a century of the club's existence, the esteemed gentlemen who held office as chairman had to lead with authority yet managed by consensus. They may have had the casting vote, in many ways they had the largest shareholding, but crucially they never had the security of a majority shareholding.

It is interesting that Charles Green also addressed Board decisions/governance/leadership:[439]

> I can assure you that there will not be any investor who owns more than 15%. I don't believe that any one person should own a football club.

The EBTs were, without doubt, a huge issue and are integral (perhaps the most important part) to the Rangers story. Of note, they were legal. Perhaps, however, they were not used in the correct way i.e. they should have been discretionary and non-contractual. Rather, it appears that they were contractual and non-discretionary. But — and it is important to make this point — it is understood that both Sir David Murray and Craig Whyte tried to arrange a settlement figure with HMRC. When we now understand that the HMRC figure may have been too high in the first place one really does wonder if HMRC was also a major contributor to this sorry story. If the correct liability had been calculated, perhaps other buyers may have come forward.[440]

We should also not lose sight of the global financial crisis that affected companies globally — not just Murray International Holdings Limited, The Rangers Football Club plc or Rangers FC. In this respect, all money was tight and in a 'credit crunch,' there was a reluctance by many banks to lend and, of note, a determination by the said backs to recoup their money. This is exactly what Lloyds wanted to do i.e. they wanted their money back and did not want the potential liability of the EBT. Therefore, the Craig Whyte option was attractive to them as he (Whyte) was willing to take on the EBT liability. In many respects, there was a perfect storm at play.

Turning to Craig Whyte, I do give him the benefit of the doubt. I do not consider that he was going to 'hang about' for the long-term, but I do believe that he thought that — by increasing revenue and decreasing costs — he could make the project work. His problem was early elimination from Europe (i.e. no addition revenue) — recognised, too, by Donald Findlay QC — and delays to the FTTT. Simply, he (Craig Whyte) ran out of money.

I also believe that Charles Green was not going to be at Rangers for the long term. I, offer, however that he provided leadership: he secured the SFL position/place for the football club; gave operational focus via The Rangers Football Club Limited; made the IPO 'happen;' and set strategic direction via Rangers International Football Club plc. His problem was, I suggest, his many associates, his links to Craig Whyte and the 'noise' that surrounded him.

During the period 14 February 2012 – 27 July 2012, three inter-related and complex themes were at play: the administration process of The Rangers Football Club; the sale of Rangers FC to Sevco Scotland Limited; and the eventual entry into the SFL Third Division of Rangers FC. In addition, there was also: the SFA Independent Committee/5-Way Agreement; the SPL

Commission; and the proposed Financial Fair Play amendments issued by the SPL. Looking back on this summer of 2012, although it appeared that 'things were made up as they went along', we had — in the context of Scottish football — not seen anything like this before. The administration process created shock for all, not just Rangers FC stakeholders: "This was Rangers — this does not happen to them." Perhaps with hindsight, many stakeholders in this drama (indeed tragedy) including stakeholders and associated clubs would now do things somewhat different. With reflection and learning by all, one does hope so.

During the period 2011 – 2015, I estimate that there were four Boards of Directors led by: Craig Whyte, Malcolm Murray, David Sommers, and Paul Murray. There were also many Directors both executive and non-executive. Moreover, the instability at Board-level caused huge problems at the strategic and operational levels. It is also not clear if there was 'vertical alignment' between Rangers International Football Club plc, The Rangers Football Club Limited and Rangers FC. Finally, I am struck by the way in which Mike Ashley was slowly gaining control at Rangers International Football Club plc, The Rangers Football Club Limited and Rangers FC. As stated, there is clearly a case study in this (Ashley) episode alone.

But in end, business folk and Rangers folk — with the help of various stakeholders' groups (particularly the social movements of fans) — won the day. Renewal and Integration commenced on 6 March 2015.

Although I do not seek to judge, blame, or make recommendations, I do hope that organisational learning has taken place with the many stakeholders involved in this story — particularly the regulators. As a result of the global financial crisis of 2007-2009, many banks have now learned from their experiences and adapted accordingly. In this respect, I do hope that the SFA and SPFL will now approach football clubs who are in distress in a somewhat different way. Was the football club really at fault here? I suggest not — yet Rangers FC was punished.

What remains clearly contentious to many (particularly non-Rangers FC supporters), however, is the ongoing status of the football club. My view is that the club i.e. Rangers FC celebrates its 150th anniversary this year.

In closing, and I say again, in that spring evening of 6 May 2011, did any of us really know what was coming 'down the tracks' in the next four years. In this respect, I do leave the last word to Paul Murray who said in his Chairman's Statement in the Interim Results of 31 March 2015:[441]

> When I resolved to do everything within my power to make sure the correct people would regain control of Rangers I had no idea how long it would take. I just knew that this fantastic Club and its history had to be protected and even in those moments when it felt as though the fates themselves were conspiring against our efforts, there were no thoughts of retreat. Rangers and the task of setting the Club back on the correct path were too important but I must say I never imagined I would become Chairman of one of our country's great institutions.

> I may be in the Chair only in the interim but the honour is no less great. Sadly, those who have held this post in recent times have failed to recognise the profound significance of being Chairman of Rangers but there is no possibility of the new Board ever under-valuing Rangers' position.

> The new Directors have been in place only a matter of weeks but have already started to repair the damage caused through recent years of neglect and disrespect for this Club, its people, and its history. The mismanagement of the Club in recent years has been simply staggering. The new Board is well advanced on funding plans, especially short to medium term which will ensure the Club has a firm foundation from which to drive on into the future. We have moved quickly to secure the short term funding position by agreeing a £1.5m unsecured interest-free loan from key shareholders. In the very near future we will present a medium – long term funding plan for the Club. This

funding will be provided by existing and new investors who now want to invest in the Club. Thereafter, the Club must quickly become self-sustaining and absolutely free from the kind of funding crises which have plagued Rangers in recent years. As the Interim Accounts prove, the new Board has inherited major problems but while campaigning for change we all knew the Club would be in need of major restructuring and repair on all fronts. We can and we will return this Club to a strong and profitable footing through strategic planning, investment, and re-engagement with all of our stakeholders. Too many of them have been lost or disenfranchised because of successive failings by a series of Directors over the last four years in particular. But they are gone now and this is a new era for this great and special Club which must be regenerated, not only for its own good but for the greater good of Scottish football. With the fans returning to support the Club we believe that there is significant potential to grow our commercial income. Let's never forget just how important Rangers is to the domestic game This Club's fans have filled the grounds of many smaller clubs throughout the country and given them income to improve their own facilities. Many of these other clubs have expressed their gratitude but we must also thank them for the warmth of their welcome. We won't forget that. Neither will we forget that Rangers' fans are the Club's most significant stakeholder and they must never again be taken for granted or treated with contempt. They have demonstrated the depth of feeling and belief in their Club and having played such a crucial part in achieving boardroom change it would be wrong, never mind foolish, to ignore them now. So I would like to take this opportunity to reinforce the new Board's commitment to them. They will have full and meaningful boardroom representation and their voice will be heard. Of course a large number of others also helped in the struggle to achieve change and they, too, have our gratitude but the supporters are the real heroes. Without them nothing would have changed and there would have been no way of recovery from the set of figures in this report. However, that is not to say the Club cannot begin to thrive again. Of course it can. We have access to significant new funding and with intelligent investment at Murray Park and at Ibrox we can all be confident of a bright future for this remarkable Club. It is clear to everyone what can be achieved when there is a strong connection between the Club's Directors and the support and this is a link which we must ensure remains strong. So the simple truth is Rangers needs every fan to invest in the future. It is only by remaining united that we will begin to prosper and regain our traditional standing in Scotland's topflight as well as re-entering the European arenas. This is what we, the Board, are working towards but achieving this will be impossible if our fans do not buy into that vision. Buying season books and match-day tickets is not just about today, it is also very much about where we want to be in a year, five years, ten years and beyond. The Board is working towards a plan which sees Rangers at the top and every single one of us has to buy into that vision. New Board members and the highly-skilled individuals required to get the Club functioning at optimum levels in the various departments are being considered and they will help find the correct balance between football, commercial, financial and fan engagement. The vision I mentioned earlier is to focus on the next seven years so that by 2022, the Club's 150th anniversary and the 50th anniversary of Barcelona we, Rangers, will be back at the very top. This means that over the next few years the finance we are putting in place now will provide the infrastructure and personnel at Murray Park to make sure Rangers are competing and winning in Scotland's topflight as well as stepping back into the European arenas again Then for the three or four years after that all our efforts will be directed towards making Rangers stronger and European regulars as our 150th year approaches. That year should be one of celebration. It is not unreasonable to expect this because Rangers have been there before so the message is that by purchasing a new season ticket you are investing in Rangers' future Winning the boardroom back was Part One of the recovery and now we face Part Two. A massive rebuild is required at every level and in every department of this huge Club of ours and we cannot and will not shy away from those tasks. Together we will regenerate every aspect of the Club and make certain Rangers will be a force again on and off the field of play. After years of mismanagement we need patience and support. We must never forget what has happened to our Club in the last four years. The new board will ensure that it never happens again. Although we are looking to the future we will also examine and act upon any evidence of past impropriety by former Directors and executives. We are all aware of the problems on the field but I would like to offer my thanks to Ally McCoist and Kenny McDowall who did all they could to give Rangers a winning team and we should take into consideration the difficulties they both faced. They had to operate against a backdrop of constant boardroom upheaval and turmoil. No one felt secure and the life was being sucked out of Ibrox and Murray Park. We have brought in Stuart McCall as Interim Manager to help get the team into the Premiership and although he faces a difficult task we believe he will do it. Stuart jumped at the challenge without fear or hesitation and that tells us a lot about the calibre of the man but even so, we cannot rush into making a final decision on the permanent position because the success of everything we are planning behind the scenes will depend almost entirely on the team's ability to compete at the very top. Only 13 men have held the position of Rangers Manager so we have a duty to take whatever time is necessary to find the right man. We would expect Stuart to be a strong candidate in that process. We will also find the right people to restructure player development and unearth talent in all corners of the football world. Sufficient amounts of money will be set aside for this vital purpose but everything we do will be to help make Rangers a premium brand again and to shape the vision. We will ensure that particular emphasis is placed on player identification and development. For too long this has been neglected at the Club. Our vision is to build a football club fit for the 21st Century but one that is founded on the traditional values and traditions of Rangers which we all hold dear. No matter what functions we perform within the Club all of us must believe in this vision and already the new Directors are engaging with staff to spread the message we are in this together. Together we are the Rangers Family and we will face our challenges and celebrate our successes together. Our focus must be on doing everything necessary to guarantee an exciting, vibrant, and much more successful future and we will also be working towards creating better working relationships with all our commercial partners, including Sports Direct. We are in the process of engaging with them because they are a large shareholder as well as being our key commercial partner. Finally, I would also like to thank the staff for their efforts and commitment in difficult times when various individuals and Directors seemed to come and go without any obvious long-term strategy. The views of staff and their contributions will be recognised and appreciated by this new Board. Remember, this is our Club, we have taken ownership of it and with our 2022 vision we will not fail.

Notes

Chapter One

[1] See: Page 11 to The Rangers Football Club plc Annual Report 2010 at: https://find-and-update.company-information.service.gov.uk/company/SC004276.

[2] See: Statement of administrator's proposal at: https://find-and-update.company-information.service.gov.uk/company/SC004276/filing-history.

[3] Wavetower Limited was a newly incorporated company formed for the purpose of acquiring The Rangers Football Club plc (and, therefore, Rangers FC) from Murray International Holdings Limited and which was 100% owned by Liberty Capital — itself, ultimately owned by the London-based businessman.

[4] This is a key point: a company (Wavetower Limited) bought shares in another company (The Ranges Football Club plc).

[5] See: https://www.thetakeoverpanel.org.uk/.

[6] In advance of — and throughout — the process of Whyte's purchase of The Rangers Football Club plc, a sum of approximately £49M was owed to HMRC in respect of an outstanding tax bill. The tax bill related to a claim by HMRC for unpaid taxes over a period of several years dating back to 2001. The case related to the use of Employment Benefit Trusts (EBTs) to pay players and other staffs. This became known as 'The Big Tax Case'. At this time, HMRC believed The Rangers Football Club plc/Murray International Holdings Limited misused the scheme and avoided paying significant sums in tax.

[7] See: Craig Whyte completes takeover of Rangers for £1 at: www.bbc.co.uk/sport/football/13292829.

[8] See: Rangers FC signals its intent to go into Administration at: www.bbc.co.uk/news/uk-scotland-glasgow-west-17015966.

[9] Ibid.

[10] Ibid.

[11] See: https://www.soccerex.com/insight/articles/2012/rangers-enters-administration and https://www.belfasttelegraph.co.uk/sport/football/scottish/battle-to-save-glasgow-rangers-from-the-abyss-28715068.html.

[12] See: Rangers Football Club enters administration at: https://www.bbc.co.uk/news/uk-scotland-glasgow-west-17026172.

[13] Ibid.

[14] See: Rangers liquidated as CVA formally rejected at: www.scotsman.com/sport/football/rangers/in-full/rangers-liquidated-as-cva-formally-rejected-1-2353211.

[15] See: Section 14.27 of Statement of administrator's proposal at: https://find-and-update.company-information.service.gov.uk/company/SC004276.

[16] See: Charles Green completes purchase of Rangers' assets at: www.independent.co.uk/sport/football/scottish/charles-green-completes-purchase-of-rangers-assets-7851528.html.

[17] Sevco Scotland Limited was formed on 29 May 2012 as a means for Charles Green to acquire the assets of Rangers Football Club plc.

[18] See: Green Consortium Buys Rangers Football Club at: https://news.sky.com/story/green-consortium-buys-rangers-football-club-10478277.

[19] See: Charles Green completes purchase of Rangers' assets at: www.independent.co.uk/sport/football/scottish/charles-green-completes-purchase-of-rangers-assets-7851528.html.

[20] See: See Notice of court order ending Administration dated 12 Nov 2012 at: https://find-and-update.company-information.service.gov.uk/company/SC004276.

[21] See: Rangers newco refused SPL entry after chairmen vote at: www.bbc.co.uk/sport/football/18703183.

[22] See: Raith & Clyde criticise Rangers newco Division One Plan at: www.bbc.co.uk/sport/football/18656012.

[23] See: Press Statement, SPL website, 27 July 2012: "We are pleased to confirm that agreement has been reached on all outstanding points relating to the transfer of the Scottish FA membership between Rangers FC (In Administration), and Sevco Scotland Ltd, who will be the new owners of The Rangers Football Club. *A conditional membership will be issued to Sevco Scotland Ltd today, allowing Sunday's Ramsdens Cup tie against Brechin City to go ahead.*" Note: there is incorrect and misleading language here. Rangers FC was not in administration — *it was The Rangers Football Club plc that was in administration.*

[24] See: Rangers: Conditional membership allows cup tie to go ahead at: ww.bbc.co.uk/sport/football/19012042.

[25] See: https://www.theguardian.com/football/2012/jul/28/rangers-uncharted-waters-fears.

[26] See: http://www.scotzine.com/2012/07/in-full-rangers-newco-statement-on-sfa-membership/.

[27] See: Rangers' SFA membership rubber-stamped at: www.bbc.co.uk/sport/football/19120224.

[28] See: Rangers: Conditional membership allows cup tie to go ahead at: https://www.bbc.co.uk/sport/football/19012042.

[29] See: JOINT STATEMENT ON BEHALF OF THE SCOTTISH FA, THE SCOTTISH PREMIER LEAGUE, THE SCOTTISH FOOTBALL LEAGUE AND SEVCO SCOTLAND LTD AT: https://spfl.co.uk/news/joint-statement-2012-07-27.

[30] See: Rangers get SFA green light at: https://www.skysports.com/football/news/11788/7944396/rangers-get-sfa-green-light.

[31] See: Rangers: Dave King company buys 15% of Glasgow club at: www.bbc.co.uk/sport/football/30661103.

[32] See: Dave King's consortium wins control of Rangers boardroom at: www.bbc.co.uk/sport/football/31759573

[33] Ibid.

[34] See, for example, https://www.formpl.us/blog/research-bias

[35] Interested readers may refer to: Grint, K. (2005). Problems, problems, problems: The social construction of leadership. Human Relations. 58 (11): 1467-1494.

[36] See: RFC 2012 P.L.C. Full Group Accounts (made up to 31 May 1986) at: https://find-and-update.company-information.service.gov.uk/company/SC004276.

[37] See: The Rangers Football Club Limited Full Accounts (made up to 30 June 2013) at: https://find-and-update.company-information.service.gov.uk/company/SC425159/filing-history?page=4

[38] This Interim Report to Creditors was not required to be filed at Companies House. Hence it is not on the filing history there. Source: personal correspondence with Mr Simon Shiperlee of Duff & Phelps.

[39] See: Administrator's Progress Report at: https://find-and-update.company-information.service.gov.uk/company/SC004276.

[40] See: Succulent Lamb or Inaccurate Spam? Rangers and the Media (page 101) to Franklin, W. S., Gow, J. D. C., Graham. C., & McKillop, A. (Eds.). (2013). Follow We Will THE FALL AND RISE OF RANGERS. Edinburgh: Luath Press Limited.

[41] All shares in The Rangers Football Club Limited are owned by Rangers International Football Club plc. The Rangers Football Club Limited operates Rangers FC.

[42] Interested readers may refer to: Baron de Jomini, A. (2016). The Art of War. New York: Dover Publications Inc; Clausewitz, C. V., & Maude, F. N. (1997). On War. Ware: Wordsworth Editions Limited; and United Kingdom Defence Doctrine. (2014). Joint Doctrine Publication 0-01. London: Ministry of Defence.

[43] Interested readers may refer to: Czarniawaska, B. (2014). Social Science Research: From Field to Desk Paperback. London: Sage Publications Limited.

[44] In this book, it is argued that Renewal commenced from 6 March 2015.

[45] See: https://www.exeter.ac.uk/media/universityofexeter/humanresources/documents/learningdevelopment/the_change_curve.pdf

[46] See: From Crash to Cash... and beyond (page 29) to Franklin, W. S., Gow, J. D. C., Graham. C., & McKillop, A. (Eds.). (2013). Follow We Will THE FALL AND RISE OF RANGERS. Edinburgh: Luath Press Limited.

Chapter Two

[47] See: Chapter 24 (page 278) to Smith, P. (2012). For Richer For Poorer. RANGERS: THE FIGHT FOR SURVIVAL. Edinburgh: Mainstream Publishing Limited.

[48] Interested readers may refer to: Franklin, W. S., Gow, J. D. C., Graham. C., & McKillop, A. (Eds.). (2013). Follow We Will THE FALL AND RISE OF RANGERS. Edinburgh: Luath Press Limited; Mac Giolla Bhain, P. (2012). Downfall: How Rangers FC Self Destructed. Edinburgh: Frontline Noir; Smith, P. (2012). For Richer For Poorer. RANGERS: THE FIGHT FOR SURVIVAL. Edinburgh: Mainstream Publishing Limited; and O'Donnell, S. (2019). Tangled Up in Blue. Worthing: Pitch Publishing Limited.

[49] See: Chapter 23 (page 265) to Smith, P. (2012). For Richer For Poorer. RANGERS: THE FIGHT FOR SURVIVAL. Edinburgh: Mainstream Publishing Limited.

[50] See: INTRODUCTION (page 9) to Smith, P. (2012). For Richer For Poorer. RANGERS: THE FIGHT FOR SURVIVAL. Edinburgh: Mainstream Publishing Limited.

[51] See again Mac Giolla Bhain, P. (2012). Downfall: How Rangers FC Self Destructed. Edinburgh: Frontline Noir; and Smith, P. (2012). For Richer For Poorer. RANGERS: THE FIGHT FOR SURVIVAL. Edinburgh: Mainstream Publishing Limited.

[52] See: Chapter 12 (page 138) to Smith, P. (2012). For Richer For Poorer. RANGERS: THE FIGHT FOR SURVIVAL. Edinburgh: Mainstream Publishing Limited. Smith notes: "Towards the end of Murray's time in charge, the weariness was becoming apparent."

[53] See: Rangers eventually land their man as Dutchman becomes highest paid manager in Scotland. The Herald. 17 February 1998.

[54] See: Chairman's Statement (pages 2-3). The Rangers Football Club plc Annual Report (1998) available at: https://find-and-update.company-information.service.gov.uk/company/SC004276.

[55] See: Rangers' future in hands of bank. The Sunday Herald. 8 August 1999. In detail:

Rangers Football Club who face a vital European tie on Wednesday which could make or break their season financially have mortgaged their future to the Bank of Scotland. The bank has secured a charge over the loss-making club which gives them first claim on all of the Scottish champions' income and assets should Rangers fail to meet loan repayment obligations. One financial analyst, who has closely studied football clubs, described this as "unprecedented in more than 100 years of Rangers' history". But Chairman David Murray dismissed it as insignificant and normal business practice. Rangers lost £7 million in the seven months to December last year, after spending more than £30m on players and more than £20m on wages. The year before the club had made a profit of £6m. Murray has said the Ibrox side must not be a net spender in the transfer market, but in the run-up to this season — and a hoped-for success in the European Champions' league — manager Dick Advocaat spent a further £5m on new players Michael Mols and Claudio Reyna. The Bank of Scotland secured the floating over all Rangers' income and assets in February. This is understood to be part of a complex deal which saw the bank pay more than £20m to increase its stake in Murray's holding company, Murray International, from 5% to 11.5%, which also gave the bank a 7% stake in Rangers. Murray, personally and through his company, owns 62% of the club. The chairman said last night that the bank was now the second biggest investor in Murray International. The charismatic entrepreneur — who, in his 10 years in control, has transformed Rangers from a struggling and unambitious club into one of the biggest in the world — intends to move the club out of Murray International into a new company, Rangers Sport, in an effort to protect his main business.

[56] See: Chapter 23 (page 265) to Smith, P. (2012). For Richer For Poorer. RANGERS: THE FIGHT FOR SURVIVAL. Edinburgh: Mainstream Publishing Limited.

[57] See: BBC Documentary, Rangers — the men who sold the jerseys (https://www.bbc.co.uk/programmes/p00szrhq). In detail, Roger Isaacs states that the Murray International Holdings Limited net debt (to 31 January 1999) reduced from £69M to £57M. Thereafter, Murray International Holdings Limited embarked on a period of rapid expansion and borrowed money (financed by bank) to acquire assets and property over next 10 years. In detail he (Isaacs), commenting on the scale of growth of debt, asks: "when does responsible risk taking become reckless gambling?" Of note, Isaacs suggests that the level of borrowing strategy (i.e. the reliance on debt) was high risk.

[58] See: Chairman's Statement (pages 2-3). The Rangers Football Club

plc Annual Report (1999) available at: https://find-and-update.company-information.service.gov.uk/company/SC004276.

[59] See: Chapter 23 (page 265) to Smith, P. (2012). For Richer For Poorer. RANGERS: THE FIGHT FOR SURVIVAL. Edinburgh: Mainstream Publishing Limited.

60 See: Rangers' triple whammy. The Herald. 31 March 2000.

[61] See: Chapter 23 (page 266) to Smith, P. (2012). For Richer For Poorer. RANGERS: THE FIGHT FOR SURVIVAL. Edinburgh: Mainstream Publishing Limited.

[62] See: Rangers eyes move to full market listing. Financial Times. 31 March 2000.

[63] See: Moving places John McClelland. Financial Times. 3 October 2000.

[64] See: Adam steps down from his director's role with Rangers. The Herald. 3 October 2000.

[65] See: Chairman's Statement (pages 2-3). The Rangers Football Club plc Annual Report (2000) available at: https://find-and-update.company-information.service.gov.uk/company/SC004276.

[66] It is understood that David Murray had a long and established relationship with the Bank of Scotland and Gavin Masterton, its former Treasurer and Managing Director (Masterton retired in 2001 when the Bank of Scotland merged with Halifax).

[67] See: Chairman's Statement (pages 2-3). The Rangers Football Club plc Annual Report (2001) available at: https://find-and-update.company-information.service.gov.uk/company/SC004276.

[68] See: Glasgow Rangers chairman steps down. Financial Times. 6 July 2002.

[69] See: Murray in over his head. Scotland on Sunday. 14 July 2002.

[70] See: Financial Results (page 6) to The Rangers Football Club plc Annual Report (2002) available at: https://find-and-update.company-information.service.gov.uk/company/SC004276.

[71] See: Chairman's Statement (pages 2-3). The Rangers Football Club plc Annual Report (2003) available at: https://find-and-update.company-information.service.gov.uk/company/SC004276.

[72] See: Directors Cut. The Sunday Herald. 11 January 2004.

[73] See: Murray's mint not so sweet for Rangers: The owner of Ibrox is worth £450m, but club debts are a thorn in the side of his multi-million empire. The Observer. 30 May 2004.

[74] See: Back in the hotseat: Rangers owner resumes hands-on role. The Daily Mirror. 2 September 2004.

[75] See: Put your; where your; mouth; is; He may be the man largely responsible for Rangers' crippling debt, but David Murray has answered his critics by pledging £ 50 million of his own money. The Sunday Herald. 5 September 2004.

[76] See: INTRODUCTION (page 11) to Smith, P. (2012). For Richer For Poorer. RANGERS: THE FIGHT FOR SURVIVAL. Edinburgh: Mainstream Publishing Limited.

[77] See: Bank backs my empire. The Herald. 12 November 2004.

[78] See: BBC Documentary, Rangers — the men who sold the jerseys (https://www.bbc.co.uk/programmes/p00szrhq).

[79] See: Rangers supporters must feel like breaking out the blindfolds. The Herald. 21 October 2003.

[80] See: Celtic feast on Murray's folly. The Herald. 5 January 2004.

[81] See: McLeish guilty of unsettling tried formula; Khizanishvili gamble backfired completely. The Herald. 17 December 2004.

[82] See: Pressure mounts on desperate McLeish; Hearts defeat compounds woes. The Herald. 26 September 2005.

[83] See: Chairman's Statement (pages 2-3). The Rangers Football Club plc Annual Report (2005) available at: https://find-and-update.company-information.service.gov.uk/company/SC004276.

[84] See: Chapter 23 (page 269) to Smith, P. (2012). For Richer For Poorer. RANGERS: THE FIGHT FOR SURVIVAL. Edinburgh: Mainstream Publishing Limited.

[85] See: Jobs fear as Rangers bag a Pounds 48m deal. The Daily Mail. 10 March 2006.

[86] See: Rangers owner says he might sell team in next three years. Associated Press International. 13 July 2006.

[87] See: Three British Clubs Are Raided in Transfer Investigation. The New York Times. 17 July 2007.

[88] See: UK detains five in soccer corruption probe. FT.com. 28 November 2007.

[89] See: Chairman's Statement (pages 2-3). The Rangers Football Club plc Annual Report (2007) available at: https://find-and-update.company-information.service.gov.uk/company/SC004276.

[90] Insider.co.uk analyses the audited records of Murray International Holdings Limited – the 'parent company' of The Rangers Football Club plc – from 2007 to 2013. See: Revealed: How Murray

International Holdings' accounts outline Lloyds 'incentives' to Sir David Murray before and after Craig Whyte Rangers sale. 7 June 2017. In detail:

Financial year to 31 January 2007
Walter Smith had returned to Rangers in early 2007, and Sir David said the absence of Champions League football in 2006/07 had "adversely impacted the club's financial performance." The debt to assets ratio at MIH rose to 69 per cent in the 2007 year, up from 63 per cent the prior year, with debts to Bank of Scotland totalling £677.9 million with the group having added £239.4 million of new borrowing in the year. Sir David said: "Bank of Scotland continues to provide these facilities under a relationship which extends from lender to partner throughout our activities. We look forward to developing our partnership further as we explore new ways to capitalise on our combined skills and resources."

[91] See: Global financial crisis: five key stages 2007-2011. The Guardian. 7 August 2011.

[92] See: Chairman's Statement (pages 2-3). The Rangers Football Club plc Annual Report (2008) available at: https://find-and-update.company-information.service.gov.uk/company/SC004276.

[93] Insider.co.uk analyses the audited records of Murray International Holdings Limited – the 'parent company' of The Rangers Football Club plc – from 2007 to 2013. See: Revealed: How Murray International Holdings' accounts outline Lloyds 'incentives' to Sir David Murray before and after Craig Whyte Rangers sale. 7th June 2017. In detail:

Financial year to 31 January 2008
In the MIH 2008 accounts to January, signed off on 28 November 2008, Sir David was still outwardly positive in his assessment of group performance, though by late 2008 the global banking crisis was reaching its peak. Rangers was also reported to have had a "remarkable year", making it to the group stages of the UEFA Champions League, reaching the final of the UEFA Cup and domestically winning the Scottish Cup and CIS Insurance Cup. MIH noted in the 2008 accounts it had taken a £34.2m impairment provision against the remaining goodwill which arose in the clubs 2004 rights issue. The loan to asset ratio with Bank of Scotland also rose to 70 per cent.

[94] See: Lloyds TSB seals £12bn HBOS deal at:
http://news.bbc.co.uk/1/hi/business/7622180.stm.
[95] See: Bank bailout: Alistair Darling unveils £500billion rescue
package. *The Telegraph. 8 October 2008.*
[96] See: Chairman's Statement (pages 4-5). Murray International
Holdings Limited Annual Report (2008) available at: https://find-and-
update.company-
information.service.gov.uk/company/SC192523/filing-history?page=2
[97] See: Lloyds HBOS merger gets go-ahead at:
http://news.bbc.co.uk/1/hi/business/7823521.stm
[98] See: BBC Documentary, Rangers — the men who sold the jerseys
(https://www.bbc.co.uk/programmes/p00szrhq).
[99] See: No pressure from bank to cut salaries or staff. Scotland on
Sunday. 11 January 2009.
[100] See: Sir David Murray steps down as chairman of Rangers at:
https://www.theguardian.com/football/2009/aug/26/david-murray-
rangers-chairman.
[101] See: Cash crisis may force Rangers to sell players, says Walter
Smith at: https://www.theguardian.com/football/2009/oct/26/rangers-
walter-smith-finances. In detail: "Players may be sold unless quick
buyer is found and Manager says Lloyds Bank is keeping club afloat."
[102] See: Walter: The bank is running Rangers. The Sunday Mail. 25
October 2009. In detail:

HBOS appointed Donald Muir to the Gers board nine days ago and
the bank now has a major say in the running of the club. Muir will call
the shots as they try to reduce a £30million debt and find someone to
buy out owner Sir David Murray. Mail Sport understands Muir
outlined his plans at a board meeting last week and the Ibrox
hierarchy were left shocked. The bank will continue to seek buyers for
as many players as they can during the January transfer window. After
watching his side draw 1-1 with Hibs yesterday, Smith said: "As far as
I'm concerned the bank is running Rangers. Sir David has stepped
down and a representative of the bank has been placed on the board.
It's not a situation anybody wants the club to be in."
[103] See: Rangers fans threaten Lloyds boycott over club's financial
straits at: https://www.theguardian.com/football/2009/oct/29/rangers-
lloyds-scotland-football. In detail: "Supporters groups promise to
remove business from Lloyds and Rangers majority shareholder urged
to sell up quickly."

[104] See: https://www.belfasttelegraph.co.uk/sport/football/scottish/no-bids-yet-for-club-insist-rangers-28500563.html
[105] See: Rangers' debt is small beer in relation to Murray's firm. The Times. 31 January 2009.
[106] See: Rangers Empire Falling into Ruin. Rangers limp into two vital games crippled by debts that dictate a bleak financial future. The Sunday Times. 1 November 2009.
[107] See: Rangers owner kicks accounts into long grass. The Sunday Times. 1 November 2009.
[108] See: How Murray International Holdings' accounts outline Lloyds 'incentives' to Sir David Murray before and after Craig Whyte Rangers sale at: https://www.insider.co.uk/news/revealed-how-murray-international-holdings-10575967.
[109] See: Murray International Holdings Limited Annual Report 2009 available at: https://find-and-update.company-information.service.gov.uk/company/SC192523.
[110] This strategy (business model) is echoed by Graham Spiers in his 18 January 2015 article How the mighty Glasgow Rangers have fallen. See: https://www.theguardian.com/football/2015/jan/18/how-the-mighty-glasgow-rangers-have-fallen.
[111] Insider.co.uk analyses the audited records of Murray International Holdings Limited – the 'parent company' of The Rangers Football Club plc – from 2007 to 2013. See Revealed: How Murray International Holdings' accounts outline Lloyds 'incentives' to Sir David Murray before and after Craig Whyte Rangers sale. 7 June 2017. In detail:

Financial results for 17-months to 30 September 2009
In September 2009, the MIH accounting period was extended from 31 January 2009 to 30 June 2009.
The 2009 accounts covering 17 months made for grim reading. The metals business had moved from profit to loss "almost overnight" and the value of property assets had also fallen. Bank of Scotland, and its new owners Lloyds Banking Group, had conducted a financial restructuring of MIH prior to the financial statements being audited – a process Sir David said had been completed "to our mutual satisfaction." MIH noted in the 2009 accounts the funding arrangements for Rangers "will remain unchanged as a result of the group financial restructure," and Sir David stated the club would

continue to have an independent credit line though its debt facilities would remain "separate from and without recourse to the group." He added: "Importantly, and despite speculation to the contrary, Rangers does not and never has cross guaranteed the debt obligations of the group." Independent corporate restructuring specialist Donald Muir was appointed as a director of Premier Property Group on 12 October 2009. Later the same week, 16 October, Muir joined the board of The Rangers Football Club Plc. Rangers had racked up operating losses of £11.7m in the 2009 year to June, though Sir David said: "Despite this, further funds were invested in the playing squad" to win the SPL 2009 title and "secure direct participation in the financially lucrative UEFA Champions League and then retaining the SPL title in 2010." However Sir David added in the absence of significant TV revenue from football, such as secured by the English Premier League from Sky, a "new financial reality is being imposed" and warned player wages and transfer fees would need to be "more realistic in order to balance the books and ensure the long term future of the club."

Lloyds Banking Group renewed the MIH banking facilities in the 2009 year which involved "segregating" the group's banking arrangements into a series of sub-facilities applicable to each of its operating divisions. The bank also increased its stake in MIH, subscribing to approximately £150m of the issued share capital "while reducing the debt levels by a similar quantum". This restructuring was completed on 21 April 2010. Lloyds debt-for-equity swap served to reduce the Murray family's holding in MIH to 76 per cent, down from 88 per cent previously.

Bank of Scotland subsidiary Uberior Investment's stake in MIH rose to 12.07 per cent following the debt-for-equity swap.

[112] See: Chairman's Statement (page 2). The Rangers Football Club plc Annual Report (2009) available at: https://find-and-update.company-information.service.gov.uk/company/SC004276.

[113] See: How Murray International Holdings' accounts outline Lloyds 'incentives' to Sir David Murray before and after Craig Whyte Rangers sale at: https://www.insider.co.uk/news/revealed-how-murray-international-holdings-10575967.

[114] See: How the Rangers takeover ended up in the dock at: https://www.bbc.co.uk/news/uk-scotland-40117731

[115] See: 16 things we learned from the Craig Whyte fraud trial. At: https://www.bbc.co.uk/news/uk-scotland-40110475

[116] See: Rangers attract 'tentative' sale enquiries as finance worries continue at:
https://www.theguardian.com/football/2009/oct/25/rangers-sale-enquiries-spl

[117] See Annual Return (2009) at: https://find-and-update.company-information.service.gov.uk/company/SC004276.

[118] See: The Rangers Football Club plc Annual Report (2009) available at: https://find-and-update.company-information.service.gov.uk/company/SC004276.

[119] See: Rangers offer is expected within days at:
https://www.scotsman.com/sport/rangers-offer-expected-within-days-1731063

[120] See: Rangers enter talks on possible takeover at:
http://news.bbc.co.uk/sport1/hi/football/teams/r/rangers/8553269.stm

[121] See: Takeover interest in Glasgow Rangers. RTE News. 8 March 2010.

[122] See: Glasgow Rangers takeover talks under way. Business World (Digest). 9 March 2010.

[123] See: Andrew Ellis uncovered. Scotland on Sunday. 14 March 2010.

[124] See: Rangers face HMRC investigation over offshore payments to players at:
https://www.theguardian.com/football/2010/apr/27/rangers-hmrc-investigation-offshore-payments (27 April 2010).

[125] Insider.co.uk analyses the audited records of Murray International Holdings Limited – the 'parent company' of The Rangers Football Club plc – from 2007 to 2013. See Revealed: How Murray International Holdings' accounts outline Lloyds 'incentives' to Sir David Murray before and after Craig Whyte Rangers sale. 7 June 2017. In detail:

Financial year to 30 June 2010
The 2010 accounts, signed off on 17 December 2010, also included a note on the group's use of employee benefit trusts, described in the accounts as a "tax query" raised by HM Revenue & Customs.
The MIH directors, acting on professional tax advice, were of the view it was "reasonable not to provide amounts in respect of this matter."

[126] See: Taxman at the Gates. Evening Times. 27 April 2010.

[127] In the BBC Scotland Newsnight programme (Newsnight - Craig Whyte - 17 Oct 2012), Whyte offers that the 'ruinous EBT' schemes started the chain of events. If it had not been for that, The Rangers Football Club plc would not have been sold for a pound. He argues that the previous Board of Directors could have built up a surplus of cash to deal with tax case – they did not. They buried their head in the sand. See: https://www.youtube.com/watch?v=NivEmMik-Sg

[128]See: Rangers discussed administration before Whyte at: https://www.bbc.co.uk/news/uk-scotland-glasgow-west-39704580. In detail:

The Board of Directors of Rangers discussed putting the club into administration months before it was bought by businessman Craig Whyte. According to former financial director Donald McIntyre, the size of the club's financial liabilities meant it would have been "remiss" not to do so. Speaking from the witness box where he was giving evidence for a second day of the Trial of Craig Whyte in 2017, Mr McIntyre discussed the financial obligations faced by Rangers in the months leading up to the sale of the club to Mr Whyte in May 2011. He said Rangers faced a potential bill from HMRC of about £50m, which had been described as the "Big Tax Case". Defence QC Donald Findlay called the debt a "nuclear missile" that was heading straight for Rangers. He said it was "like an exocet, nothing could be done to stop it". Mr McIntyre said Rangers board members had hoped to challenge the amount owed and that counsel at the time had suggested they had a very good chance in the case. However, Mr Findlay put it to the witness that the tax bill was a "potentially terminal event" for the club. The advocate asked when Mr McIntyre first knew "the board was discussing the possibility of administration" for Rangers. Mr McIntyre said he could not be "specific of a date" but that the "subject would have cropped up" in 2010.

[129] See: Rangers Takeover Timeline. PA Newswire: Sport News. 6 May 2011.

[130] See: Murray announces Rangers no longer for sale at: http://news.bbc.co.uk/sport1/hi/football/teams/r/rangers/8742600.stm

[131] See: Chapter 6 (page 69) to Smith, P. (2012). For Richer For Poorer. RANGERS: THE FIGHT FOR SURVIVAL. Edinburgh: Mainstream Publishing Limited. Smith suggests that in 2009, Paul Murray had joined forces with Dave King and Douglas Park to lead a

buyout. The plan was vetoed by Lloyds.

[132]See: Chairman's Statement (page 3). Murray International Holdings Limited Annual Report (2010) available at: https://find-and-update.company-information.service.gov.uk/company/SC192523.

[133] Interested readers in Murray International Holdings Limited are directed to Chapters 8-9 of Smith, P. (2012). For Richer For Poorer. RANGERS: THE FIGHT FOR SURVIVAL. Edinburgh: Mainstream Publishing Limited.

134 See: There must be some mistake. Huge tax bill could kill off Rangers. The Sun. 2 April 2011.

[135] See Cooper, M. (2021). Rangers: The Lost Decade. Self-published: Amazon. Cooper suggests (page 10) that: "the FTTT which had sat before Christmas 2010 was due to restart again in April 2011 with, it was hoped, a verdict by the summer of 2011."

[136] See: https://www.realbusinessrescue.co.uk.

[137] See: http://laingrose.com.

[138] The online site, Contractor UK (https://www.contractoruk.com/), offers specialised advice in EBTs for the IT contracting community — perhaps the word 'contract' is key here.

[139] The basic idea was that the Trustees could distribute the Trust fund when it was tax advantageous to do so, perhaps when the employee was retired or a non-UK resident. In this regard, EBTs had many of the characteristics of a pension without the restrictions that UK pension legislation applied to contribution limits and the nature and timing of benefits.

[140] See: https://services.parliament.uk/bills/2010-12/financeno3.html

[141] See: HMRC wins Rangers tax case appeal at: http://wwwnews.live.bbc.co.uk/news/uk-34720850

[142] See: https://www.gov.uk/hmrc-internal-manuals/business-income-manual/bim44535

[143] See: From Crash to Cash… and beyond (page 37-38) to Franklin, W. S., Gow, J. D. C., Graham. C., & McKillop, A. (Eds.). (2013). Follow We Will THE FALL AND RISE OF RANGERS. Edinburgh: Luath Press Limited.

[144] See: BBC Documentary, Rangers — the men who sold the jerseys (https://www.bbc.co.uk/programmes/p00szrhq).

[145] See: From Crash to Cash… and beyond (page 10) to Franklin, W. S., Gow, J. D. C., Graham. C., & McKillop, A. (Eds.). (2013). Follow We Will THE FALL AND RISE OF RANGERS. Edinburgh: Luath Press Limited.

[146] See: From Crash to Cash... and beyond (page 38) to Franklin, W. S., Gow, J. D. C., Graham. C., & McKillop, A. (Eds.). (2013). Follow We Will THE FALL AND RISE OF RANGERS. Edinburgh: Luath Press Limited. Kinnon notes that – and not reported by the media/press – the player remained liable to the sub-trust for the money borrowed and his estate became liable after death.

[147] See: https://assets.publishing.service.gov.uk/media/57650ad4e5274a0da30 0008d/HMRC-v-Murray-Group.pdf

[148] Several writers suggest that in 2007 The City of London Police (Steven's Inquiry) — investigating the transfer of J A Boumsong from Rangers to Newcastle — gave material to HMRC. In 2007, the global financial crisis commenced — perhaps HMRC was under pressure to recoup all revenues for the Treasury. Rangers then entered a dispute, known informally as 'The Big Tax Case' with HMRC, regarding their use of EBTs between the period 2001 and 2010. This tax case was made public in May 2010. In January 2011, as Craig Whyte was completing his due diligence, the FTTT was about to resume to hear the last evidence of the Big Tax Case. It is understood that on 23 January 2011, Andrew Thornhill QC (he took up case in spring of 2010) offered HMRC £10M to settle. On 5 April 2011, the second half of the FTTT commenced.

[149] See: From Crash to Cash... and beyond (page 37) to Franklin, W. S., Gow, J. D. C., Graham. C., & McKillop, A. (Eds.). (2013). Follow We Will THE FALL AND RISE OF RANGERS. Edinburgh: Luath Press Limited.

[150] See How Rangers' dubious tax wheeze unravelled at: https://www.bbc.co.uk/news/uk-scotland-glasgow-west-34723209.

[151] See: Chapter 10 to Tangled Up in Blue. Stephen O'Donnell. 2019. Worthing: Pitch Publishing.

[152] See: Introduction (page 23) to Franklin, W. S., Gow, J. D. C., Graham. C., & McKillop, A. (Eds.). (2013). Follow We Will THE FALL AND RISE OF RANGERS. Edinburgh: Luath Press Limited

[153] See: Rangers Administrators Press Conference at: https://www.youtube.com/watch?v=fACV_unAFRg

[154] See: THIRTEEN (page 121) to Whyte, C. (2020). Into the Bear Pit. Edinburgh: Birlinn Limited.

[155] See: Chapters 7-11 to Smith, P. (2012). For Richer For Poorer. RANGERS: THE FIGHT FOR SURVIVAL. Edinburgh: Mainstream Publishing Company Limited.

[156] See: Certificate of re-registration from Private to Public Limited Company (31 May 1982) available at: https://find-and-update.company-information.service.gov.uk/company/SC004276.

[157] See: Chapter 7 (page 86) to Smith, P. (2012). For Richer For Poorer. RANGERS: THE FIGHT FOR SURVIVAL. Edinburgh: Mainstream Publishing Limited.

[158] At the Notes to the Financial Statements (Note 3) to the 2011 Annual Report of RFC Investment Holdings Limited, it says: "On 31 January 2011, the company sold its entire shareholding in The Rangers Football Club plc to its parent company, Murray Sports Limited."

[159] Note: Wavetower Limited (Company number 07380537) was incorporated on 17 September 2010. It changed its name to The Rangers FC Group Limited on 12 May 2011. It is, of note, still trading today.

[160] Interested readers may refer to: Malagila, J.K., Zalata, A.M., Ntim C.G. and Elamer, A.A. (2021). Corporate governance and performance in sports organisations: The case of UK premier leagues. International Journal of Finance & Economics, 26(2): 2517-2537.

[161] See: Yukl, G. (2013). Leadership in Organizations (8th Edition). Harlow: Pearson Education Limited.

[162] See: Rousing the Rangers Family (page 172) to Franklin, W. S., Gow, J. D. C., Graham. C., & McKillop, A. (Eds.). (2013). Follow We Will THE FALL AND RISE OF RANGERS. Edinburgh: Luath Press Limited.

[163] See: Chapter 23 (page 265) to Smith, P. (2012). For Richer For Poorer. RANGERS: THE FIGHT FOR SURVIVAL. Edinburgh: Mainstream Publishing Limited.

[164] See: Murray's leadership is the main reason for Rangers' success. The Times. 22 November 2008.

[165] See: 'Those wanting to buy Rangers better have cash in a piggy bank'; The new Ibrox chief, Alastair Johnston, says Celtic provide his role model for leadership. The Sunday Times. 4 October 2009.

[166] See: 'Doctor No' asked to save Rangers; Cost-cutter is given task of tackling the £30m debt at Ibrox - even if 'sacred cows' must be sacrificed. The Times. 27 October 2009.

[167] See: Murray in over his head. Scotland on Sunday. 14 July 2002.

[168] See: Celtic take opportunity to laugh at the loan Rangers: Reckless spending has left Ibrox in the red. The Observer. 1 November 2009.

[169] See: Sir David hits back as club crisis mounts. Evening Times (Glasgow). 15 January 2009.

[170] See: INTRODUCTION (page 11) to Smith, P. (2012). For Richer For Poorer. RANGERS: THE FIGHT FOR SURVIVAL. Edinburgh: Mainstream Publishing Limited.

[171] See: Introduction (page 13) to Mac Giolla Bhain, P. (2012). Downfall: How Rangers FC Self Destructed. Edinburgh: Frontline Noir.

[172] Ibid page 37.

[173] See: Rousing the Rangers Family (page 171) to Franklin, W. S., Gow, J. D. C., Graham. C., & McKillop, A. (Eds.). (2013). Follow We Will THE FALL AND RISE OF RANGERS. Edinburgh: Luath Press Limited.

[174] See: Foundations for the Future (Page 163) to Franklin, W. S., Gow, J. D. C., Graham. C., & McKillop, A. (Eds.). (2013). Follow We Will THE FALL AND RISE OF RANGERS. Edinburgh: Luath Press Limited.

[175] See: Gorilla in the room' refuses to budge for Rangers' Whyte knight. The Daily Telegraph. 4 April 2011.

[176] See: Foundations for the Future (page 163) to Franklin, W. S., Gow, J. D. C., Graham. C., & McKillop, A. (Eds.). (2013). Follow We Will THE FALL AND RISE OF RANGERS. Edinburgh: Luath Press Limited.

[177] See: Time for Followers to become Leaders (page 179) to Franklin, W. S., Gow, J. D. C., Graham. C., & McKillop, A. (Eds.). (2013). Follow We Will THE FALL AND RISE OF RANGERS. Edinburgh: Luath Press Limited.

[178] See: strategic processes – transformation and renewal (page 253-256) to: Leavy, B., & Leavy & McKiernan, P. (2009). Strategic Leadership. Governance and Renewal. Basingstoke: Palgrave Macmillan.

[179] The current ratio is a liquidity ratio that measures a company's ability to pay short-term obligations or those due within one year. It tells investors and analysts how easily, or not, a company can maximise the current assets on its balance sheet to satisfy its current debt and other payables. A current ratio that is in line with the industry average or slightly higher is generally considered acceptable.

A current ratio that is lower than the industry average may indicate a higher risk of distress or default. Similarly, if a company has a very high current ratio compared with its peer group, it indicates that management may not be using its assets efficiently. The current ratio is called current because, unlike some other liquidity ratios, it incorporates all current assets and current liabilities. The current ratio is sometimes called the working capital ratio.

[180] The acid-test ratio, commonly known as the quick ratio, uses a firm's balance sheet data as an indicator of whether it has sufficient short-term assets to cover its short-term liabilities. Unlike the current ratio, the acid test usually excludes inventories which may not always be immediately convertible to cash.

[181] Return on equity (ROE) is a measure of financial performance calculated by dividing net income by shareholders' equity. Because shareholders' equity is equal to a company's assets minus its debt, ROE is considered the return on net assets. ROE is considered a gauge of a corporation's profitability and how efficient it is in generating profits.

[182] The debt-to-equity (D/E) ratio is used to evaluate a company's financial leverage and is calculated by dividing a company's total liabilities by its shareholder equity. The D/E ratio is an important metric used in corporate finance. It is a measure of the degree to which a company is financing its operations through debt versus wholly owned funds. More specifically, it reflects the ability of shareholder equity to cover all outstanding debts in the event of a business downturn. The debt-to-equity ratio is a particular type of gearing ratio.

[183] See Chapter 23 (page 271) to Smith, P. (2012). For Richer For Poorer. RANGERS: THE FIGHT FOR SURVIVAL. Edinburgh: Mainstream Publishing Limited.

[184] See: strategic processes – transformation and renewal (page 253-256) to: Leavy, B., & Leavy & McKiernan, P. (2009). Strategic Leadership. Governance and Renewal. Basingstoke: Palgrave Macmillan.

[185] We are seeing, in all economic sectors, significant corporate learning as a result of Covid-19.

[186] See: strategic processes – transformation and renewal (page 253-256) to: Leavy, B., & Leavy & McKiernan, P. (2009). Strategic Leadership. Governance and Renewal. Basingstoke: Palgrave Macmillan.

[187] See: strategic processes – transformation and renewal (page 253-256) to: Leavy, B., & Leavy & McKiernan, P. (2009). Strategic Leadership. Governance and Renewal. Basingstoke: Palgrave Macmillan.

[188] See: We were the People (pages 107-108) to Franklin, W. S., Gow, J. D. C., Graham. C., & McKillop, A. (Eds.). (2013). Follow We Will THE FALL AND RISE OF RANGERS. Edinburgh: Luath Press Limited.

[189] See: Murray in over his head. Scotland on Sunday. 14 July 2002.

[190] See: INTRODUCTION (page 12) to Smith, P. (2012). For Richer For Poorer. RANGERS: THE FIGHT FOR SURVIVAL. Edinburgh: Mainstream Publishing Limited.

[191] See: https://www.exeter.ac.uk/media/universityofexeter/humanresources/documents/learningdevelopment/the_change_curve.pdf.

Chapter Three

[192] See: Craig Whyte's Rangers 'villainy' remains at:
https://www.bbc.co.uk/news/uk-scotland-40176560

[193] See: One (pages 8-9) to Whyte, C. (2020). INTO THE BEAR PIT.
Edinburgh: Birlinn Limited.

[194] See: Rangers face 'pure carnage' says Butcher. The Daily
Telegraph. 15 February 2012.

[195] See: Rangers fraud trial: Craig Whyte 'portrayed as pantomime
villain' at: https://www.bbc.co.uk/news/uk-scotland-glasgow-west-
40129976.

[196] The Merchant House Group plc (MHG
) (Company number 04034645) Annual Report for the year ended 31
December 2008 stated that Liberty Capital owned 15.54% of share
capital of MHG plc (page 7). In addition, Merchant Turnaround plc
(Company number: 07116894) was part of MHG (Craig Whyte was
Director and Secretary of Merchant Turnaround plc. Phil Betts was
also a Director of this company). Merchant Corporate Recovery plc
(Company number 06805838) was also part of MHG (Craig Whyte
was Director and Secretary of Merchant Corporate Recovery plc).

197 One does wonder, then, if this was the reason that Sir David
Murray announced that Murray International Holdings Limited was
no longer "actively marketing its controlling stake in the club for sale"
i.e. Andrew Ellis could not secure the funds for his takeover.

[198] David Gilmour – who worked in Guernsey for a trust company that
had administered an EBT scheme for Rangers – had suggested the
deal to Andrew Ellis.

[199] See: Three (page 24) to Whyte, C. (2020). INTO THE BEAR PIT.
Edinburgh: Birlinn Limited.

[200] Ibid.

[201] See: Three (page 27) to Whyte, C. (2020). INTO THE BEAR PIT.
Edinburgh: Birlinn Limited.

[202] See: Six (page 49) to Whyte, C. (2020). INTO THE BEAR PIT.
Edinburgh: Birlinn Limited. By the time of his purchase of the
shares in The Rangers Football Club plc, the debt had reduced from
£30M to £18M due to Champions League and Europa league
participation.

[203] See: Section 5.6 to Statement of administrator's proposal at:

https://find-and-update.company-information.service.gov.uk/company/SC004276/filing-history.
Section 5.6 to Statement of administrator's proposal at: https://find-and-update.company-information.service.gov.uk/company/SC004276/filing-history.

[204] See: Five (page 38) to Whyte, C. (2020). INTO THE BEAR PIT. Edinburgh: Birlinn Limited.

[205] See: Four (page 31) to Whyte, C. (2020). INTO THE BEAR PIT. Edinburgh: Birlinn Limited.

[206] See: Tycoon Craig Whyte confirms interest in Rangers takeover. The Scotsman. 18 November 2010 and Whyte confirms interest in buying Rangers. The Daily Telegraph. 19 November 2010.

[207] See: Revealed: How Murray International Holdings' accounts outline Lloyds 'incentives' to Sir David Murray before and after Craig Whyte Rangers sale at: https://www.insider.co.uk/news/revealed-how-murray-international-holdings-10575967. The Craig Whyte trial heard Sir David Murray had been 'incentivised' by Lloyds to sell Rangers with the promise of securing Murray International Holdings' lucrative metals business, which the court heard he picked up for a nominal £1 sum.

[208] See: Six (page 48) to Whyte, C. (2020). INTO THE BEAR PIT. Edinburgh: Birlinn Limited.

[209] See: 16 things we learned from the Craig Whyte fraud trial at: https://www.bbc.co.uk/news/uk-scotland-40110475

[210] These Directors were Donald Muir and MIH Limited Finance Director, Mike McGill.

[211] See: Craig Whyte's Rangers 'villainy' remains at: https://www.bbc.co.uk/news/uk-scotland-40176560.
In his statement, Murray said: "I do not accept that we failed to carry out due diligence on Craig Whyte. Given that he was advised by Collyer Bristow, a reputable firm of lawyers, Saffrey Champness and MCR, both reputable firms of accountants, all of whom were FCA-regulated firms, we were entitled to assume that Craig Whyte was a person of good standing."

[212] See: Chapter 4 (page 49) to Smith, P. (2012). For Richer For Poorer. RANGERS: THE FIGHT FOR SURVIVAL. Edinburgh: Mainstream Publishing Limited.

[213] See: Five (page 38) to Whyte, C. (2020). INTO THE BEAR PIT. Edinburgh: Birlinn Limited.

He says: "Perhaps my problem was applying solid business logic to a football club. I was soon to discover that this wasn't a logical business."

[214] See: Rangers in administration move over tax bill. The Daily Telegraph. 14 February 2012

[215] See Annual Return (AR 01 (ef) dated 27 January 2012) for The Rangers Football Club plc available at: https://find-and-update.company-information.service.gov.uk/company/SC004276.

[216] See: McCoist steps up as Rangers takeover looms. The Daily Telegraph. 23 February 2011.

[217] See: Statement of administrator's proposal (Section 5.2) at: https://find-and-update.company-information.service.gov.uk/company/SC004276/filing-history.

[218] See: Five (page 46) to Whyte, C. (2020). INTO THE BEAR PIT. Edinburgh: Birlinn Limited. Whyte offers that they (including Donald McIntyre) tried to put him (Whyte) off the deal.

[219] See: Rangers fans ask how patient Whyte is ready to be; Still no deal at close of play yesterday as prospective buyer meets Ibrox board. The Daily Telegraph. 1 April 2011.

[220] See: Six (page 52) to Whyte, C. (2020). INTO THE BEAR PIT. Edinburgh: Birlinn Limited. Whyte states that he told the IBC that participation in the Europa league was the minimum requirement to ensure for working capital.

[221] See: The Liquidation Game (Page321) to O'Donnell, S. (2019). Tangled Up in Blue: The Rise and Fall of Rangers FC. Worthing: Pitch Publishing Limited.

[222] See: https://www.bbc.co.uk/sport/football/12932160

[223] See: Ranger chairman admits they could go bust if no white knight is found; Johnson insists buyer must be found by Monday or tax demands could put the club into administration. The Daily Telegraph. 2 April 2011.

[224] See: The PA newswire: Sport News. 6 May 2011.

[225] See: Rival plan for Ibrox takeover. The Daily Telegraph. 20 April 2011.

[226] See Cooper, M. (2021). Rangers: The Lost Decade. Self-published: Amazon. Cooper (pages 12-13) reports on this alternative bid: "Johnston and the board desperately sought out an alternative. It arrived in the shape of a £25m bid from Dave King and Paul Murray. They offered to pay Lloyds £15m (of the £18m they were owed), buy

out David Murray's shareholding and then provide £10m to Ally McCoist for players. There would then be a share issue, underwritten by King to around £20m, to provide additional funding to the club. Unlike Whyte's offer, though, it did not involve replacing the Lloyds debt with a debt to King. King's offer also foresaw the need to maintain a working credit facility, ideally with Lloyds in the short-term, to manage the football club over a season. Whyte's offer would close off the club's credit facility leaving it entirely on Whyte's own funding. Paul Murray, among others, saw the club running out of cash very quickly under Whyte's offer." He continues "The only downside to Kings offer, and it was not a downside from a Rangers point of view, was that any potential HMRC liability would reside with the Murray Group and, thus, with Lloyds. The unavoidable conclusion is that Dave King and Paul Murray offer stood no chance as Lloyds would not have entertained any offer that did not involve the potential HMRC liability being taken on by another party. Whyte's offer involved paying Lloyds and not much else. It left little room for player investment, stadium maintenance, let alone any potential bill from HMRC." Simply put, Whyte's offer was weighed in favour of the bank rather than the club.

[227] See: https://www.bbc.co.uk/news/uk-scotland-40110475

[228] See: Ibrox saga rumbles on. The Daily Telegraph. 22 April 2011.

[229] See also Chapter 6 (page 69) to Smith, P. (2012). For Richer For Poorer. RANGERS: THE FIGHT FOR SURVIVAL. Edinburgh: Mainstream Publishing Limited. Smith suggests that in 2009, Paul Murray, Dave King and Donald Park tried to buy The Rangers Football Club plc but Lloyds said no.

[230] See: Five (page 49) to Whyte, C. (2020). INTO THE BEAR PIT. Edinburgh: Birlinn Limited.

[231] Ibid.

[232] Wavetower was 'parked' in Liberty Capital – a holding company registered in the British Virgin Islands. Liberty Capital owned a lot of Whyte's investments.

[233] See: Six (page 53) to Whyte, C. (2020). INTO THE BEAR PIT. Edinburgh: Birlinn Limited.

[234] Note: By paying off the debt to Lloyds, Craig Whyte also made sure that he inherited the floating charge which BoS had secured over the club in late 1990s allowing the new owner to become the only secured creditor. This would ensure that if all went 'south' rather

rapidly, Whyte – in theory at least – would not lose out. The Floating Charge (of 8 May 1999) was assigned to The Rangers FC Group Limited (see again Vignette by Mathew Bonnet at pages 6-7).

[235] The Rangers FC Group Limited still trades to date. It is interesting that Craig Whyte remained a Director of this company until 11 April 2014.

[236] See Cooper, M. (2021). Rangers: The Lost Decade. Self-published: Amazon. Cooper (page 17) states that the £18M debt now resided with the Rangers FC Group Limited, with the exception of one circumstance. And that is if the club suffers an" insolvency event within 90 days of an appeal in relation to the tax claim brought against it by HMRC." The circular also promised £5M for investment in the playing squad for 2011/12, £1.7M to fund improvement in the kitchens and the PA system and around £3M for the small tax bill that had been received, and not disputed, by the plc earlier in the year. In the case of an insolvency event, however, this (£9.7M) would be added to the £18M used to pay Lloyds meaning the Rangers FC Group Limited would be owed around £28m.

[237] See: https://www.bbc.co.uk/news/uk-scotland-40110475

[238] See: https://www.youtube.com/watch?v=I75_bgQSmqA.

[239] In this documentary, Daily states that Craig Whyte was a Director of MHG. There is no indication from Companies House that this was the case (see: https://beta.companieshouse.gov.uk/company/04034645).

[240] See: Former colleague 'annoyed' by Craig Whyte's Rangers bid at: https://www.bbc.co.uk/news/uk-scotland-glasgow-west-40037609

[241] See: Jury urged to convict Craig Whyte at: https://www.bbc.co.uk/news/uk-scotland-glasgow-west-40105764. The Jerome Group's parent company, Worthington, was part-owned by Craig Whyte.

[242] See: Whyte completes Rangers deal. The Daily Telegraph. 7 May 2011.

[243] See: Rangers owner suspends Bain and McIntyre. The Guardian. 25 May 2011 and Whyte of the long knives; Rangers boardroom clear out, Whyte sacks two board members at Ibrox - then suspends two more. Daily Record. 25 May 2011.

[244] See: Johnston voices concerns for Rangers' future at: https://www.bbc.co.uk/sport/football/13518277

[245] See: Whyte needs to walk the walk. The Daily Telegraph. 25 May 2011.

[246] See Section 5.7 to Statemen of administrator's proposals/Report to Creditors, dated 5 April 2012 at: https://find-and-update.companyinformation.service.gov.uk/company/SC004276/filing-history.

[247] See Section 5.8 to Statemen of administrator's proposals/Report to Creditors, dated 5 April 2012 at: https://find-and-update.companyinformation.service.gov.uk/company/SC004276/filing-history.

[248] Craig Whyte also sent a letter to all shareholders. This letter was an exchange for the waiving of the requirement buyers sometimes have to make a mandatory offer to all shareholders.

[249] See Newsnight – Craig Whyte – 17 Oct 2012 at https://www.youtube.com/watch?v=NivEmMik-Sg&t=7s

[250] See Section 5.9 to Statemen of administrator's proposals/Report to Creditors, dated 5 April 2012 at: https://find-and-update.companyinformation.service.gov.uk/company/SC004276/filing-history.

[251] See Section 5.10 to Statemen of administrator's proposals/Report to Creditors, dated 5 April 2012 at: https://find-and-update.companyinformation.service.gov.uk/company/SC004276/filing-history.)

[252] See: Sheriff officers pay visit to Rangers over £2.8m debt. The Herald. 11 August 2011 and Rangers given tax warning. The Daily Telegraph. 11 August 2011.

[253] As stated, Whyte suggests that annual costs were £45M and that annual revenue was £35M — an immediate shortfall of £10M. Clearly, European income would have helped with this significant shortfall

[254] See: Craig Whyte 'portrayed as pantomime villain' at: https://www.bbc.co.uk/news/uk-scotland-glasgow-west-40129976

[255] See: Nine (page 81) to Whyte, C. (2020). INTO THE BEAR PIT. Edinburgh: Birlinn. Whyte also comments on the Murray contracts with The Rangers Football Club plc

[256] See: Ten (page 90) to Whyte, C. (2020). INTO THE BEAR PIT. Edinburgh: Birlinn.

[257] See: Section 5.12 to Statemen of administrator's proposals/Report to Creditors, dated 5 April 2012 at: https://find-and-update.companyinformation.service.gov.uk/company/SC004276/filing-history.)

[258] See: Section 5.13 to Statemen of administrator's proposals/Report to Creditors, dated 5 April 2012 at: https://find-and-update.companyinformation.service.gov.uk/company/SC004276/filing-history.)

[259] See: Money worries stalk Ibrox corridors. The Daily Telegraph. 10 September 2011.

[260] See: Rangers 'at substantial risk of insolvency'; Bain has £480 000 of his former club assets frozen. The Daily Telegraph 14 September 2011.

[261] See: Section 5.15 to Statemen of administrator's proposals/Report to Creditors, dated 5 April 2012 at: https://find-and-update.company-information.service.gov.uk/company/SC004276/filing-history). The JAs state that arrestment order was for £528 000 on 15 September 2011.

[262] See: Rangers paying heavy price for damage done by Murray. The Daily Telegraph. 16 September 2011.

[263] See: Rangers left to ponder the power of 10. The Daily Telegraph. 26 September 2011.

[264] See: Section 9.26 to Statement of administrator's proposal at: https://find-and-update.company-information.service.gov.uk/company/SC004276/filing-history.)

[265] See: Section 5.16 to Statement of administrator's proposal at: https://find-and-update.company-information.service.gov.uk/company/SC004276/filing-history.

[266] See: Whyte ready to sue over BBC documentary. The Daily Telegraph. 21 October 2011.

[267] See: Eleven (page 104) to Whyte, C. (2020). INTO THE BEAR PIT. Edinburgh: Birlinn Limited.

[268] See: Eleven (pages 102-103) to Whyte, C. (2020). INTO THE BEAR PIT. Edinburgh: Birlinn Limited.

[269] See: Eleven (page 105) to Whyte, C. (2020). INTO THE BEAR PIT. Edinburgh: Birlinn Limited.

[270] See: Eleven (page 106) to Whyte, C. (2020). INTO THE BEAR PIT. Edinburgh: Birlinn Limited.

[271] See: Eleven (page 107) to Whyte, C. (2020). INTO THE BEAR PIT. Edinburgh: Birlinn Limited.

[272] See: Rangers face up to Ibrox credit crunch. The Daily Telegraph. 11 January 2012.

[273] See: Twelve (page 110) to Whyte, C. (2020). INTO THE BEAR PIT. Edinburgh: Birlinn Limited.

[274] See: Rangers face up to Ibrox credit crunch. The Daily Telegraph. January 11, 2012.

[275] See: Section 5.20 to Statement of administrator's proposal at: https://find-and-update.company-information.service.gov.uk/company/SC004276/filing-history.

[276] See: Rangers Trust Wants Answer at:
https://www.eurosport.com/football/spl/2011-2012/rangers-trust-wants-answer_sto3135036/story.shtml
[277] See: Whyte denies cash claims. The Daily Telegraph. 1 February 2012.
[278] See: Step aside Sir Fred Goodwin, some Rangers fans want to see Sir David Murray stripped of title; Former owner is seen as the cause of the club's woes but mortgaging of tickets so far into the future is a huge gamble.
[279] See: Former Rangers chairman wants investigation of Craig Whyte's takeover. Guardian.com. 9 February 2012.
[280] See: Section 5.22 to Statement of administrator's proposal at:
https://find-and-update.company-information.service.gov.uk/company/SC004276/filing-history.
[281] See: Chapter 2 (page 23) to Smith, P. (2012). For Richer For Poorer. RANGERS: THE FIGHT FOR SURVIVAL. Edinburgh: Mainstream Publishing Limited. Smith suggests that the 'threat of administration' was an attempt to put pressure on the tax authorities to concede in their full pursuit of the full amount and come to a compromise amount arrangement. But the administrators had been enlisted even if the final decision on administration had not yet been taken.
[282] See: Chapter 2 (pages 21-26) to Smith, P. (2012). For Richer For Poorer. RANGERS: THE FIGHT FOR SURVIVAL. Edinburgh: Mainstream Publishing Limited. Smith offers that If HMRC agreed a manageable agreement with the club, a formal insolvent procedure could be averted. So, Duff & Phelps advised to seek protection of a moratorium from HMRC action whilst a CVA proposal was made of creditors. If this could be done in one-month, it would still allow for Rangers FC to play in European football. It was anticipated that it would be the following week before formal move into admin took place, with a 10-day grace period between the NoI and the deadline for following it through. But, at 2.50 pm on 14th February 2012, Duff & Phelps confirmed the bleak news that the process was complete. An unpaid tax bill of £9M had forced the issue. HMRC had made a legal bid to appoint their own administrators forcing a rapid change of pace by Whyte.
[283] See: Morrow, S. (2015). Power and logics in Scottish football: the financial collapse of Rangers FC. Sport, Business and Management. 5 (4): 325-343. DOI:10.1108/SBM-08-2012-0029.

[284] See: Rangers in administration move over tax bill; Old Firm club face £50m investigation by HMRC. The Daily Telegraph. 14 February 2012.

[285] See: Rangers call for lifeline from rising tide of debt; Old Firm football club lodges legal papers of its intention to appoint an administrator. The Daily Telegraph. 14 February 2012.

[286] See: Rangers face 'pure carnage' says Butcher; Administration will mean cuts in jobs and salaries. Points deduction all but hands league title to Celtic. The Daily Telegraph. 15 February 2012.

[287] See: Murray's futile attempt to 'live the dream' has caused the nightmare; Rangers' woes ultimately can be traced back to the former owner's grand plan to chase European glory. The Daily Telegraph. 15 February 2012.

[288] See: Taxman deepens crisis at Rangers; Old Firm giants fighting for survival after entering administration over £9m bill Tax dispute sees Rangers enter administration. The Daily Telegraph. 15 February 2012.

[289] See: Rangers administrators to probe 'invisible' £24m loan. The Daily Telegraph. 17 February 2012.

[290] See: Chairman's Statement (page 4). Murray International Holdings Limited Group of companies' accounts made up to 30 June 2011 available at Companies House (Company number SC192523).

[291] See: Eleven (page 101) to Whyte, C. (2020). INTO THE BEAR PIT. Edinburgh: Birlinn Limited.

[292] See: Chapter 1 (page 19) to Smith, P. (2012). For Richer For Poorer. RANGERS: THE FIGHT FOR SURVIVAL. Edinburgh: Mainstream Publishing Limited.

[293] See: Eight (page 78) to Whyte, C. (2020). INTO THE BEAR PIT. Edinburgh: Birlinn Limited. Whyte comments on the Murray contracts with The Rangers Football Club plc: "retail, marketing, internet and administering the tax deal."

[294] See: Whyte was disqualified as a director; BBC documentary claim confirmed by Rangers Owner says tax dispute is 'dark cloud' over the club. The Daily Telegraph. 1 December 2011

[295] See: Eleven (page 102) to Whyte, C. (2020). INTO THE BEAR PIT. Edinburgh: Birlinn Limited.

Chapter Four

[296] See: https://find-and-update.company-information.service.gov.uk/company/SC004276.

[297] See: https://insolvency-practitioners.org.uk/

[298] And I did so in advance of the ongoing 'issues' with Duff & Phelps and the Crown Office.

[299] This Report was not required to be filed at Companies House. Hence, it is not in the 'filing history'. It was obtained directly from Duff & Phelps via private correspondence.

[300] The first Rangers Administrators Press Conference at Ibrox Stadium on Thursday 16 February 2012 is at: https://www.youtube.com/watch?v=fACV_unAFRg. Paul Clark states that their (i.e. he and David Whitehouse) appointment as JAs was approved by the Court of Session and agreed by HMRC. Of note, he states that the JAs are Officers of the Court and are accountable to the Court. As such, and as JAs, they have a statutory duty to act in the best interests of the creditors and stakeholders of the Company (i.e. The Rangers Football Club plc).

[301] See: Rescuing Rangers: From Whyte to Green (page 47) to Franklin, W. S., Gow, J. D. C., Graham. C., & McKillop, A. (Eds.). (2013). Follow We Will THE FALL AND RISE OF RANGERS. Edinburgh: Luath Press Limited.

[302] See Section 6.1 to Report to Creditors dated 5 April 2012 at: https://find-and-update.company-information.service.gov.uk/company/SC004276.)

[303] The JAs note Murray Park. It is now called Auchenhowie or The Rangers Training Centre.

[304] See Section 7.4 to Report to Creditors dated 5 April 2012 at: https://find-and-update.company-information.service.gov.uk/company/SC004276.)

[305] Bob Downes was Deputy Chairman of the Environmental Protection Agency and Professor Niall Lothian was the past President of the Institute of Chartered Accountants in Scotland.

[306] See: SFA to launch inquiry into Rangers' affairs. Governing body to probe potential rule breaches. Ticketus say it did not lend £24m for season tickets. The Daily Telegraph. February 18, 2012.

[307] See: Taking on the Establishment: Rangers and the Scottish Football Authorities (pages 81-82) to Franklin, W. S., Gow, J. D. C.,

Graham. C., & McKillop, A. (Eds.). (2013). Follow We Will THE FALL AND RISE OF RANGERS. Edinburgh: Luath Press Limited.

[308] See: Raith Rovers director appeals for calm after Rangers threats. The Courier. 27 April 2012.

[309] See: SFA panel admits 'rushed' decision; Drysdale concedes 10.30 at night was not the best time to release findings on such a 'contentious case'. The Daily Telegraph. 27 April 2012.

[310] The panel members were Lord Carloway, Allan Cowan and Craig Graham. Cowan was previously Chairman at Partick Thistle FC and Graham was Chairman of East of Scotland League side Spartans and a partner at KPMG.

[311] See: McCoist is cautiously optimistic; Ibrox manager 'delighted' that transfer embargo has been lifted but knows that the club face new sanctions. The Daily Telegraph. 30 May 2012. The administrators were, however, advised by Richard Keen QC that they had strong grounds for a legal appeal and yesterday Lord Glennie agreed with the lawyer's argument that a ban on the registration on players was not a sanction available to the Judicial Tribunal. He also awarded Rangers the costs of their appeal. Now the SFA will have to decide on another punishment - with the options being a fine, termination or suspension of membership of the governing body of Scottish football, expulsion from the game or a ban from next season's Scottish Cup. The matter will be considered by the appeals panel, rather than the judicial tribunal. However, since Lord Carloway stated that it would have been too harsh to have suspended or excluded Rangers from membership of the SFA or to have expelled them from football - and since they have already been fined the maximum of £100,000 - it appears that expulsion from the Scottish Cup is now the significant option, although the absence of the Ibrox club is likely to reduce the value of the tournament in the eyes of its sponsors. McCoist, meanwhile, said: "At least now I have a chance of finding players for next season and that is great news for the club, the squad and the fans - even if the last year has made me cynical about believing anything I hear."

[312] See Rangers accused of misleading SFA on secret deals. Mail Online 2 March 2012 at: https://www.dailymail.co.uk/sport/football/article-2109018/Rangers-accused-misleading-SFA-secret-deals.html. In detail, Rangers stand accused of failing to properly register players after a former director

322

revealed secretive payments had been consistently excluded from contracts lodged with the SFA. The embattled Ibrox club are awaiting the outcome of the First Tier Tax Tribunal which will determine the legality or otherwise of Employee Benefit Trusts. Regardless of whether Rangers are hit with an additional bill of £49million from the so-called 'big tax case', it appears such payments were kept 'off the books' - in direct contravention of SFA registration rules.

[313] See: Rescuing Rangers: From Whyte to Green to Franklin, W. S., Gow, J. D. C., Graham. C., & McKillop, A. (Eds.). (2013). Follow We Will THE FALL AND RISE OF RANGERS. Edinburgh: Luath Press Limited. Calvin Spence states that all thoughts of verifying the accuracy of Adam's claims or awaiting the outcome of the FTTT were hastily discarded in the rush to condemn Rangers and moralise about 'sporting integrity'. He suggests that football authorities succumbed to clamour for retribution against Rangers.

[314] See O'Donnell, S. (2019). Tangled Up in Blue. Worthing: Pitch Publishing Limited. O'Donnell (page 323) offers that players agreed to take 75% wage cut saving £1M/month in hope that further redundancies and failure to complete the season could be avoided. In return, the players got a 'minimum release contract', which would allow them to leave for discounted transfer fees once they reverted to full salary at the end of May.

[315] See: Where are all the Rangers Men? to Franklin, W. S., Gow, J. D. C., Graham. C., & McKillop, A. (Eds.). (2013). Follow We Will THE FALL AND RISE OF RANGERS. Edinburgh: Luath Press Limited. Colin Armstrong notes (page 71) that on 9 March 2012, Whittaker, Naismith and Davis agreed to take a 75% pay cut but there was clearly more being discussed behind the scenes. Whittaker and Naismith refused to transfer their contracts under Transfer of Undertakings (Protection of Employment) legislation – this denied Rangers FC of any transfer fee. The club did, however, get a fee for Davis but there was a significant feeling of betrayal as others left.

[316] See Section 8.13 to Report to Creditors dated 5 April 2012 at: https://find-and-update.company-information.service.gov.uk/company/SC004276.

[317] See: From Crash to Cash…and beyond to Franklin, W. S., Gow, J. D. C., Graham. C., & McKillop, A. (Eds.). (2013). Follow We Will THE FALL AND RISE OF RANGERS. Edinburgh: Luath Press Limited. David Kinnon

(page 41) offers: As is usual in insolvency proceedings, the prospect of a sale of assets at a discounted or distressed value attracted a number of persons with no discernible interests in Rangers as a club but with interest in the property asset as a redevelopment opportunity.

[318] Gary Withey – The Rangers FC Group Limited Company Secretary – was also a Partner at Collyer Bristow.

[319] See: Thirteen (page 130) to Whyte, C. (2020). INTO THE BEAR PIT. Edinburgh: Birlinn Limited. Whyte elaborates on this theme. Lord Hodge claimed the season ticket deal to be void i.e. they did not have a claim. In Scotland, a personal right (a seat was a right) could not be sold. Duff & Phelps wanted that judgement because without it, the business would be unsellable i.e. no one would have taken on this liability.

[320] Section 5.9 to Interim Report to Creditors dated 10 July 2012.

[321] Sections 5.10 – 5.17 to Interim Report to Creditors dated 10 July 2012.

[322] Sections 5.20 – 5.25 to Interim Report to Creditors dated 10 July 2012.

[323] See Taking on the Establishment: Rangers and the Scottish Football Authorities to Green to Franklin, W. S., Gow, J. D. C., Graham. C., & McKillop, A. (Eds.). (2013). Follow We Will THE FALL AND RISE OF RANGERS. Edinburgh: Luath Press Limited.

[324] See: Rangers forced to put bid announcement on hold as SPL clubs vote on financial fair play. Mail Online. 11 April 2012. See also: https://spfl.co.uk/news/financial-fair-play-2012-04-11; and https://spfl.co.uk/news/tougher-financial-fair-play-rules-introduced-2012-05-30.

[325] Sections 5.28 – 5.46 to Interim Report to Creditors dated 10 July 2012.

[326] Sale and Purchase Agreement to document the sale of a business and its assets from one legal entity to another.

[327] Sections 5.34 to Interim Report to Creditors dated 10 July 2012.

[328] See: SPL: Clubs set new financial fair play rules at Hampden meeting at: https://www.bbc.co.uk/sport/football/18263819. 30 May 2012.

[329] Sections 5.39 – 5.48 to Interim Report to Creditors dated 10 July 2012.

[330] It is understood that on 7 May 2012, Bill Miller had been given a period of 'exclusivity' by Duff & Phelps. He had been given

assurances that New Co Rangers would play in SPL. When authorities stuttered, the 'No to New Co' fan-led campaign was gaining ground. In the end, fans won.

[331] Duff & Phelps had received several offers but Charles Green offered a binary i.e. an option if CVA failed. This was very attractive to Duff & Phelps.

[332] See Section 4.20 to Proposal for a Company Voluntary Arrangement by the Joint Administrators of The Rangers Football Club plc to its Creditors and Shareholders dated 29 May 2012 at: https://find-and-update.company-information.service.gov.uk/company/SC004276).

[333] Ibid.

[334] See: Fourteen (pages 132-144) to Whyte, C. (2020). INTO THE BEAR PIT. Edinburgh: Birlinn Limited.

[335] There is a discrepancy here: in INTO THE BEAR PIT., Whyte (page 134) suggests £7.5M. In Section 4.19 - 4.20 to Proposal for a Company Voluntary Arrangement by the Joint Administrators of The Rangers Football Club plc to its Creditors and Shareholders dated 29 May 2012 (at: https://find-and-update.company-information.service.gov.uk/company/SC004276), Duff & Phelps state £8.5M (£8.3M + £200 000 for exclusivity).

[336] See: Rescuing Rangers: From Whyte to Green to Franklin, W. S., Gow, J. D. C., Graham. C., & McKillop, A. (Eds.). (2013). Follow We Will THE FALL AND RISE OF RANGERS. Edinburgh: Luath Press Limited. Calvin Spence opines that in terms of Green's consortium, opposition and suspicion mounted especially as he would not disclose details of members of his consortium. Suggestions included: Arif Massod Naqvi, Imran Ahmad, Allesandro Celano and Blue Pitch Holdings.

[337] See: Smith, P. (2012). For Richer For Poorer. RANGERS: THE FIGHT FOR SURVIVAL. Edinburgh: Mainstream Publishing Limited. Smith (p14) states that Green's consortium had 20 backers (UK, Middle East and Africa and Southeast Asia). The first sight of Green was on 13 May 2012 (St Johnstone FC v Rangers FC). Green said that not one investor should own more than 15%.

[338] See: Green: I shafted Whyte to get Gers. Bombshell as ex-chief in £50m bid for club. The Sun. 4 April 2013. In detail: Craig Whyte claims he and business pal Aidan Earley, 44, were behind the Sevco 5088 company which Green used to take over the club. But Green

says he was just telling Whyte porkies so he could get the businessman's shares — a plan he says was changed when the club was liquidated. Green revealed Whyte, from Motherwell, is now demanding £1million a year for LIFE — or a quarter of Green's own shares in the club. In his plush office at Ibrox stadium in Glasgow, he said: "At the point the Company Voluntary Agreement failed and we moved into the newco realm, the shares and the rest of his indemnity didn't matter. What he believes now, in his mind — and it could only be in Craig Whyte's mind — is that he is entitled a quarter of my shares. Whyte also wants one million quid a year for life. It is not going to happen." It is understood Whyte's legal team are preparing to apply for a High Court writ to serve on Ahmad and Green. He reckons with taped conversations and claims of signed documents, he has a strong case to win back control at Ibrox. Whyte's claims of his buy-out involvement with Green will stun Rangers fans. They centre on Sevco 5088 — where Green was a director — which paid £5.5million to buy Gers from liquidation in June last year. Whyte will argue that he and Aidan Earley were the moneymen behind the move. Green transferred the assets — including Murray Park and Ibrox — to new company Sevco Scotland just days after sealing the deal. Whyte claims the assets were transferred ILLEGALLY because Green did not have the permission of Sevco 5088's backers — himself and Earley.

[339] It is, however, not clear who Whyte's other investors were.

[340] The Rangers Football Club Limited subsequently announced an independent inquiry into his takeover (See Chapter Five).

[341] See: https://media.rangers.co.uk/uploads/2017/10/Annual-Report-Inside-2013.pdf

[342] See Section 4.30 to Proposal for a Company Voluntary Arrangement by the Joint Administrators of The Rangers Football Club plc to its Creditors and Shareholders dated 29 May 2012 at: https://find-and-update.company-information.service.gov.uk/company/SC004276).)

[343] Details of the ongoing liquidation process can be found at: https://www.bdo.co.uk/en-gb/rfc-2012-plc

[344] This is also reported on the Wikipedia website. Another consortium, led by former Rangers manager Walter Smith, made a last-minute bid for the assets. This was rejected by Duff & Phelps, who already had a binding agreement to sell them to Charles Green.

Walter Smith's consortium, including Scottish businessmen Douglas Park and Jim McColl, made a £6million offer that was also turned down. Charles Green then offered Walter Smith a role and the opportunity for his consortium to invest in the club. On 19 June 2012, Walter Smith and his consortium pulled out from trying to acquire the relaunched club. Smith's consortium was originally hostile to Charles Green's consortium but stated that "We wish the new Rangers Football Club every good fortune." In addition, On 20 June 2012, it was reported that two Glasgow businessmen, housebuilders and property developers Allan Stewart and Stephen McKenna were preparing a bid for the club worth about £11m. On 25 June, McKenna had a bid of £8.7m rejected. Prominent former Rangers player John Brown had been involved in the bids and made a further attempt to take control by leading a supporter buyout of Green's consortium. Brown left his position as transfer scout after a meeting with Green and told 5,000 demonstrating supporters at Ibrox Stadium not to renew their season tickets, in order to "starve" them of funds and force them out. Brown challenged Green to show the title deeds to Ibrox and Murray Park, because he suspected that Craig Whyte or Ticketus retained an interest in the assets. Brown also accused Green of "surrendering" to a plot by Celtic chief executive Peter Lawwell, alleging that Lawwell wanted a weak Rangers in the SPL to boost Celtic's own revenues.

[345] See: Taking on the Establishment: Rangers and the Scottish Football Authorities to Franklin, W. S., Gow, J. D. C., Graham. C., & McKillop, A. (Eds.). (2013). Follow We Will THE FALL AND RISE OF RANGERS. Edinburgh: Luath Press Limited.

[346] See: Progress Report to Creditors dated 24 August 2012 at: https://find-and-update.company-information.service.gov.uk/company/SC004276).

[347] See: https://www.acas.org.uk/tupe. TUPE regulations protect employees' rights when they transfer to a new employer. A TUPE transfer happens when: an organisation, or part of it, is transferred from one employer to another; a service is transferred to a new provider, for example when another company takes over the contract for office cleaning.

[348] See: https://www.exeter.ac.uk/media/universityofexeter/humanresources/documents/learningdevelopment/the_change_curve.pdf

[349] Ibid.   327

Chapter Five

[350] See: History of Rangers FC at:
https://en.wikipedia.org/wiki/History_of_Rangers_F.C.
[351] See:
https://en.wikipedia.org/wiki/2012%E2%80%9313_Rangers_F.C._sea
son
[352] See: https://find-and-update.company-
information.service.gov.uk/company/SC425159/filing-history?page=3
[353] See Page 6 to Annual Report to 30 June 2013 at: https://find-and-
update.company-
information.service.gov.uk/company/SC425159/filing-
history?page=3. In detail: "In August 2012, Rangers Retail was
formed as a joint venture with major sports retailer SportsDirect.com

In detail: "In August 2012, Rangers Retail was formed as a joint
venture with major sports retailer SportsDirect. SC425159/filing-
history?page=3
[353] See Page 6 to Annual Report to 30 June 2013 at: https://find-and-
update.company-
information.service.gov.uk/company/SC425159/filing-
history?page=3. In detail: "In August 2012, Rangers Retail was
formed as a joint venture with major sports retailer SportsDirect.com.
In detail: "In August 2012, Rangers Retail was formed acom with the
aim of developing the Club's retail, merchandising, apparel and
product licensing business. The partnership enables the Club to utilise
the huge buying power and resources of SportsDirect.com. This new
structure means the Club has a controlling interest in its retail
operation and can now give supporters the opportunity to buy direct
from the Club and in doing so continue to invest in its future."
[354] Further information on IPOs can be found at:
https://www.barclays.co.uk/smart-investor/investments-
explained/shares/understanding-initial-public-offerings-ipos/.
[355] See: https://find-and-update.company-
information.service.gov.uk/company/SC437060/filing-history?page=4
[356] See: https://www.rangers.co.uk/investor-
information/3xiJwTahGEhZWGZAUcKMy1

[357] Rangers Retail Limited was incorporated on 13 July 2012 as SDI Newco No 1 Limited. It changed its name to Rangers Retail Limited on 14 August 2012.

[358] See: https://media.rangers.co.uk/uploads/2017/10/Annual-Report-Inside-2013.pdf

[359] See From Crash to Cash...and beyond to Franklin, W. S., Gow, J. D. C., Graham. C., & McKillop, A. (Eds.). (2013). Follow We Will THE FALL AND RISE OF RANGERS. Edinburgh: Luath Press Limited.' in Follow We Will The Fall and Rise of Rangers.

[360] He was, however, somewhat confrontational with the football authorities in Scotland. For example: Green must make peace in Scotland. Irish Daily Mail. 11 January 2013 Friday; and Murray: Charles can help change. Evening Times. 11 January 2013.

[361] The IPO Prospectus included: development of club, acquisition and development of land surrounding Ibrox Stadium, new sponsorship partners on improved financial terms and the objective of playing football at the highest European level.

[362] Evening Times 9 August 2012.

[363] The Sun 21 August 2012.

[364] See: Malcom in the muddle; man at top still posted missing as the crisis goes on. Daily Record and Sunday Mail. 12 April 2013 (in this article Keith Jackson raises several issues including: Craig Whyte; police raiding properties in an attempt to gather evidence which may prove illegality occurred when Whyte bought the club in May 2011; links between Whyte and Green; tensions between Green and McCoist; a charge of racism by the SFA; a player sacked after being hoaxed by some obsessive internet extremist; a Chief Scout being dismissed and wrongly accused of malpractice; a physiotherapist axed without the Manager's consent; and the possibility of a dispute with the SFA over whether or not the club should be allowed to operate at all); and Leader needed to calm troubled waters before Rangers are engulfed. The Herald. 17 May 2013.

[365] See: https://www.bbc.co.uk/sport/football/22043867

[366] See: https://www.bing.com/newtabredir?url=https%3A%2F%2Fwww.bbc.co.uk%2Fnews%2Fuk-scotland-glasgow-west-22064369

[367] See: https://www.bbc.co.uk/sport/football/22096954.

[368] See: https://www.bbc.co.uk/sport/football/22138094.

[369] See: https://www.bbc.co.uk/sport/football/22220035.

[370] See: https://www.bbc.co.uk/sport/football/22231397.

[371] See: Ibrox remains in flux, with parties inside and out jockeying for position. 28 April 2013. Sunday Herald; Murray clings on as directors close in at Ibrox. The Herald. 17 May 2013; and Fractured still by the factions. Sunday Herald. 19 May 2013.

[372] See: Walter ready to walk. Scottish Star. 8 May 2013; and Gers fans threaten backlash if Walt's removed. Scottish Express. 30 May 2013.

[373] See: Reasons to be cheerful to the fore at Ibrox. The Herald. 6 May 2013.

[374] See: Murray hangs on as Rangers hit self-destruct. The Daily Telegraph. 8 May 2013.

[375] See: Rangers shareholders try to overthrow chairman Malcolm Murray in bid to snatch control of boardroom. The Daily Record. 16 May 2013.

[376] See: Murray clings on as directors close in at Ibrox. The Herald. 17 May 2013.

[377] See: Leader needed to calm troubled waters before Rangers are engulfed. The Herald. 17 May 2013.

[378] See: Rangers: Club chairman Walter Smith urges board 'unity'. The Scotsman. 30 May 2014.

[379] Harper McLeod was a source of constant debate. A glowing testimonial from Peter Lawwell (Celtic Chief Executive Officer) was removed from Harper McLeod website. There were also suggestions that McKenzie had been particularly confrontational during negotiation over the 5-Way agreement.

[380] See 7. RFC 2012 P.L.C. (Formerly The Rangers Football Club plc) (In Administration) Final Progress Report to Creditors 27 September 2012 at: https://find-and-update.company-information.service.gov.uk/company/SC004276/filing-history. In detail:

SPL Commission

5.3 As has been widely publicised, the SPL appointed a Commission to investigate the Company's use of Employee Benefit Trusts and any breaches of the SPL's rules that may have arisen thereon. As stated in the JAs' recent press release, based on legal advice, their opinion is that, as confirmed by the SPL's solicitors, the Commission is appointed under the contract between the SPL and its member clubs.

In the Company's case, this contract was terminated when the Company ceased to be a member of the SPL. The JAs do not, therefore, propose for the Company to participate any further in the Commission's activities as this would not appear to be in the interests of the Company's creditors.

[381] See: We Were the People to Green to Franklin, W. S., Gow, J. D. C., Graham. C., & McKillop, A. (Eds.). (2013). Follow We Will THE FALL AND RISE OF RANGERS. Edinburgh: Luath Press Limited.

McKillop offers that the RFFF would use at least some of £538 000 to appoint a QC and solicitor to represent Rangers at the SPL-appointed Commission chaired by Nimmo Smith. A statement released on 17 Jan 2013 announced that RFFF would underwrite costs of protecting Rangers' 54 league titles. A QC would fight Rangers corner at the evidence stage.

[382] Page 93 to Cooper, M. (2021). Rangers: The Lost Decade. Self-published: Amazon.

[383] See: https://find-and-update.company-information.service.gov.uk/company/SC425159/filing-history?page=3

[384] See: Power struggle puts McCoist under pressure; Former chief executive Green returns to Rangers. The Daily Telegraph. 5 August 2013.

[385] See Page 94 to Cooper, M. (2021). Rangers: The Lost Decade. Self-published: Amazon.

[386] See: Controversial Green shown the exit after just 18 days back at Rangers. The Daily Mail. 21 August 2013.

[387] See: Green exit unlikely to avert EGM; EXCLUSIVE Former Rangers CEO quits in middle of conference call Mather and Murray at the centre of power struggle. The Daily Telegraph. 21 August 2013.

[388] See: IBROX EGM DATE UNCLEAR. The Daily Telegraph. 3 September 2013.

[389] See: TWIST IN RANGERS STRUGGLE. The Daily Telegraph. 6 October 2013.

[390] The requisitioners were Paul Murray, Malcolm Murray, Scott Murdoch, and Alex Wilson.

[391] See Page 98 to Cooper, M. (2021). Rangers: The Lost Decade. Self-published: Amazon.

[392] See: Fans' anger as Rangers announce £14.4m loss. The Scotsman. 1 October 2013.

[393] In relation to the Ahmad legal action, the former Commercial Director had his preliminary hearing in the Court of Session in Edinburgh. He claimed that he was owed £3.4M as part of a bonus on £67M worth of commercial business. His claim was based on a letter written by the former Chief Executive Officer Charles Green. Ewan Campbell, representing Ahmad, said in the preliminary hearing that Green had "applied authority" when he wrote the letter given that he was Chief Executive Officer at the time. Alan Summers, the Rangers QC, said in reply that the letter was an "independent, unilateral exercise of power by a CEO." He added that the argument made by Ahmad's legal team was "breathtaking in its audacity". The judge said that a procedural hearing would be held in December.

[394] See: Former Rangers director Paul Murray wins court battle to postpone annual general meeting. The Daily Record. 14 October 2013.

[395] See: Rangers saga takes another twist. The Scotsman. 17 October 2013.

[396] See: Rangers: Craig Whyte may be involved – Johnston. The Scotsman. 17 October 2013.

[397] See: Rangers fans' groups call for boardroom answers. The Scotsman. 21 October 2013.

[398] See: Somers: I don't know Charles Green, Craig Whyte. The Scotsman. 6 December 2013.

[399] See: Rangers chairman brands Murray's group fanatics. The Scotsman. 7 December 2013.

[400] See: Rangers: Sons of Struth group in investment call. The Scotsman. 9 December 2013.

[401] See: Rangers boardroom contenders gear up for AGM fight. Scotland On Sunday. 15 December 2013.

[402] See: Rangers AGM: 'Back McCoist' call from fans' group. The Scotsman. 17 December 2013.

[403] See: Graham Wallace Q&A. The Daily Record. 17 January 2014.

[404] See: Rangers AGM: 'Back McCoist' call from fans' group. The Scotsman. 17 December 2013.

[405] Note 15. Contingent Liabilities. On 15 April 2013, the Board of RIFC plc announced that it was commissioning an independent examination and report relating to allegations made by Craig Whyte, the previous owner of Rangers Football Club plc, concerning RIFC's former Chief Executive and former Commercial Director.

[406] See: Page 103 to Cooper, M. (2021). Rangers: The Lost Decade. Self-published: Amazon.

[407] Ibid. Page 105.

[408] See: https://media.rangers.co.uk/uploads/2017/10/164581-Rangers-Annual-Report-as-printed.pdf

[409] See: https://find-and-update.company-information.service.gov.uk/company/SC425159/filing-history?page=3

[410] https://en.wikipedia.org/wiki/2014%E2%80%9315_Rangers_F.C._season#cite_note-1

[411] See: Page 115 to Cooper, M. (2021). Rangers: The Lost Decade. Self-published: Amazon.

[412] https://en.wikipedia.org/wiki/2014%E2%80%9315_Rangers_F.C._season

[413] Extensive analysis is offered at pages 110-111 to Cooper, M. (2021). Rangers: The Lost Decade. Self-published: Amazon.

[414] https://en.wikipedia.org/wiki/2014%E2%80%9315_Rangers_F.C._season

[415] Ibid.

[416] See pages 110 – 111 to Cooper, M. (2021). Rangers: The Lost Decade. Self-published: Amazon.

[417] See Rizvi has introduced potential investors to Rangers at: https://www.bbc.com/sport/football/29227423

[418] See pages 110 – 111 to Cooper, M. (2021). Rangers: The Lost Decade. Self-published: Amazon.

[419] Ibid.

[420] See Rangers: Graham Wallace resigned as Rangers' chief executive just two days after failing to stop Mike Ashley's takeover; Ashley's £2m loan offer was accepted and Wallace followed his sole ally Philip Nash out of the club. Independent.co.uk. 27 October 2014 at: https://www.independent.co.uk/sport/football/scottish/rangers-graham-wallace-resigned-as-rangers-chief-executive-just-two-days-after-failing-to-stop-mike-ashley-s-takeover-9820539.html

[421] See https://media.rangers.co.uk/uploads/2017/10/164581-Rangers-Annual-Report-as-printed.pdf; and Rangers International Football Club reports £8m pre-tax loss for 2014 year https://www.insider.co.uk/company-results-forecasts/rangers-

international-football-club-reports-9873724.
[422] See page 114 to Cooper, M. (2021). Rangers: The Lost Decade. Self-published: Amazon.
[423] See page 109 to Cooper, M. (2021). Rangers: The Lost Decade. Self-published: Amazon.
[424] https://media.rangers.co.uk/uploads/2017/10/164581-Rangers-Annual-Report-as-printed.pdf
[425] See page 117 to Cooper, M. (2021). Rangers: The Lost Decade. Self-published: Amazon
[426] See Douglas Park launches bid to save Rangers... Motor group chief drives bid to rescue Ibrox club. Mail Online at: https://www.dailymail.co.uk/sport/football/article-2888091/Douglas-Park-launches-bid-save-Rangers-Motor-group-chief-drives-bid-rescue-Ibrox-club.html.
[427] See, for example, @BBCSport tweet of 14 March 2022: The sanctioning of Chelsea owner Roman Abramovich in the wake of Russia's invasion of Ukraine has forced English clubs to confront questions. Who should be allowed to own its top clubs?
[428] See page 122 to Cooper, M. (2021). Rangers: The Lost Decade. Self-published: Amazon
[429] See page 123 to Cooper, M. (2021). Rangers: The Lost Decade. Self-published: Amazon

Chapter Six

[430] See Rangers administrators ordered to pay £3.4m over 'duty breach' at: https://www.bbc.co.uk/news/uk-scotland-58820790.

[431] See Global giant sues for £25million in Rangers debacle at: https://www.pressreader.com/uk/scottish-daily-mail/20210820/281986085634548.

[432] See Rangers liquidators aim to slash millions more off tax bill as they dispute massive £51m of debt at: https://www.thescottishsun.co.uk/sport/football/8178367/rangers-liquidatiors-aim-slash-millions-off-tax-bill-debt/.

[433] See Rangers lose court battle with Sports Direct and forced to disclose Castore deal details that could cost them millions. at: https://www.thescottishsun.co.uk/sport/football/8180399/rangers-court-sports-direct-disclose-castore-deal-millions/.

[434] See Crown Office once again faces legal action of Gers prosecution at: https://www.pressreader.com/uk/the-herald-on-sunday/20211121/281865826731219.

[435] See Inquiry into wrongful prosecution of Rangers administrators at: https://www.bbc.co.uk/news/uk-scotland-56014280.

[436] See, for example, https://www.bdo.co.uk/en-gb/rfc-2012-plc.

[437] See again The Herald newspaper, 13 June 2012: "Rangers Football Club Born 1872, died 2012." It is also interesting that the same newspaper told us — on 5 March 2022 — that "Rangers celebrate 150th anniversary." Perhaps there is some editorial confusion in this newspaper.

[438] See: CHAPTER 7 (page 79) to Smith, P. (2012). For Richer For Poorer. RANGERS: THE FIGHT FOR SURVIVAL. Edinburgh: Mainstream Publishing Limited.

[439] See Glasgow Rangers takeover deal agreed at: https://edition.cnn.com/2012/05/13/sport/football/football-rangers-administration/index.html

440 See Rangers liquidators want to cut millions of tax bill at: https://www.thetimes.co.uk/article/rangers-liquidators-want-to-cut-millions-off-tax-bill-q8hqv9w5h

[441] See https://media.rangers.co.uk/uploads/2017/10/Interim-December-14_14_clean.pdf

Printed in Great Britain
by Amazon

10599101R00220